Let's imagine a *place* that sets
your business up for any future.

A place that champions flexibility
without diluting *culture*.

A place that brings *purpose*,
values and behaviours to life.

A place that balances
work and *wellbeing*.

A place that elevates everyone's
experience of work.

All whilst driving profits,
productivity and *performance*.

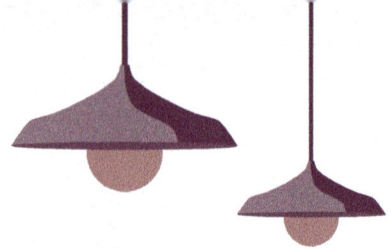

© 2023, Melissa Marsden

All rights reserved. No part of this book may be reproduced in any form or by any means, electronic or mechanical, including photocopying, recording or by any information or retrieval, without prior permission in writing from the publisher. Under the Australian Copyright Act 1968 (the Act), a maximum of one chapter or 10 per cent of the book, whichever is the greater, may be photocopied by any educational institution for its educational purposes provided that the education institution (or the body that administers it) has given a remuneration notice to Copyright Agency Limited (CAL) under the Act.

Marsden, Melissa. COMUNiTI

ISBN: 978-0-646-87410-4
First published in 2023 by: Melissa Marsden
Project management: @em.lystudio
Editing: Melissa Marsden, Ann Maynard
Sub-editing: Claire Hey
Proofreading: Prue Kingsford-West
Creative direction, design & illustration: @em.lystudio
Cover photography: Shae Style Photography

Distribution enquiries: melissa@melissamarsden.com.au
Media enquiries: melissa@melissamarsden.com.au
Project enquiries: admin@comuniti.com.au

This is proudly a COMUNiTI and Melissa Marsden product,
www.melissamarsden.com.au
www.comuniti.com.au
Instagram @melmar, @wearecomuniti
LinkedIn @melissamarsden @comuniti

DISCLAIMER
The content of this book is to serve as a general overview of matters of interest and is not intended to be comprehensive, nor does it constitute advice in any way. The author or COMUNiTI will not be liable for any loss or damage suffered by any person arising out of the reliance on any information from this book. This book is a compilation of one person's ideas, concepts, ideologies, philosophies and opinions. You should carry out your own research and/or seek your own professional advice before acting or relying on any of the information displayed in this book. The author, COMUNiTI and its related entities will not be liable for any loss or damage (financial or otherwise) that may arise out of your improper use of, or reliance on, the content of this book. You accept sole responsibility for the outcomes if you choose to adopt and/or use the ideas, concepts, ideologies, philosophies and opinions within the content of this book. Every effort has been made to reference copyright holders; should there be any inaccurate acknowledgements, please contact the publisher.

The writing of this book and the projects featured within its pages, have been created in Meanjin, the lands of the Turrbal and Jagera people.

This book tells a story of strengthening cultures and instilling a sense of belonging through our connection to the places in which we work, a place of learning. A knowing that our First Nation peoples have always understood. Their relationship to their culture and to their sense of belonging, is in their connection to place, to Country; the land they live on, the sea that surrounds them and the strength that comes from community. I pay my respects to Elders past and present, extending that respect to all the Traditional Owners of Country throughout Australia, a place that I am grateful to call my home.

In the learning borne of country is the light that nourishes the world.
— Ambelin Kwaymullina, Aboriginal lawyer

the next workplace

DESIGNING DYNAMIC ENVIRONMENTS THAT INSPIRE HUMAN POTENTIAL

Melissa Marsden
FOUNDER AND DIRECTOR AT COMUNiTI

contents

INTRODUCTION — 11
   Who Am I? — 13
   What is a Workplace Strategist — 19
   Design Thinking Principles — 23

CHAPTER 1: REIMAGINING THE FUTURE OF WORK — 31
   Corporate Strategy and How It Impacts Your Workplace Design — 33
   Case Study: Davidson — 36
   Why Do Brands Need Purpose? — 52
   Why Do I Need an Office? — 54
   The Five Levels of Autonomy — 60
   The Evolution of Work — 64
   Reimagining The Future of Work — 67
   What Does the Future of Work Look Like? — 68
   Social Competencies are the New Human Currency — 70
   The Shifting Nature of Work: The Impact of Technology — 72
   Workplace Styles: What are the Options? — 76
   Workplace Management Technology: Enabling Data-Driven Design — 84
   Who Do You Need to Engage With? — 89
   Worksheet: Strategy Kickoff — 94
   Chapter Huddle — 95

CHAPTER 2: USE YOUR SPACE TO TELL YOUR STORY — 97
   Discovering Your Organisation's Purpose — 104
      Defining Your Brand — 106
      What is Your Brand Story, and How is it Showing up in Your Business? — 109
   Case Study: Plantation Homes — 110

Worksheet: Define Your Story — 120
Worksheet: Discover Your Organisation's Personality — 122
How Your Brand Leads Your Culture — 124
Case Study: Hall Chadwick — 126
Culture is The System That Shapes the Dynamics of The Organisation — 148
    The insights of Culture Surveys — 149
Activity: The Five Words Your Team Would Use to Describe Your Culture — 152
What Your Workplace Design Says About Your Culture and Values — 154
Why Your Story Is the Foundation and Reflection Point for All Decisions — 158
Chapter Huddle — 160

CHAPTER 3: BRINGING YOUR VALUES TO LIFE IN THE WORKPLACE (The Secret to Success Lies in Influencing Behaviour) — **163**

Nudge Theory: What Is It and How to Use it — 168
Spaces Designed to Influence Value-Aligned Behaviours — 172
How Your Values Define the Behaviours of Your People — 174
    There are three ways behaviours are influenced by design — 176
Worksheet: Define Your Values — 181
Translating Values into Behaviour — 186
Case Study: Mapien — 190
Designing for Deep Work — 208
Chapter Huddle — 213

CHAPTER 4: WELLBEING AT WORK — **215**

A Fruit Box is Not Wellness — 217
The Elements of Wellbeing at Work — 220
The Impact of Socialisation at Work — 222
    Designing Workplaces for Connection — 226
Designing a Wellness Strategy — 234

How Hybrid Work Contributes to Wellbeing	236
Working from home is making us lonely	239
Work-life balance is a fine line we walk	241
Locational divides introduce a new dynamic	243
Case Study: ENTAIN	244
The Financial Case of Designing for Wellbeing	260
Social Detriments of Health	262
The Amount of Time We Spend Indoors	263
The Cost of People to a Business	264
WELL Building Standard	268
Worksheet: Spaces for Wellbeing	272
Worksheet: Is your workplace suffering from Presenteeism?	273
Chapter Huddle	274

CHAPTER 5: DESIGNING THE EMPLOYEE EXPERIENCE — 277

The Art of Placemaking: Creating an Experience	278
Case Study: Fathom	282
The Layers of Employee Experience	292
The Three Environments of Employee Experience	294
How Our Workplace Environment Impacts Our Experience of Work	303
How to Create an Outstanding Workplace Experience	306
Worksheet: How to Create an Employee Empathy Map	307
Designing for "Me"	308
Generations in The Workplace	308
Personality Profiling	310
Neurodiversity	315
Diversity & Inclusivity	319
The Four Types of Worker	325

Worksheet: Identify Your Personas	330
Making the Workplace a Place to Be, with a Hospitality-Led Approach	331
So How Do We Design the Employee Experience?	336
Worksheet: How to Create a Journey Map	338
Case Study: EDMI	340
Supporting Your People Through Change	358
Creating a Vision for Your Journey	358
Communication On the Journey	359
Engaging Your People Throughout the Journey	360
What Experience Do You Want to Create?	362
Chapter Huddle	364

CHAPTER 6: LET'S PUT IT INTO ACTION — 367

Start With a Clear Plan for Success	369
What Are You Trying to Achieve? Write it Down	372
What Does Your Future Look Like? Get Specific	374
What Does the Picture Look Like Now? Establish The Baseline	375
How Are You Going to Get There? Break It Down	376
How Will You Know You've Succeeded? Measure It and Adapt	378
Worksheet: How Well Prepared Are You to Maximised Your Opportunity?	
Ten Questions you Should Answer Before Engage the Market	380
Assemble Your Support Team	384
Preparing Your Workplace Market Brief	396
Worksheet: The Eleven Questions You Need to Ask Your Prospective Designer	398
The Two Big Questions Every Client Wants to Know. How Much & How Long?	403
How long does it take to design and build a workplace?	403
Money, Money, Money! How Much Does a New Workplace Cost?	410
Your Story Is the Reflection Point for Every Decision	416

DIVE IN AND WATCH THE RIPPLES OF CHANGE

Expand your impact with *The Next Workplace*

Reading this book is the first step in creating a dynamic workplace that will set your organisation up for any future. The real power in this book comes from putting the learnings into action and engaging your people.

To support you in this transformational journey, I've curated a number of supporting resources to assist you in expanding your impact, from an online community where you can connect with like-minded people exploring the future of work, to downloadable worksheets, checklists and templates to guide your journey to creating your next workplace.

You can find them all at:
www.melissamarsden.com.au/TheNextWorkplace_resources
or scan the QR code below:

introduction

LET'S INSPIRE OUR HUMAN POTENTIAL

Your workplace, the physical environment in which your company operates, is the most influential element in your business. It impacts each and every employee; it guides behaviour, enables or compromises the operations of your business, and opens or restricts communication flow, information transfer, speed and efficiency. When it's done consciously, your workplace will build and transform the culture, foster community, encourage a sense of belonging, and reinforce the values the company holds so dear. And yet too many leaders back-burner workplace design, treating it like a nice-to-have instead of a vital imperative. In doing so, they miss out on the enormous untapped potential surrounding them as they sit at their desk each day. I want to change that.

This book will introduce you to new ways of seeing, appreciating and embracing the opportunities within the four walls of your workplace. I will show you what's possible and how workplace design can transform your business. The space you refer to as "your office" can shift from being a liability on your balance sheet, an inconvenient cost of doing business, to an investment that you welcome, celebrate, and confidently go "all-in" on to take your business to the next level. I will teach you to expect more from your space instead of accepting what has always been. Your workplace should inspire your people, not purely house them in rows of workstations from Monday to Friday. It should enhance performance, increase productivity, improve efficiency and strengthen culture, delivering business returns.

THE SHIFT IS AVAILABLE TO YOU NOW.

We'll also look beyond the office. While this book is about workplace design, it is more broadly about work; how we work, where we work, who we work with, and the tools we need to work productively and happily.

The pandemic transformed our whole world of work – from why we *go* to an *office* through to our idea of the role work fulfils in our lives. It forced us to reevaluate our priorities, our own sense of personal purpose and how it aligns to the organisations we work for, and reconsider the purpose of an *office*. Work is no longer performed in one place; it is not a solo venture, nor does it *require* everyone to be in the same space. While we don't yet know how our workplaces will continue to evolve, as organisations embrace new hybrid ways of working, what you will find in this book is the founding principles from which you can explore what work is in your business and how your workplace will need to adapt to support this continuing evolution. You have the opportunity to position your business to thrive in these new conditions while others are scrambling to *make it work*.

My goal in writing this book is to break down your preconceptions of what a workplace *should* be and liberate your thinking to imagine what is possible. These *shoulds* are often the result of years of unconscious immersion in soul-depressing cubicles and uninspiring environments.

They are so pervasive, so ingrained, that most clients can't conceive the unbridled transformation possible for them until we've had a few meetings.

HOW ABOUT YOU?

If you stripped away all the suppositions of what an office is, the ones we have built up over years of working in one, what could your workplace look like? How would it feel? What could it deliver? And how would your business be different as a result?

Often when I begin working with clients, they are dazzled by the idea (and the dollar signs) of reining in their leasing footprint through increased efficiency in planning and workstyle design, resulting in reduced rent, operational maintenance, and fit-out costs. What continues to blow them away is not the immediate return to their bottom line but the extraordinary change deep within the organisation's fabric.

Transformation awaits...

just some of the outcomes my clients have experienced

They see business processes that were slow and stagnant become agile, adaptable and progressive.

They see the mindsets of even the most entrenched employees shift towards new opportunities and possibilities.

They acquire new clients and partners who are inspired and aligned, enhancing the enjoyability of their work and streamlining their workflow and communication.

They see increases in cross-functional communication, collaboration and knowledge-sharing, resulting in cross-service delivery, increased client engagements and significant increases in their revenue.

Their employee attraction and retention improves, and so does their applicant pool. It brims with prospective hires who are deeply aligned to the organisation, who subscribe to its purpose, brand promise, culture, and values, and are just as committed and rewarded by their achievement as the business.

They can race to embrace new opportunities that previously would have been beyond the business's physical, mental and emotional capabilities.

These outcomes are possible for your company too. You have an opportunity to look to the future to see what potential awaits you and your team – and I want this for you! I want your employees to love coming to work each day, excited about the opportunity, knowing that their contribution is making a difference to the organisation, the clients your organisation touches, the community around you, and the world at large. I want you to see this book as a roadmap for creating the best practice workplace environment for your people and, later, as a guide for checking in to see if your organisation is still doing things the right way.

In the chapters to come, you'll find a fresh perspective, a new viewpoint and an alternative reality to imagine what *your* workplace of the future looks like – one that reflects your organisation's unique requirements, departmental mixes, roles, service delivery streams, culture, values, behaviours, worldview, and the difference you want to make. This is your moment to embrace expansive reinvention and the opportunity to think big, make a radical change and embrace a new world of work that is not confined to a desk within four walls.

It will shift your thinking, enabling you to see how your business objectives can be stifled or liberated by the shape of your space, aligning, enabling and inspiring your human potential.

This book is filled with data-led, evidence-based thinking and research from the world's leading people and culture consultancies, trainers, and educators. I also share my first-hand experiences of working with clients like you – the challenges they faced, the internal pushback they felt, and the wins they enjoyed, firstly with their people and then the inevitable effects on their business performance and profitability.

WHATEVER YOUR STARTING POSITION, MY PROMISE IS THAT YOU WILL EXPAND YOUR UNDERSTANDING OF THE IMPACT THAT YOUR ENVIRONMENT HAS ON YOU, YOUR PEOPLE, AND YOUR BUSINESS' PERFORMANCE.

Who am I?

Through practical, actionable steps, you can move your organisation into the future, knowing that you are designing a place that inspires the human potential within us all.

Over the past twenty years, I have worked with organisations to help them express who they are and what they do through their workplace design.

Inspired by cultural transformation, organisational psychology and neuroscience, and in constant pursuit of delivering conscious environments that support the physical, mental, and emotional wellbeing of their occupants, I have evolved an approach unique to the work we do at COMUNiTI – a workplace strategy and commercial design studio, where we reimagine workplaces to bring brands to life, connect people and empower teams to perform at their best. We draw together design philosophies and scientific research to develop a methodology that delivers unparalleled environments for our clients.

And while I'd love to say my collaborative approach came to me wrapped in a bow, the truth is that it was forged by my frustration with "the way things were done" in the workplaces of the clients I've worked with.

Early in my career, I was expected to create workplaces for my clients using a brief that told me little more than the size of the space they had leased and the number of offices and workstations they wanted to wedge into it. There was little communication and even less reflection about what changes could serve them best. I got so fed up with it that I began to go rogue. I'd find ways to uncover more of who they were as an organisation, what they did, their values, who worked for them and what they needed to succeed. Then I'd incorporate that research into the work I did for them and smile when they reached out months later to tell me how much had changed.

It took fifteen years of trial and error to create the systems, processes, engagement surveys, and workshop structures I now use to delve into the depths of an organisation to truly understand and support them in creating a workplace that works. Our conversations enable them to understand their business better and position me to help them express their brand, culture, and purpose in every element of its physical construction. More importantly, I design a space that supports people in getting their job done. And now, with this book, I can start that conversation with you.

We'll start with a reasonable amount of crystal ball gazing before diving deeper into the core of your business. The initial chapters are filled with research, anecdotes, and stories of transformation to help you see the opportunities before your organisation. They are the *why* and the *what*. Each chapter centres on one of the five pillars that underpin the workplace dynamics in every organisation and how these pillars can be activated through the structural design of your physical environment:

WORKPLACE DYNAMICS OF EVERY ORGANISATION

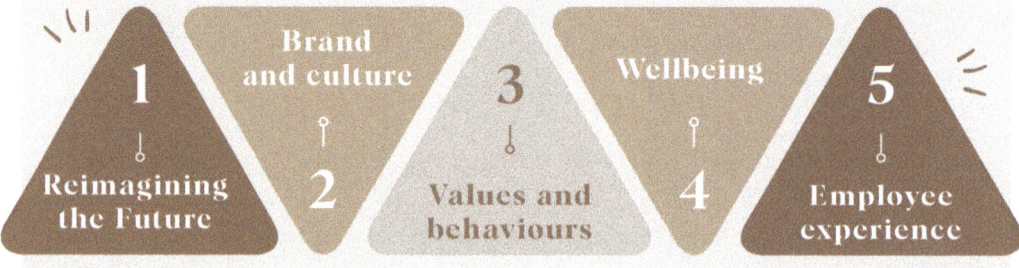

I aim to inspire you with a vision of the possible future before your organisation and the impact that conscious workplace design will have. The book's final chapter brings it all together and explains the *how* – what you need to know to take action.

While I firmly believe that everything I have written between these covers is essential for us all to know, I'm also well aware that you may prefer to dip in and out of each section, topping up your knowledge tank and exploring new opportunities. You can use this book as a reference guide to support your journey, seeking greater clarity, guidance or perspective – or you can read it cover to cover! Whichever sounds like you is just fine, and I encourage you to work with this book in a way that works for you.

Now, let's be clear: this book will not deliver you a brand spanking new sparkly office! There are a lot of steps required, and if you want to optimise this opportunity, you can't do it alone. You will need the expertise of critical specialists to make this happen.

THIS BOOK WILL LEAVE YOU INFORMED AND CONFIDENT ENOUGH TO HARNESS OPPORTUNITIES TO MAKE YOUR WORKPLACE WORK FOR YOU, YOUR BUSINESS, AND YOUR PEOPLE.

While there are spaces in the pages of this book to capture your thoughts and complete the exercises, you may prefer to do this on a printable version, or perhaps even multiple times or with your team. So I've created a resource library for you on my website to access all the tools and templates mentioned in the book. Head over to **melissamarsden.com.au/TheNextWorkplace_resources** to find them.

No matter where you are in your workplace journey, be it ready to sign a new lease or *five years off contemplating that nightmare again!* every chapter of this book will offer you inspiration you can embed into your organisation. This book is not solely about *building* a workplace for the future; it is about *designing* a workplace for the future. And with that comes the opportunity to transform a vast array of aspects already within your workplace, outside of the physical construction of the *office*.

So what does your future look like?

What is a workplace strategist?

Design thinking is being actively implemented into today's management practices to the point where entire MBAs have been developed to teach design strategy, creating the world's next generation of innovative leaders focused on moving beyond just profits to a sustainable, ethical world. It's truly meaningful.

As workplace strategists, we use creative design principles combined with an analytical business brain. We create a holistic strategic framework to understand who you are, how you work, what you do, what your people do, what that looks like, how they interact, move, communicate… so that the design of your space transcends the aesthetic and enables your organisation to create a haven that embraces something truly meaningful to your business, connecting you to your community.

Driven by the need to understand your business in finite detail, a Workplace Strategist wants to understand your Business Strategy: your vision for the company, your mission, and your values. Then, using design, they will bring these things to life so that you can start to see the results of this strategy in action.

This starts the same way as every other good strategy: with planning. Most of what a workplace strategist does happens before a designer puts pen to paper. The research into the organisation and its people informs the opportunities and resolves the challenges, identifying optimal space needs, workflows, locations, size, floor plates, and outcomes.

COLLABORATION AND OPEN COMMUNICATION ARE ESSENTIAL TO SUCCESSFULLY IMPLEMENTING A WORKPLACE STRATEGY.

We work within the organisation to gain a deeper understanding of the business, uncover the potentially unknown challenges, and highlight the opportunities through fresh eyes and a different perspective.

The outcome is an articulated brief that encapsulates the essence of the business, implementing and embracing the business strategy to form a space that communicates the vision and values of the organisation inherent to your community, enabling you to achieve them.

WHEN YOUR STAFF ARE HAPPIER, THEY ARE ENGAGED. WHEN THEY ARE ENGAGED, THEY PERFORM BETTER. WHEN THEY PERFORM BETTER, YOUR CLIENTS ARE HAPPIER.

Increased productivity = Increased Profitability = ROI. So taking a more holistic approach is not just more meaningful; it's more ethical, more sustainable and more profitable.

Wondering what the difference is between an

Architect vs Interior Designer vs Workplace Strategist

ARCHITECT

Architects are responsible for the design of the building – outside in. The form a building takes, its position on the site, and how it responds to "place" influencing the surrounding community. They are responsible for the creation of the structure, the way all the services within operate, and ensuring its compliance for occupancy.

INTERIOR DESIGNER

Interior designers are responsible for the design of the internal space – inside out. They are focused on designing space for people and their experience of that space, combining materiality, style, traffic flow and essential services. Responding to and applying the brief to the given area, they extract the drivers of the design and apply them to the space.

WORKPLACE STRATEGIST

Workplace Strategists bring together historically disparate disciplines of people [HR] and property [Facilities], combined with the commercial acumen to ensure that strategic business objectives are optimised. They look to enhance employee behaviours, relationships, and performance, through researching, collating, and analysing the data within your business, from growth forecasts to workforce planning. This data provides the insights required to determine everything from your workplace style to the square meterage you require to the relationship of spaces on the floor.

> *Design is not just what it looks like and feels like. Design is how it works.*

— STEVE JOBS

Design thinking principles

When I first started in the design industry, I was fascinated by how businesses ticked, what made them work, and how the office fitout they occupied reflected those things. So I became extremely frustrated when each new office project began with a simplistic brief that offered little more than the required number of offices and workstations to be fitted onto a floor.

Clients were coming to me having already leased the space and seemed concerned only with the business hierarchy, symbolised by who got an office and who got a workstation. There was no consideration for any other element of their business, no thought given to creating an environment that inspired or excited their employees, and little regard for their wellbeing or ability to contribute beyond their in-cubicle attendance.

I was flabbergasted! These clients had missed what little opportunity they had to influence the shape and size of their space. They saw their workplace as one giant box with a series of smaller boxes within it. There was no imagination about what was possible. It was a classic case of *this is the way we've always done it!*

I'm a rather stubborn person and wasn't particularly fond of this approach. I'm also highly ingenious when it comes to helping a client see a better way. So, I introduced additional *value-adds* to my projects. In the beginning, these included a workplace employee survey to understand the employees' perspective of the workplace and an observational study to see for myself the behaviours, workflow patterns and use of the workplace. Over time, these value-adds became an entire service offering for my clients, ensuring that they no longer missed these opportunities in their workplace.

What these tools enabled me to do was to change the conversation. Instead of discussing the number of workstations and offices the client wanted, we shifted our attention to discussing what was essential to the organisation, where they saw themselves in five years, what the departments in their organisation were, what they did and who they interacted with. We discussed the type and style of work they did and questioned whether the space catered to their needs.

I had established the beginnings of what we now call "workplace strategy." While I may have been working within the parameters of a space that has already been defined, we discussed the possibilities of what could be contained within that space, away from workstations and offices, to spatial tools that would enable their people to optimise their business and enhance performance.

I was creating the foundation for my unique approach to workplace design: one that builds a solid understanding of who I am working with and what will serve them best. I don't interact with just my key representative in the organisation (although this is also a given!).

I WORK WITH THE CLOSELY HELD VALUES AT THE HEART OF THE ORGANISATION:

1. Who they are, where they came from, and what brought them to this point

2. The purpose, vision and values of the business, what is important to them, what matters most

3. The people, what they do, how they work, and the clients who come to them for help

When I have a deeper understanding of the organisation, what makes them tick, their workflow processes, communication flows and challenges, I get far-reaching insight into the possibilities before us. This level of understanding enables me to make informed decisions about the natural teaming on the floor, how a seemingly insignificant wall placement could create a physical roadblock for communication, or whether the space is undermining the motto emblazoned on the company wall. Using the data I have collected, I unlock more impactful solutions to a problem that has plagued the client for years.

This immersion and the ability to bring a fresh and creative perspective to your workspace and your whole approach to business is the most important opportunity that sits before us.

I often explain what I do as taking a client's business, tipping it upside down, shaking everything out and then carefully putting it all back together in a way that works for them now. This approach can seem extreme, but the results tell the story. My approach enables us to examine every element from every side before putting it back into the box: What is its function? Do we still use it? Do we need it? We can then place it back into the space in a position that works with all the other aspects of the business or leave it on the sorting table as it no longer serves the organisation, their goals, or the future they have imagined for themselves. You and your business deserve a workplace that aligns with, supports, and serves you.

One of our core values at COMUNiTI is to be *Rebels with a Cause*. It gives us permission to challenge the status quo, ask the tough questions, and dig deep to find our courage to call out the elephant in the room to create a better outcome for everyone involved. I want you to have the knowledge so you can find the courage to challenge the status quo in your organisation and design a better workplace.

BE A REBEL WITH A CAUSE.

Throughout this book, you'll also note my strong passion for invoking an organisation's brand essence, far beyond the token feature wall colour or pride of place logo, to something far more integrated and fused into the fabric of space. Something that you can *feel* when you walk in, a *knowing* sense of what this organisation is all about.

LET YOUR SPACE TELL YOUR STORY, WHAT MATTERS TO YOU, YOUR STYLE, AND HOW YOU DO BUSINESS.

You'll also learn the power that spatial design has on influencing behaviour and how you can encourage this to reflect the values of your organisation with careful curation. The way a space is arranged, the proximity of spaces, the furniture selections, and even the material and finishes are all highly influential.

USE THE POWER OF SPATIAL DESIGN TO POSITIVELY INFLUENCE HOW PEOPLE ACT, ENGAGE AND COMMUNICATE IN YOUR ENVIRONMENT.

Another overarching principle that you will find in this book is centred around data. When I work with organisations, we invest significant time in gathering information because when we unpack it, organise it and analyse it, we find the answers that will shape our recommendations. With good data, decision-making is straightforward because it is substantiated, and the path forward is clear. You are already sitting on a goldmine of information, covering everything from your employees' demographics to how they work. You just need to unlock it.

SEE DATA AS THE KEY TO YOUR DECISION-MAKING.

These are the design thinking principles that I will share with you in each chapter of this book. Over the years, I've refined my approach – what has worked, what hasn't, and what has given me the most significant insights into the clients I work with – and each time, I have found that it comes back to people. When we understand the people within the organisation, their relationships, behaviours, roles, activities to be performed, communication channels, information flow, work preferences, generational alignments, personalities… that's when we can create a truly transformational experience through the workplace. •

I want you to be empowered by this knowledge, too. I want to interrogate your thinking and invite you to look at your business and your people from another angle. To see data as a key to decision making. To turn the challenges and problems you've continually faced in your business upside down and see if there is a better solution you have not considered before.

Shall we begin?

CHAPTER ONE

reimagining the future of work

Many people feel that an office is an office is an office. But *your office* is your unique opportunity to tell everyone – your staff, peers, clients, suppliers, competitors, EVERYONE – who you are, what you care about, and what you stand for. In my twenty years of experience, I can honestly say that no two workplace environments have ever been the same, just as no two companies can be the same. Sure, they have shared elements, but how these elements come together is distinctly different. Their ratios, sizes and styles create a unique dynamic and provide physical cues about how people behave in that environment. Many underlying factors begin to bleed into an organisation's culture over time; people, personalities, changes in the work style, the influence of technology, the type and location of clients, and the demands required to service these clients all sculpt a culture that can easily hurt an organisation instead of helping it.

Workspace design is a holistic, three-dimensional jigsaw puzzle influenced by an organisation's culture, purpose, and vision. Understanding these surrounding factors shows you a complete picture specific and unique to the organisation. It informs how you can provide the spaces necessary to enable supportive behaviours and see them flourish.

Corporate strategy and how it impacts your *workplace design*

If you knew that a decision you were making for your business could constrain its future potential, would you move forward with it? *Of course not*, you might be thinking. But, surprisingly, business leaders unknowingly make decisions like these every day for their two most expensive business assets: their property and their people.

When leaders define their corporate strategy, the last people they would consult are their workplace designers. And fair call. Traditionally the role of the designer has been *to put this many little boxes into the big box*. However, a new style of design philosophy is evolving. It takes a more holistic approach to create a workplace that embodies your organisation's strategic plan and infuses every element of the physical environment, creating a space that influences and guides the behaviours needed to execute that vision.

- Departments — People — Communication processes
- Work type and style — Cultural nuances — Rituals, policies and procedures
- The story of your business evolution — Your vision for the future — ★

OUR WORK ENVIRONMENTS ARE NOT MERELY AN ATTEMPT TO CREATE A FURNITURE SHOWROOM.

They must be responsive and specific to your organisation's particular style of collaboration, communication and connection. They must adequately balance the need for social versus individual work settings, noisy versus quiet spaces. This ratio is determined by several factors that tie back to "what behaviour do you want to see?"

As technology only further influences our world, it has transformed how we work. No longer do we need to physically attend our place of work to be working. Remote working has rapidly become the norm, whether from home, from a client's office, the bus, train, or a café.

IN TURN, OUR REASONS FOR ACTUALLY GOING "TO WORK" HAVE CHANGED.

We go to work to connect with our colleagues on a social level, connect with our organisation and the culture, immerse ourselves in the atmosphere of what we are all about, and remind ourselves of why we do what we do. We look to connect, share information, ideas and stories, and find support and answers to questions we may struggle with on our own.

JUST AS OUR NEED TO PHYSICALLY CONNECT WITH OUR WORKPLACE HAS CHANGED, SO MUST THE WORKPLACE'S DESIGN.

No longer can it be purely a kit of parts consisting of meeting rooms, desks and offices. We need so much more to facilitate the meaningful social interactions we seek out. We need spaces to collaborate, connect and focus. However, we also need spaces to relax, recharge and work. Our needs have changed, and so too must our work environments.

> "The physical office is a garden for cultivating relationships which bloom over "how was your weekend?", quick coffee catchups and shared workplace experiences."
>
> – UNWORK

A WELL-CONSIDERED AND PLANNED WORKSPACE CAN CREATE A CULTURE RESPONSIVE TO YOUR COMPANY'S STRATEGIC VISION AND DRIVE TANGIBLE OUTCOMES IN HOW YOUR PEOPLE ENGAGE WITH YOUR BUSINESS.

So when presented with an opportunity to take over an existing space, massage your business into an existing fitout (and receive a healthy financial incentive for doing so), you should be aware that you may inherit more than a office. It may make perfect sense on paper, but there is a hidden cost that influences the way your business operates.

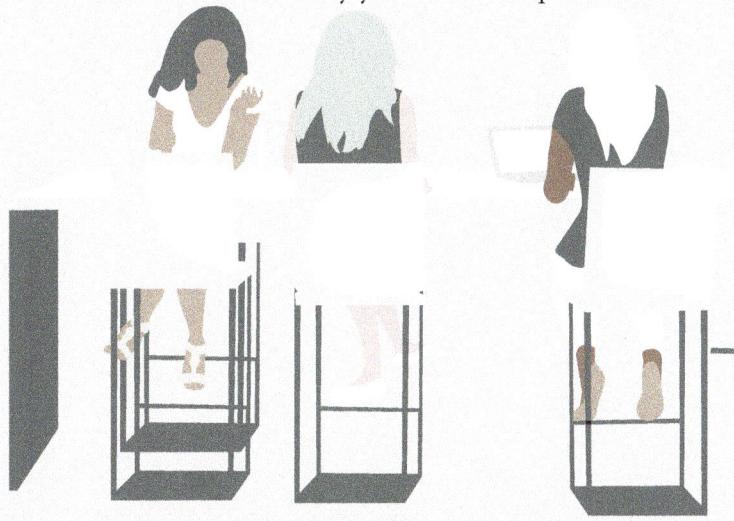

case study
Davidson

Our workplaces speak to and drive the behaviours within them. Our workspaces influence all of our interactions, internally and externally, and shape how people engage with the company itself. They impact people's work and their performance, efficiency and efficacy. When Davidson, a workplace performance company specialising in business advisory, search and recruitment and technology consultancy, decided to create their first purpose-built environment, they had been in business for thirty years. Never did they dream that the offices they occupied had been diminishing their ability to execute their corporate strategy.

When working with Davidson we started by unpacking the organisation's strategic goals and objectives, the key drivers underpinning the work they did and how they wanted to enable their people to work to the best of their ability.

Creating a collaborative work environment was at the strategic core of how Davidson saw their ability to deliver the best outcomes to their clients. They wanted to see the wealth of knowledge that existed within their business shared across their various business units; to see the growth of their staff through the mentorship of more tenured employees; to embody a culture of cross-disciplinary collaboration to enhance their customer experience, and deliver a far superior service. However, their previous workplaces had failed to provide this environment. Instead, their employees were constrained by their spaces – offices, meeting rooms and workstations – resulting in a series of siloed departments that didn't share information or communicate. Their work environment was constraining the cross-disciplinary growth inherent within the organisation solely because of the structure of the physical workplace.

Infusing a variety of collaborative spaces to facilitate everything from informal small group discussions to more robust and animated problem-solving sessions became our key focus when designing Davidson's new space. The plan we devised included a work area that fans the building perimeter, enabling complete visibility across the entire business and providing transparency, access and, most importantly, giving younger staff the chance to "learn through osmosis" from more experienced team members. We added a central café space that brings the entire business together, facilitating impromptu and serendipitous conversations, sparking new ideas and ways for teams to collaborate. All of this actively enables the desired knowledge sharing across departments, enhancing Davidson's clients' experience.

Tune into Episode 68 of the *Work Life By Design* podcast for the rest of the chat.

Executive Director Bruce Davidson shared his thoughts on the process in Episode 68 of the *Work Life by Design Podcast*, Enhancing Workplace Performance:

What we were seeking to do was create collaborative spaces, to create greater connection between our people, more visibility of each other all the time. People have lunch in the café because they want to sit in there and connect. We've got a library where I find people literally lying down and making a phone call as they might at home with a friend, and yet they're talking to a client. The yarning circle has become a metaphor, where we go to sit down and have a chat, where anyone can say anything.

It's the sort of space that makes you want to come to work, and while we still do as much as many organisations do, people are choosing to come or not to come depending on their needs. I'm perfectly sure we've got a whole lot more people coming into our space because of the nature of the way you designed it.

But the success of this workplace design goes so much deeper than finishes and aesthetics. It goes right to the heart of how this came about; how their purpose, values, and behaviours informed the process. What Davidson needed was a space to achieve, shaping the employee experience and providing cues for behaviour, encouraging top talent and cultural alignment. Here's how we transformed a brief for a functional workplace into an award-winning space ideal for collaboration, connection and experience.

> IT'S THE SORT OF SPACE THAT MAKES YOU WANT TO COME TO WORK.
>
> – BRUCE DAVIDSON, EXECUTIVE DIRECTOR

the task

Davidson invested in creating a purpose-built space they could call their own for the first time in their thirty-year history. The brief was a simple one, to create an authentic workplace that optimised the potential of their people and created a fantastic employee experience. Doing justice to this brief required some deep diving to get to the very heart of the organisation's values, what they meant to the team and the founder, and how this could be woven into the design fabric.

the inspiration

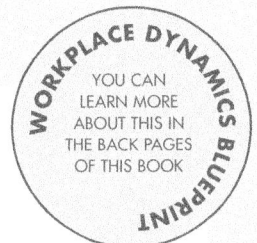

Like many of our projects, we began with our signature Workplace Dynamics Blueprint™, a comprehensive strategic process that enables us to engage with the business at a deeper level and understand the essence of what it meant to be part of Davidson. Through this, we uncovered the pillars of their culture, values and passion for people, and helped them communicate those things through every element of the workplace. Our unique process added enormous value to the brief in taking Davidson from "just another office" to creating an environment authentic to them.

Their social pillars of Diversity, Equality, Inclusivity and Community sit at the heart of this project, brought to life by extracting the essence of the communities they work with. Davidson has a long-standing friendship with the Yalari Mob (a not-for-profit organisation offering quality, secondary education scholarships for Indigenous children from regional and remote communities) who harness a strong stance against domestic violence and a commitment to improving diversity and inclusion. These commitments, coupled with Davidson's long-standing values and the desire to help every person, team and organisation to optimise their potential, now show up in their environment in a way everyone can feel.

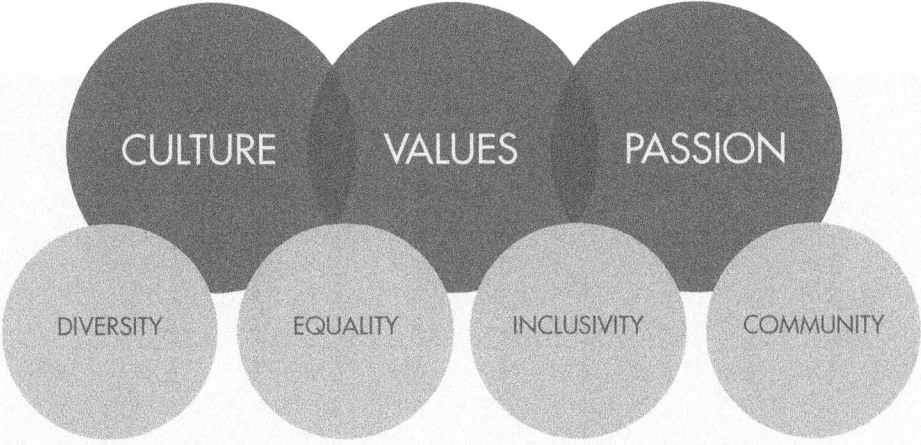

The entry space is a welcoming multipurpose area that encourages casual conversation and invites you to make yourself at home while waiting.

CASE STUDY – DAVIDSON

the solution

Davidson are a fellow ambassador of enhancing workplaces through employee experience, making a positive difference and changing lives. This is a direct alignment between our respective corporate visions to create a space that reflects our deep passion for designing workplaces people love and establishing a community where people feel connected.

Davidson's passion is evident in how their people show up and engage every day. A visible distinction has been observed in how their people dress; they come to work with pride in themselves and their workplace.
Their passion for humanity, wellbeing and making a positive difference in the lives of others and continuing to encourage and promote these behaviours were at the core of the project.

The circular lounge in the café is a direct nod to the Yarning Circles of the Yalari Mob, reflective of the Indigenous gathering point. From the outset, this space was intended to reflect the strong alliance with the Yalari Mob and to represent their communication traditions and sense of belonging. The café space was inspired by Campsite 4 to express their ethos of going that step further, the grit and determination to do what's hard, and the desire to serve sitting at the heart of the business. It is the first space staff enter and a place for all to celebrate together. The space is not closed and confined but open and connected to the work environment, making it a gathering place that encourages others to join with visibility across the business.

Employee diversity informed the floorplan, with the space ensuring individual preferences for how and where to work were balanced with mental and emotional wellbeing. All personalities and preferences are supported and celebrated by incorporating collaborative, communal spaces, individual phone booths, quiet lounge areas, and a wellness room.

The layout of the space also reflects this, with quieter activity spaces pulled to the extremities of the workspace and communal and activated workspaces scattered throughout the work area. We focused on emotional wellbeing to ensure the design gave the best to people and got the best in return. It is demonstrated by ensuring spaces enable serendipitous interactions that lay the foundations for solid individual and cross-functional employee relationships. The general work area supports tacit learning through peer-to-peer conversation and osmosis. Furniture typologies and spatial design encourage movement throughout the day, supporting physical wellbeing and diverse preferences in ways of working.

The Yarning Circle is a nod to Indigenous culture and the strong alliance that Davidson have with the Yalari Mob. This space reflects the organisation's pillars while also encouraging open and collaborative communication.

Below: At the heart of the workplace, the café is a multipurpose space that encourages incidental connection and informal meetings, supporting the establishment of relationships across the organisation.

Above: Open to the space, the café is integral to the workplace, offering alternative and informal work settings.

the detail

Embracing the curved nature of the floor plate and offset core, the workspace enables an uninterrupted view, connecting the entire business without barriers. This connectivity allows for natural osmosis to occur, engaging the skill and knowledge of the team, learning from one another.

Supported by a variety of space styles, employees are encouraged to optimise their work performance by engaging with the suitable space for the task, offering enhanced flexibility. The materiality embraces the essence of Davidson: honest, authentic and trusted, executed through the sealed concrete, exposed services and signature "D" shape, partnered with their signature navy blue and a splash of orange.

The holistic approach to this space reflects that design is not achieved through excellence in a single area; it requires a considered approach from multiple viewpoints to create a balanced and harmonious space that supports the needs of the people who work there. By incorporating the values that Davidson holds dear and weaving this into the very fabric of design, we provide subtle cues and inspiration for how people should behave and a clear roadmap for attracting like-minded talent.

The Library offers a "home away from home" space for employees to relax or have a casual conversation. The space takes on a calming feeling, through the soft lounges, books and colour palette.

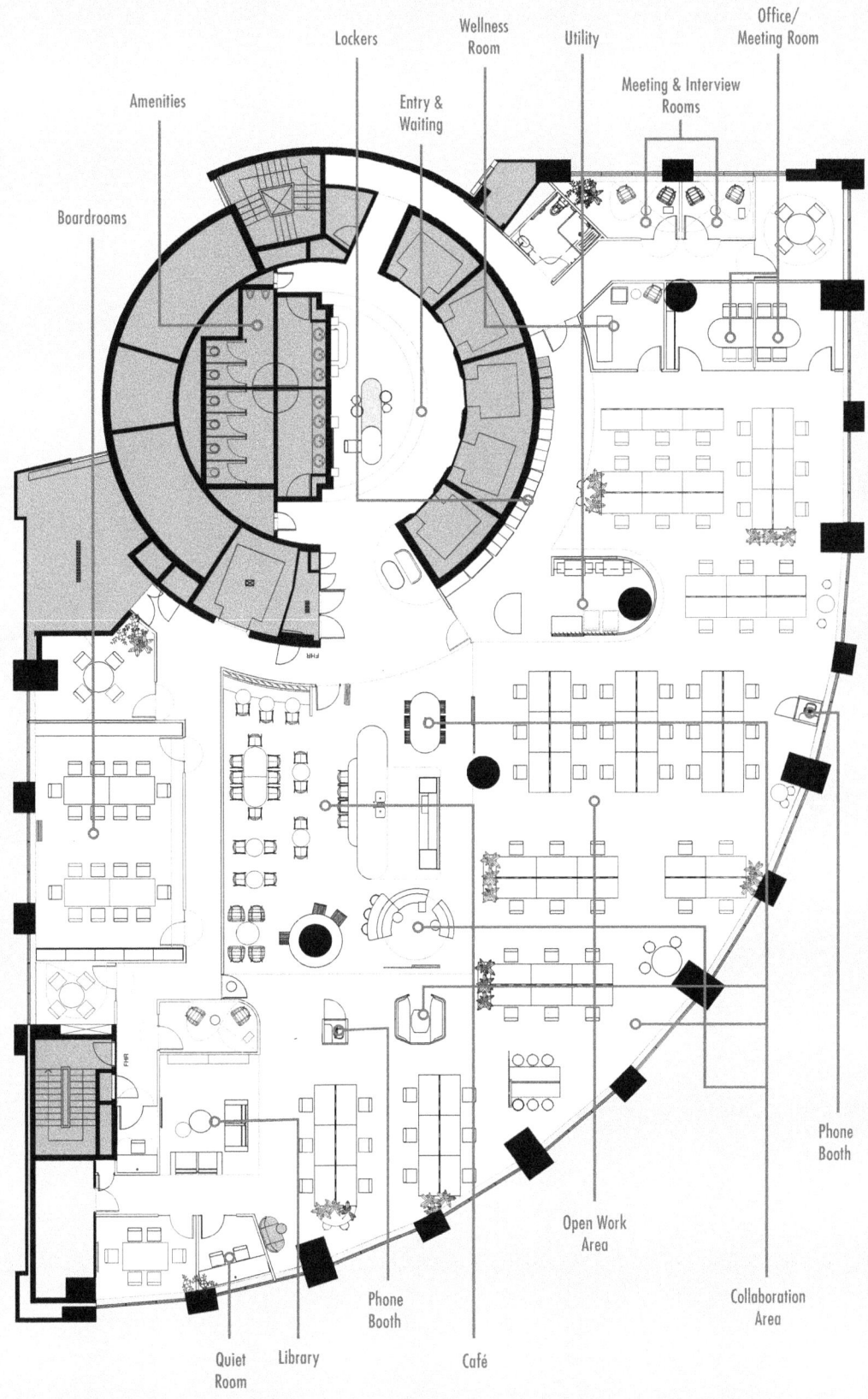

Left: High-backed booths provide collaborative meeting spaces with a layer of privacy in the open environment.

Below: Collaborative workspaces enable easy access for teams to meet and problem solve spontaneously.

Below: Colour, shape and pattern are layered into the space, functionally connecting the environment to the broader Davidson brand.

The boardrooms are flexible spaces that can be used as two individual rooms or opened up to facilitate large training events. The walls incorporate whiteboards, enabling functional use of the space for collaborative work.

Davidson's extensive art collection was carefully curated into the space, enhancing key areas such as this waiting area.

Below: The journey to the boardroom offers a glimpse into the workplace via operable panels inspired by the Prayer Wheels of Nepal.

The pathway to the boardrooms reflects Davidson's commitment to enhancing workplaces

CASE STUDY – DAVIDSON

Why do brands need *purpose?*

Purpose is not just for the social enterprise or the not-for-profit.

The values and purpose of an organisation inform everything from the top down.

Purpose informs your brand.

It's important to remember that when we talk about a brand, we aren't referring to your logo, feature colours or words on the wall; we are talking about how you want people to feel when they do business with you – the experience you provide for both clients and employees.

Your brand leads your culture.

When the brand experience is infused into the very fabric of the environment, it guides your organisation's culture, which then radiates through the actions of your people. This culture, in turn, defines what your organisation values and holds dear. These values are the guideposts that will help you attract and retain top talent, make decisions, and form the kinds of behaviours that reinforce how you want your organisation and people to operate.

Why do I need an office?

We used to need the office for the simplest reason: as a physical structure with all necessary equipment and office supplies where the whole team could do work. But with the introduction of more mobile and flexible technology, this need has been eliminated.

Technology is affecting the way that we do business. We can work anywhere, any time. More than that, we have experienced the effects of being kept away from the office but still being able to do our job. Thanks to extended lockdowns due to the pandemic, we realised the workplace's role in our mental, emotional, and social wellbeing.

WE NOW SEE THAT OUR WORKPLACES CONTRIBUTE TO OUR MOST BASIC HUMAN NEED FOR CONNECTION AND BELONGING. WE DON'T GO TO WORK TO DO OUR JOBS. WE GO THERE FOR MUCH MORE.

Collaboration

The workplace presents countless opportunities for us to connect with people socially. It increases our wellbeing, and it also helps us in our work. We need to collaborate with our colleagues because we can't solve complex problems and challenges individually. We need an environment where we can bounce ideas off each other and develop innovative solutions. Two heads are always better than one!

Connection to each other

We still like going to our workplace because we want to interact with people. We want to connect with them and be part of a community with shared ideas and values. Our workplace is where we feel like we belong. And that sense of belonging creates a sense of wellbeing.

Connection to the organisation

The workplace allows the organisation to align the team with its purpose, vision and goals; to help them feel like they are part of something bigger than themselves, to invite them to be part of something important. It provides a platform to communicate these ideas and create a space that encourages learning, collaboration, creativity, respect, and more.

Learning and development

Whether in the form of structured, formal training sessions or casually overhearing the conversations of colleagues, our work environments are places that support personal and professional development. Activities that are difficult to replicate in a virtual environment.

AND TO FACILITATE THIS,
our workplaces require a new environment.

OUR PEOPLE ARE LOOKING FOR NEW AND DIFFERENT THINGS FROM THEIR EMPLOYERS.

HERE ARE THREE WAYS TO MAXIMISE THIS OPPORTUNITY:

1

Create a space that supports your people.

Provide them with the optimum environment for performing different tasks. The boundary between work and life has become blurred due to technology and work flexibility, meaning we are connected twenty-four hours a day. The workplace needs to transition us through the different requirements of our day. It needs to support us no matter the activity or task we have to do: sitting, standing, quiet, collaborative, groupthink, individual work, meeting, brainstorming. An optimal workplace environment enhances our synergy for different types of work that we need to perform.

2. Instil the organisation's culture and values.

The workplace is an opportunity to embed the culture of your company, influencing how people think and feel. It is a way to positively shape your people and align them with your values through physical cues that reinforce the desired behaviours. It is a place that connects your people to the greater purpose of the organisation.

3. Allow for restoration.

There is a shift away from the days of work being strictly a work environment. You know those rows of cubicles, the Dilbert-style ones? Workplaces of the future are a lot less rigid, embracing green spaces, relaxation and meditation rooms, creating a sense of physical, mental and emotional wellbeing amongst employees. Our homes used to be our retreat and relaxation spaces, a sanctuary at the end of a workday. But now, workplaces need to provide those retreat spaces as well. Our minds and bodies require this restoration, and our workplaces must adapt to provide this.

Purpose

We want to make a valuable contribution through our work; we want it to be *meaningful*.

AS HUMAN BEINGS, WE NEED THAT SENSE OF PURPOSE. IT DRIVES US TO DO GOOD WORK, EVEN ON DAYS WHEN WE DON'T FEEL LIKE IT.

For some people, that purpose is why they get up every morning – and the workplace can contribute to that sense when it feels like a space of shared goals.

If we have learned anything from the pandemic, it's that our workplaces are much more than a physical space for us to go about our business. They play an integral role in our working lives, fostering community and a sense of connectedness with our peers and the organisation as a whole.

As such, the design of our workplaces now requires us to look at them in a different way. Rather than simply accommodating our workforce, we need to dig deeper and uncover the tasks, activities, connectivity, and performance outcomes we desire, and then create environments to facilitate them; agile, flexible spaces that emanate the business' purpose, embody its values, and enable its people.

WE NEED TO UNDERSTAND WHY. WHY DO WE GO TO WORK EACH DAY, AND WHAT DOES OUR WORKPLACE MEAN TO US?

As leaders, we need to ask:

- **WHAT DOES THIS ORGANISATION STAND FOR?**
- WHAT IS ITS PURPOSE?
- **HOW DO WE CONNECT THAT PURPOSE TO OUR PEOPLE?**
- HOW DO WE USE OUR SPACE TO COMMUNICATE THAT IDEA?

It comes down to having a shared sense of purpose, vision and values. Create a collective understanding of what you're here to do and encourage connections between people through a supportive workplace design.

THE FIVE LEVELS OF AUTONOMY

The global shift to remote working in early 2020 in response to the pandemic created a new working reality that was foreign to many. And as thousands of organisations scrambled to find guidance, they turned to companies that were already operating a remote and distributed workforce model; organisations such as Automattic, the creators of WordPress.

Automattic works almost exclusively online with 1,170 employees in seventy-five countries[1] and no office. In a pandemic-free world, they *"get the whole company together once a year for seven days so that Automatticians can create bonds that influence them all year long"[2]* and an additional seven days for each team to strategise and bond.

Matt Mullenweg, CEO of Automattic, shared his model of distributed work with five levels of autonomy in April 2020*, to explain the shift in organisational mindset and operation at each level to achieve "Nirvana."

Mullenweg refers to his workforce as distributed over remote, as he believes that "remote" implies that a central place of work remains.

Let's take a closer look at each level

UNABLE TO BE DONE REMOTELY

This level refers to work that employees cannot do anywhere other than the workplace. For example, baristas, construction workers, dentists, massage therapists. Individuals who need to be hands-on to do their job.

NON-DELIBERATE ACTION

This level is where the majority of businesses were pre-COVID. Work was done onsite, with company equipment, on company time. Remote work could be done for a day or two if required, with most tasks being put off until people were back in the office. Remote access to systems and email was clunky and not very user friendly.

RECREATING THE OFFICE ONLINE

This is where many organisations landed following the shift to remote working. The typical office day was just recreated online. While technology was provided to support this remote work with access to Zoom, Team, Slack, and various other software, the work process had not been reimagined to respond to the new environment. Companies just replaced physical meetings with virtual ones.

Days get disrupted with constant interruptions, and employees are expected to be online from nine to five. Some organisations even resorted to installing screen logging software, essentially spyware, on employee computers to monitor when they were online. Certainly not instilling any level of trust there!

REMOTE-FIRST OR DISTRIBUTED ADAPTATION

Here, organisations are genuinely adapting to the remote-first distributed team model. They invest in better equipment with noise-cancelling headphones, ring lights and pro-microphones to enhance video calls. They also begin to embrace new asynchronous communication (see Level 4 for the real deal) and work methods that reduce or eliminate the need for meetings.

Communication becomes predominantly text-based, which Automattic have embraced, with their whole recruitment process carried out via Slack – not one phone call!

Mullenweg recommends that, if a meeting is required, employees get specific about the topic and set an agenda with a mere fifteen-minute time limit. (It forces participants to be succinct.) Invitees should be kept to a minimum, and agreed deliverables should be set before ending the call.

If the meeting is purely to communicate information, employees are encouraged to use email or another channel to distribute it. Participants also utilise live documents to record action items, such as Google Docs, so that everyone can see and check the notes.

ASYNCHRONOUS WORKING

Asynchronous working empowers people to work in a way that works for them. It respects the nature of the work to be performed and the most suitable communication method required; if it's not urgent, employees use Slack, Teams or chat. If it's urgent, they make a phone call. It enables people to work in flow and respond to their natural body clock, enhancing creativity, innovation, and decision-making.

Individual performance is measured by what team members produce, not when or how. Trust emerges as the foundation of the organisation. Decision-making improves through slower, more deliberate consideration, and everyone is empowered.

The global talent pool is embraced and not limited to the geographical location of a physical workplace. Employee retention goes up, and training and coaching increase.

Mullenweg believes that organisations who get good at "passing the baton" can get three times the work done of a traditional nine-to-five operation.

When you have people working across a global network of employees in every time zone, you have created a twenty-four-hour workforce.

NIRVANA

Mullenweg believes it's always a good idea to have the ultimate end in mind, even if it's not attainable, in his words, "Nirvana." At this level, an organisation outperforms any "in office" organisation. Everyone has time for the things that matter to them: wellness, family, friends. Employees are optimised and bring their highest self and creativity to their career.

Here employees have complete control over their work environment, the chair they sit in, the desk they sit at, the view outside, the lighting, temperature and the people around them. In a workplace created by the organisation, these elements are mostly beyond the control of the individual, and as Mullenweg points out, these all impact our performance and productivity.

In Nirvana, employees have complete control over their environment. This "workplace nirvana" is a far cry from the typical workday as we've come to know it.[2]

Whilst Mullenweg's views of creating "Nirvana" may be the ultimate for their organisation, this model is not the ideal nor possible for many organisations and employees, due to work style, delivery models and personal preferences. As you'll learn in the coming chapters whilst we may no longer need to "go" to work, great value remains in our ability to be physically present and connect on a human to human level, thus supporting the need for organisations to retain and reimagine a physical workplace.

Where does your organisation sit?

The evolution of work

Before we dive into how work is evolving and how our workplaces need to adapt accordingly, I want to take a brief look back at how our current concept of work and its rhythms came to be. As it's important for us to learn from the past, in order to inform our future state.

As far back as history goes, humans have toiled in the fields from sun up to sundown, six days a week, resting only on the sabbath. With the rise of the Industrial Revolution, we carried this same work ethic from the fields into the factories, achieving substantially greater output thanks to machine technologies such as steam and spinning machines. It wasn't until 1812, with the introduction of gas lighting, that we could work longer and longer hours, increasing the workday to ten- to sixteen-hour shifts.

It was in the 1820s that middle managers led by reformist Robert Owen campaigned for the eight-hour workday, seeking more time for socialisation and enjoying their newfound middle-class wealth, introducing the 8:8:8 ratio: eight hours' labour, eight hours' recreation, eight hours' rest.

It was Henry Ford, in 1926, who truly revolutionised the eight-hour workday, announcing that his factories would run around the clock, hiring thousands more workers to run three shifts of eight hours each.[3] He doubled wages to five dollars a day and shortened the working week from six to five days, popularising the forty-hour workweek. It paid off. Ford increased the productivity of his factory and doubled its profit in two years.[4]

As machines became enhanced by computers, physical labour was supplemented by knowledge work and factories transformed into offices, and we simply shifted the same work rhythms into new environments. Because the tools of our trade, our computers, were large and expensive pieces of equipment that many households could not afford, we were required to commute to a workplace to "work." However, today, the same cannot be said to be true.

A century from Ford's revolutionisation of the eight-hour workday, we no longer need to commute to a workplace to work. Our tools are light, compact, portable and connected, enabling us to be adaptable, flexible and highly mobile. Yet many businesses still subscribe to a Monday to Friday, nine to five, workweek that requires employees to attend a "workplace."

The opportunity in looking back at this point in time, is to see that the pandemic has marked history, transforming our way of working. Just as the shift from factories to offices did and the Industrial Revolution before that. Yet as history recalls, we simply lifted and shifted our old routines and work rhythms, applying them to a new environment, rather than reimagining a new future. This is our opportunity to redesign a new way of working. One that works for a new environment.

WORK IS AN ACTIVITY WE DO, NOT A PLACE WE GO

> "We shape our buildings and afterwards our buildings shape us."
>
> — WINSTON CHURCHILL

Reimagining the future of work

A silver lining has shone through the pandemic, the abrupt shift to remote work awoke us to the outdated work rhythms and structures that no longer serve us. We have been exposed to our conditioned thinking, our acceptance of "this is how it has always been done," and forced to recognise that there are other, better ways of working.

We have the opportunity to assess what it was about our work environments that made them work, the value they brought to our organisation and the impact that they had on our people. They are not just physical containers where we sit people down to "work" Monday to Friday; they are much more. They are the spaces that communicate each organisation's greater purpose, the impact they want to make on their community and the world around them. They are the space that ties employees together, connecting them to this greater purpose and enabling them to see their contribution in a larger plan. All of these things are possible with the right design.

Your workplace stands as a physical representation of the brand experience your organisation wants everyone to feel. It connects your people to the organisational values, drives behaviours and supports the delivery of your corporate strategy. You have been given the opportunity to reimagine how they can be shaped in the future to optimise their true value and the contribution they make to your people's lives.

What does the future of work look like?

There is a massive shift in the way workplaces are designed today, and numerous factors contribute to this. With technology disrupting work as we know it, the skills required to operate in this new world are far more empathetic and social than ever before. Below are four trends influencing the design of the future workplace and advice for how you can evolve with it.

TECHNOLOGY IN THE WORKPLACE

Embrace technology… NOW. We're in an age where virtual reality (VR) is creeping into the workplace, "work" is more flexible and mobile than ever, and everything from the whiteboard to the furniture is now "smart" thanks to the integration of technology. Technology keeps advancing faster every day, and if you don't adapt, you will find yourself left behind.

The same can be said for the design of your workplace. You must be open to technological improvements and remain up-to-date with furniture, office equipment, devices, and other advancements. You must also be forward-looking and consider how your workplace can continue to adapt to the adoption and integration of new technology. You never know what's next – the rise of voice solutions might bring a massive shift in the years to come.

DATA-DRIVEN DESIGN

Data-informed design will become a high-value asset to businesses aiming to adapt to a fast-paced, changing environment. As change continues to shape the workplace, previously siloed data becomes available to workplace strategists. These valuable information sources can help them make strategic decisions geared towards the growth of your business.

Infusing technology into data gathering will uncover business needs and dilemmas of the future, giving strategists insights on major issues. Data gathered through advanced technology can provide more information and accuracy, resulting in a more accurate diagnosis of problems and trouble spots, enabling better design solutions. Prioritise data collection and analysis in your business, and be open to what you may uncover.

COLLABORATION

Do you need to set up a ping pong table in your office? Well, Google did it, didn't they? The good news (or perhaps the bad) is that you don't need a ping pong table. What you need is what that table symbolises – collaboration or the catalyst of deeper relationships. It symbolises new ideas, friendships, mentorship, knowledge, casual collision, multidisciplinary collaboration and much more.

Collaboration shapes the way workplaces are designed and, more importantly, experienced. Embrace collaboration and you will promote creativity and drive productivity, because casual interactions can bring personal and business growth. A well-designed office can spark spontaneous conversations in the workplace, which lead to effective collaboration, deeper relationships, better wellbeing, and higher performance.

NEXT-GEN WORKPLACE

An inevitable culture shift is happening now, is forecast to grow and gain momentum. This culture shift is caused by the tilting scales of Baby Boomers gradually exiting the workforce versus Gen Z entering it in droves. Gen X and Millennials are taking a firm hold on the workplace, shaping it to reflect their values and ideals.

These values and ideals, such as sustainability, socialisation and flexibility, will hold greater weight when the brightest and best search for their next workplace. It's no longer just about the work and the tasks; it's now about purpose, meaning and culture too. Think about how you can integrate these causes and convictions into your workplace.

Disruption is certain. Now is a time of profound change in how office design affects and supports work. The guidance that a strategist can give an organisation is more valuable now than ever, and this work has only just begun. So, will you be pushed behind by this change, or will you ride with it, see it as an opportunity for growth and act on it? Are you ready for the future of work?

Social competencies are the new human currency

You may believe that your value at work is derived only from your experience, and that your digital and social competencies don't play a part in defining your success or your worth.

But with the exponential increase in the power of technology, the skills that cannot be replaced by artificial intelligence (AI) or automation, is our ability to be human, show empathy, connect and care. These soft skills will enable us to make a more valuable contribution in the future, as collaboration, compassion, and entrepreneurial skills make us uniquely human. These human skills are also less likely to be disrupted by artificial intelligence.

Organisations that embrace AI to automate codifiable and diagnostic tasks will free up the time of their people to be deployed towards other more valuable social tasks; an investment in building and strengthening social connections. Swinburne's Centre for the New Workforce identified in their 2019 report Peak Human Potential—Preparing Australia's Workforce For The Digital Future[5] that 38 percent of workers preferred to learn on the job over other learning formats. The report describes the need to develop these tacit learning environments, where knowledge can be shared and new skills acquired by observing the actions of colleagues:

A worker experimenting with new technologies and developing insights is 'tacit' learning in action. So too, is collaborating with others in ambiguous and dynamic environments on divergent problems. These tacit approaches to learning become even more important in the face of rapidly accelerating technologies because they can create new value faster.[5]

We can design our physical workplace environments to support and facilitate this implicit learning ability through collaborative work practices.

What business processes could your organisation automate in the future? What impact would that have on your people's time to create more valuable work by engaging in socially competent activities? How is your environment facilitating tacit learning?

In March 2019, McKinsey did a study that found 46 percent of current work activities in Australia would be displaced by automation by 2030. Swinburne's report identified that an overwhelming 51 percent of people are worried about losing their job to automation and AI. This equates to more than seven million Australians.

The opportunity for employers is to become a learning organisation, achieving a competitive advantage by embedding learning into the workforce, as 56 percent of working Australians expect that their work in the next five years will require skills they currently do not have. They found that the more digitally disrupted the industry, the more workers preferred to learn at work.

According to Sean Gallagher, Director of Swinburne Centre for the New Workforce and author of the report, "learning and work need to converge." By creating environments where we're facilitating on-the-job learning in a more tacit approach and identifying where AI, automation and digital disruption can be embraced, organisations can deliver greater value.

SO HOW DOES YOUR ORGANISATION THINK ABOUT THE OPPORTUNITIES THAT TECHNOLOGY WILL BRING IN THE NEXT FIVE TO TEN YEARS?

AND HOW IS YOUR ORGANISATION PREPARING YOUR PEOPLE WITH THE NEW SOCIAL SKILLS THEY WILL REQUIRE TO REMAIN RELEVANT IN THE FUTURE WORKPLACE?

The shifting nature of work
The impact of technology

The pandemic shocked the world in 2020, accelerating a way of working that had previously only been considered for a select few. The opportunity to work remotely and flexibly in a destination of our choosing and in a way conducive to family life was a luxury few were afforded.

As we packed up our belongings and carried them into our homes, we adapted to a way of working that some global corporations were already adopting. In January 2020, Twitter had already restructured their workplace managers to report to People and Culture, with a new focus on creating a "remote experience" for workers.[6] The pandemic only shifted the timeframe of this initiative from months to days.

What this transformation of work "place" has brought with it is the opportunity for organisations to reconsider the requirement for a physical workplace location, the role it plays and the impact it has on creating culture, connection and collaboration, when the physical activity of "work" has been demonstrated to be possible in a remote scenario.

This shift to embracing technology to work remotely has lifted the barrier; no longer constrained to geographical location, employees can now embrace the tree/sea change earlier, and employers have been provided global access to talent for their organisations to tap into the best of the best, no matter where they are in the world.

This shift has, in turn, brought with it a new set of challenges for organisations that are not prepared to manage remote teams. It is not purely about the individuals in management roles, but the organisational structures and processes that support them, from culture to recruitment, training and performance management systems.

Organisations that have traditionally operated on a presenteeism management model will likely struggle more and revert earlier to embracing the workplace as a management tool, in contrast to their counterparts who have adopted a *remote-first* or *distributed* work culture. In remote-first cultures, employees are attracted and recruited in a manner conducive to the autonomy of working in isolation. Systems, processes and training are constructed around supporting individuals, and other ways of developing culture are instilled into the organisation's fabric with the adoption of technology instead of being reliant on people's physical proximity.

As we've already discussed, organisations such as Automattic have, since their inception, embraced remote working with employees based across the world. Their autonomy-based employment model requires you to be a self-starter, invested in continual learning and challenging the status quo. These principles are not formed overnight. They are embedded in the company over the years, often from inception, and lay the foundation for the successful execution of an *office-free* organisation.

While technology has enabled distributed and remote-first work cultures, which have been dominating our thoughts since the early days of 2020's lockdowns, technology will bring other significant impacts (and opportunities) to our workplaces into the future.

With the rapid development of new technologies such as AI (artificial intelligence) infusing day-to-day tasks, the sci-fi projections seen in the movies no longer seem that distant from reality.

Bleeding into our everyday life, we are interacting with AI from Google searches and Xero's financial reconciliations, all the way through to ordering your dinner via Uber Eats. Our lives are being automated, enhanced and made more frictionless through AI. With that in mind:

1. What opportunities does automation present in your business?

2. What processes could be automated?

3. What will be changed, reduced, eliminated? How might your teams expand, contract, or be outsourced?

NOW, THE BIG QUESTION IS: HOW DOES THIS AUTOMATION IMPACT YOUR GROWTH, YOUR HEADCOUNT AND, MOST IMPORTANTLY, THE PHYSICAL WORKPLACE YOUR BUSINESS REQUIRES?

Organisations from accountants to architects are all being forced to rethink the role of automation in their business, the skill sets of the people employed, and the space required to support these new ways of working. It may also change the nature of our business and see us move into new sectors, new products and services to stay relevant and viable.

With AI replacing more and more of our menial tasks, the human skills that AI cannot replicate will need our workplaces to take on a new shape that supports these skills.

SPACES TO BRAINSTORM, CONNECT, COLLABORATE AND CREATE WILL BECOME THE CENTRAL NEED OF A BUSINESS, MAKING A TRANSFORMATIONAL SHIFT IN THE RATIOS OF OWNED VERSUS SHARED SPACE IN OUR WORK ENVIRONMENTS.

Workplace styles
– what are the options?

TRADITIONAL

MODERN

OPEN PLAN

HYBRID

REMOTE

ABW/AGILE

Where do you aspire to be?

When setting out to create your new workplace, many styles are available, sitting on a continuum from the more traditional through to a fully remote workplace.

Here I've outlined the options, giving you a general overview of what they are and how they work, industries that typically gravitate towards them and some of the pros and cons that come with them.

I'll preface this with the reminder that each organisation is different. You should make these decisions based on collating a data set from within your organisation that informs how your people work, so you can design a workplace that works for your people and your business.

	TRADITIONAL	OPEN PLAN	MODERN
OVERVIEW	Highly built form with lots of offices and a few workstations	The inverse of traditional	Open plan style work environment supplemented by a range of additional spaces to support both collaborative and quiet work activities
	Centres around individual owned spaces as opposed to shared "we" spaces	Predominantly workstations in an open design with limited offices for senior management	
			Large café/kitchen space
	Small tea point	Small tea point	
	Reception space	Reception space	Reception – manned or unmanned
	Meeting spaces for clients	Meeting spaces for clients	Meeting spaces for clients and for employees

OVERVIEW

ABW/AGILE	HYBRID	REMOTE
Modern style of work environment that provides a range of workspaces to suit a wide variety of tasks ranging from individual concentrative work through to brainstorming and robust conversations	Smaller workplace environment providing a physical presence for the organisation and to support employees in coming together	No physical workplace
	Empowers employees to work from a range of locations in addition to the workplace, including home, coworking space, local café, etc	Employees all work remotely
Employees choose workspace subject to the task to be performed	Workplace is designed to support a greater level of social interactivity, due to the nature of engagement occurring when in the space, ie more meetings, collaboration as opposed to individual work	Requires an entirely different business model to support the effective operation from recruitment, through to systems and processes and team structure and communication
Teams are located into Neighbourhoods to provide a sense of "home"	Supports employees who want to work five days in office	
Workpoints are provisioned on a ratio of people/workpoint determined by operational need	Workplace environment is constructed from a range of spaces supporting a variety of tasks with a higher ratio of collaboration and meeting style spaces supporting the nature of the work being undertaken "in the office" as opposed to "from home"	
	Deep, concentrative work to be typically carried out away from the office	
Large café/kitchen space	Office becomes a place of socialisation – internally and externally	
Reception – manned or unmanned	Large café/kitchen space	
Meeting spaces for clients and for employees	Reception – manned or unmanned	
	Meeting spaces for clients and for employees	

	TRADITIONAL	OPEN PLAN	MODERN
WORKPOINT OWNERSHIP	Allocated seating	Allocated seating	Allocated seating
COMPONENT PARTS	Offices Workstations Meeting rooms	Offices Workstations Meeting rooms	Offices Workstations Meeting rooms Collaboration spaces Quiet spaces Breakout spaces
INDUSTRY*	Legal, traditional finance-style businesses	Engineering, utilities, government, recruitment, accounting	Creative industries [marketing, advertising etc], technology, more progressive organisations
TECH	Doesn't require a lot of flexibility Tend to see fixed onsite servers and desktop computers	Doesn't require a lot of flexibility Tend to see fixed onsite servers and desktop computers	Doesn't require a lot of flexibility Shift to cloud based data storage and systems management

	ABW/AGILE	HYBRID	REMOTE
WORK SPACE OWNERSHIP	Unallocated seating; allocation of team/department/neighbourhoods	Unallocated seating; allocation of team/department/neighbourhoods	N/A
COMPONENT PARTS	Workstations Meeting rooms Collaboration spaces Quiet spaces Breakout spaces	Workstations Meeting rooms Collaboration spaces Quiet spaces Breakout spaces Home office setup	Home office setup
INDUSTRY*	Banking, fund management, utilities, more progressive organisations that have identified a mobile workforce that spend significant time away from the office	Many industries are now looking to this style of working off the enhanced flexibility identified by the pandemic – who still desire a "face to face" element of the work they do and a physical locational presence	Global software development organisations such as Automattic & Gitlab have been the pioneers in this space
TECH	Requires allocation of mobile technology to enable flexibility in work location Requires cloud based data storage, applications and systems management Consistent Wi-Fi throughout premises	Requires allocation of mobile technology to enable flexibility in work location Requires cloud based data storage, applications and systems management Consistent Wi-Fi throughout premises Workplace management tools to support booking systems and occupancy management	BYO device Requires cloud based data storage, applications and systems management

	TRADITIONAL	OPEN PLAN	MODERN
PROS	Supports deep individual, concentrative work	Cost effective real estate solution due to reduced area required with smaller footprint per person Knowledge of what's happening due to overhearing conversations	Cost effective real estate solution due to reduced area required with smaller footprint per person Knowledge of what's happening due to overhearing conversations Supports individuals with additional workspaces to suit the desired task required Supports a collaborative culture and development of community through social connection
CONS	Prohibitive to collaboration, team building and cross functional knowledge sharing Costly to adapt the space to support growth Prohibitive to flexible and adaptable work styles	Can be noisy, unsupportive of deep, concentrative work due to surrounding conversations, phone calls etc Clear hierarchy of management, undermines an egalitarian culture	Is more expensive than open plan to fitout due to additional spaces and furniture styles

	ABW/AGILE	HYBRID	REMOTE
PROS	Cost-effective real estate solution due to reduction in floor area required to support headcount	Further reduces real estate requirements due to increased head count per sqm due to utilisation of "other" work environments	Ability to access a pool of global talent without restriction to location
	Agility and flexibility in supporting organisational growth and contraction through behavioural management and workpoint ratios	Agility and flexibility in organisational head count growth due to work style behaviours	No real estate costs
	Agility in team based environments to assemble and dissolve based on project and workforce requirements	Empowers employees to work where and how best supports their work needs	Empowers autonomous individuals who want to work from anywhere
	Empowers employees to work where and how best supports their work needs		Supports asynchronous work styles
CONS	Is more expensive to fitout on a $/sqm rate, however often offsets the lettable area required	Is more expensive to fitout on a $/sqm rate due to the required workspace styles – more meeting rooms, breakout and collaboration spaces, furniture etc	Social capital, and organisational culture require a management program to be implemented to support ongoing development
	Requires a change management process to be implemented and managed to support behavioural transition	Requires a holistic approach to work style and new team routines, rituals, workflows and rules of engagement to be implemented supporting team culture and social capital	Transition to this style of environment from a 'physical' work environment is a large shift and requires a completely different business model – see page 54.
	Requires a change in management style from "presenteeism" based management given team mobility		

*The types of industries categorised here are typical in nature and do not represent all organisations of these industries

Workplace Management Technology – enabling data-driven design

With the progressive shifts that continue to evolve in our world of workplaces, our ability to observe, analyse and interpret how our people are engaging with them is paramount in enabling us to optimise their ongoing performance.

Here is where the use of workplace management technology comes in. This technology can enable everything in your organisation, from booking a workpoint to ordering a coffee. However, it's not just the enhancement of the user experience that occurs here; it's also the data insights that these systems are continuously collecting, enabling you to better understand and in turn predict the needs of your people and the organisation, and as a result the ongoing use and likely adaptation of your space.

Typically a combination of both software (apps, cloud platforms) and hardware solutions (beacons, sensors, switches), technology enables organisations to manage the utilisation of the workplace. The integration of this technology within the workplace also allows organisations to gather real-time data insights into how the space is being used, and by whom.

Everything from access to the building to meeting rooms and desk booking in its simplest form, through to enhanced integrations enabling automatic meeting room recognition and meeting commencement, can be monitored and managed.

HERE ARE A FEW SCENARIOS TO GIVE YOU CONTEXT ON THE TYPE OF DATA COLLECTED.

Let's say you want to know which meeting rooms are in hot demand. The technology can provide you with data on:

- When are peak demand periods
- How many people are in each meeting
- Which technology is being utilised to perform the meeting
- Whether a meeting room designed for ten people regularly only has four to six people using it

Perhaps you want to keep track of occupancy levels throughout the day and week. Monitoring the ebbs and flows of traffic through the workplace can give you a sense of the organisation's rhythm, such as:

- How many people are in the office on a given day
- Are particular teams in the office on particular days
- What time of day are people in the office
- Where do people prefer to sit

Maybe you've noticed that the collaboration space with the stand-up table and the expensive interactive whiteboard is hardly ever used, but the working lounge with the whiteboard and screen is always full. The technology can support exact data on:

- How regularly does each space gets used
- For what duration
- What technology is being utilised
- The number of people utilising it at each meeting

These are just some examples of what insights can be observed through the use of workplace management technology.

BUT WHY WOULD WE WANT THIS INFORMATION?

When we have this level of insight into how our workplaces are being used, we know how to enhance them. We are armed with accurate data that can support us in further optimising the space for the people using it. We can engage in meaningful conversations about why people are using a space in a particular way, given our collected data.

In the past, this data has either been collected from conversations between employees and consultants/facilities teams/managers or through manual observation and recording. The challenge with this is it's time-consuming and intensive, but when asking people how they use their space, it's very subjective. Often employees can inform you that they spend 90 percent of their day at their desk; however, when you monitor their actual utilisation of their desk over two weeks, the results present a very different picture, often one closer to only 50 percent of their time at their desk.

It's taken you two weeks to gather this information, and it is only a snapshot in time.

Through this technology, you gain an accurate, indisputable bank of data over an extended and ongoing period. This data enables you to make informed and educated recommendations on how to optimise how the space is performing to better support the needs and performance of your people.

LET'S TAKE THE MEETING ROOM DATA SET AS OUR EXAMPLE:

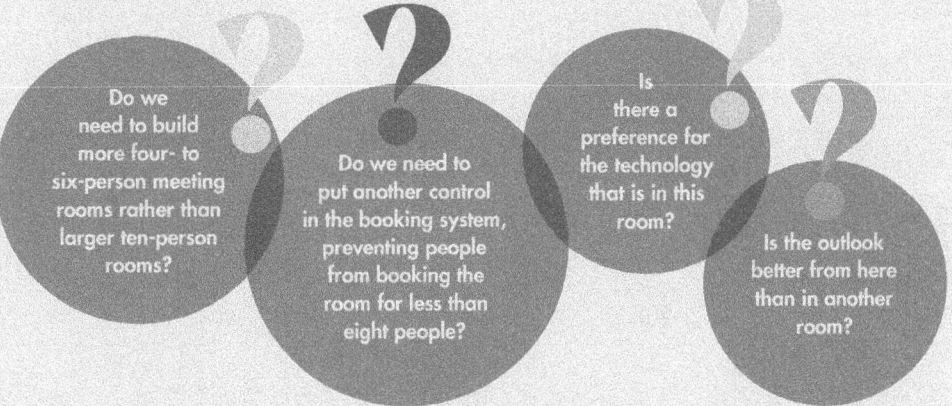

These are all possible reasons why that room gets booked over another. However, we would not have been able to identify it without having this data. Now you can start to ask more questions and make an informed decision on how to address it.

If we start looking at the desk-booking system, we might see data that leads us to ask questions.

"We can see that most people are coming in on a Wednesday, putting our desk availability under considerable strain. Can we talk with Team X about moving their team office day to Tuesday to alleviate this pressure?"

"We've noticed that as our headcount has grown over the past twelve months, our workplace utilisation has only shifted slightly. Based on our pending lease expiry in the next two years and the current data, should we recommend the Board exercise the two-year extension on the lease without requiring additional space?"

Let's take the collaboration setting now. If one setting gets utilised more than another, it will make sense to consider removing the furniture setup and replacing it with another in higher demand. Sure, the cost of the furniture may be a deterrent. Still, if we consider the rent we are paying on an underperforming space and the productivity impact on our people not having the correct tools to do their job, surely that makes for a sound economic argument.

All of this data can support you in making educated and informed decisions about your real estate portfolio and optimising your work environment. It can inform team and neighbourhood planning, future workplace design, leasing decisions and workforce management, aside from the fundamental ability to enable your people to have confidence that there will be a desk for them in the office when they arrive.

Looking ten years into what the future holds is no easy task when we don't have a crystal ball. There is a lot to consider as you have already read. This means that mapping out what your organisation and the future of work in general, will look like for you requires more input than you alone can provide.

YOU MUST BRING TOGETHER THE BRAINS TRUST IN YOUR BUSINESS TO LOOK AT THIS FROM SEVERAL ANGLES AND DEVELOP A VISION FOR THE FUTURE.

Every business is unique. While you may be an accounting, legal or engineering firm in a market of other accounting, legal or engineering firms, several elements are unique to your business that create your individual identity. Your purpose, vision, values, people, departments and clients are distinctive to your business, so it's essential to have clarity on these individual elements to develop a vision for your workplace that will work for your organisation.

Creating this vision is a "top-down" approach. Without the input and buy-in from the senior leaders in the business, the desired workplace and accommodation strategy will falter as the leaders are not wholeheartedly supporting the transformation that is about to take place.

This means that the first person on the agenda is the CEO, General Manager, or Managing Director. Alignment with the broader strategic plan for the organisation, their vision of the future, where the business will be operating, how it will be doing business and who it will be serving all play a part in the vision for the workplace. They will likely have a strong position on the workplace style they wish to explore and feel that the organisation can embrace and that employees are willing to adapt to.

Next on your list is the CFO, the money (wo)man. They will be in control of the budget and formulate one that aligns with the business, forecast projections of the various business units and have a clear understanding of the financial impacts or capital raising required to deliver the project. They are also likely to be heavily invested in the leasing negotiations, so bringing them onboard early will ensure that all parties are on the same page. The likelihood of disheartening conversations about money and scope at the later project stages gets minimised. We now have a corporate vision, and we know our budget.

The next step is to get clear on the people who will be occupying this space. Depending on your business, this department could go by a few titles: office manager, human resources, people and culture, employee experience, community, or perhaps even something more creative! Engaging with this team will enable you to understand the people operating in this space, the interdepartmental interaction between groups, personality types, generational profiles and specific operational requirements. This is also where clarity about the organisation size and projected growth will come from, along with insights into palatable

workstyle models that will ultimately affect your decisions and final lease area requirements.

One department that often goes overlooked in establishing the stakeholder group required to inform the future needs of the office is the IT department. IT are often thought of as a service provider within organisations and involved only once the workplace solution is determined to "plug everything in." But without the integration of the appropriate networks, tools and equipment, many workstyle models will fail due to the lack of mobility inherent in the technology solution of an organisation. By bringing the IT team to the table early, you can be informed about current equipment limitations, software constraints, network security concerns, adaptability of existing service contracts, and budgetary challenges in rolling out the required new tech that can cripple a beautifully envisioned workplace solution. Without the right tech, you are creating a "dumb" workplace.

THE FINAL GROUP YOU NEED TO ENGAGE IN THIS JOURNEY IS… EVERYONE!

This is the most opportune time to create a cultural shift in how your organisation works together and iron out any issues in team communication, facilities, tools and general operation of your environment. You may have an excellent handle on this, but you will be surprised by what you may learn by asking people what they think and want. Often this is where I see the strongest resistance in leadership against engaging with the broader organisation, out of fear that they will be required to act on all the requests made.

The opportunity here is to provide your people with a voice, create a channel to communicate, and for leaders to understand deeper concerns within the company to make informed decisions. Not every request needs to be actioned, however it can be acknowledged and responded to.

THE INSIGHTS GATHERED FROM THIS LEVEL OF ENGAGEMENT OFFER THE OPPORTUNITY TO TRULY TRANSFORM YOUR ORGANISATION AND MOVE THE ENTIRE BUSINESS FORWARD COLLECTIVELY.

Throughout the process of creating your workplace, there will be information required by your consulting team and decisions to be made, so it's worth establishing a stakeholder group to address these. This group may be formed with the afore mentioned leaders or several other department heads.

Either way, this group will be responsible for executing the project vision and ensuring that all decisions are moved forward in alignment with this vision. The underlying theme we are trying to tease out is this:

- **OUR WORKPLACES ARE A BUSINESS ASSET.**

- **THEY ARE THE CONTAINER THAT ENABLE PEOPLE TO PERFORM.**

So what is the work that we want them to do, and how do we want them to feel when doing it? What experience do we want to have at work?

Enlisting the expertise, insights and perspectives of a diverse range of people across all facets of the business minimises the possibility of overlooking a critical element of the business operations; it also ensures the opportunity to create an optimised workplace that transforms the company for the future is exponential. •

Your workplace *is a space* that connects your organisation, your *communities* and your *people*

— MELISSA MARSDEN

Strategy Kickoff

ALL THE ANSWERS TO YOUR WORKPLACE STRATEGY EXIST WITHIN YOUR ORGANISATION...

you just need to unlock them.

Start collating the following information so that you have a clear picture of your current workplace.

- **EMPLOYEE LIST**
  Include the following:
  - Age
  - Gender
  - Department
  - Tenure

- **ORGANISATION CHART**
  Understand the various departments in your business and how they relate to one another – how does communication and information flow?

- **FLOOR PLANS OF YOUR EXISTING FITOUT**
  And the current seating plans for your teams/departments.

- **STYLE OR BRAND GUIDES**
  What is the visual language of your business? Colour, tone, aesthetic.

- **EXISTING CULTURE**
  Map out the history and culture of the business.
  What are the organisations values? What is your story? (See chapter 2)

- **GROWTH PROJECTIONS**
  Are you expanding or contracting? Does this vary across the business?

Chapter Huddle

**THE PAST INFORMS THE FUTURE.
UNLOCK THE DATA IN YOUR ORGANISATION.**

YOUR WORKPLACE IS AN *ASSET* – NOT A LIABILITY ON YOUR BALANCE SHEET.

It's a unique opportunity to tell your story; who you are, what you care about, and what you stand for. Your space is the physical representation of the brand experience your organisation wants everyone to feel. It can connect your people to the organisational purpose and values, influence behaviour, and enable the successful execution of your corporate strategy. And, most importantly, it can enable or hinder the performance of your most expensive asset: your people.

YOUR WORKPLACE CAN DIRECTLY IMPACT YOUR BOTTOM LINE.

It does so by driving significant returns on your investment by enabling cross-functional communication, increased communication, and enhanced performance by providing the right "tools."

THE DESIGN OF YOUR WORKPLACE CAN INFLUENCE THE MINDSET OF YOUR PEOPLE AND OF YOUR BUSINESS AS A WHOLE.

It can take slow, rigid and outdated companies and transform them into agile, adaptable and responsive organisations. Think of the physical design of your space as a reflection of the heart and mind of your business.

ALL THE DATA AND INSIGHTS YOU NEED TO INFORM THE FOUNDATIONS OF YOUR WORKPLACE STRATEGY EXIST WITHIN YOUR BUSINESS.

You just need to know how to unlock them. Doing so will equip you to create a well-considered and planned workspace that can radiate your culture, connect people to the organisation's purpose and align behaviours to the values, influencing how people "show up." Your workplace can encourage a culture responsive to your company's strategic vision and drive tangible outcomes in how your people engage with your business.

WITHOUT THE EXECUTIVE LEADERSHIP TEAM ONBOARD, YOUR STRATEGY WILL FALTER.

Successful workplace strategy execution requires consultation and buy-in from every level of the organisation, starting at the top.

THE FUTURE OF WORK IS HERE. HOW ARE YOU GOING TO MAKE YOUR WORKPLACE WORK FOR YOUR BUSINESS?

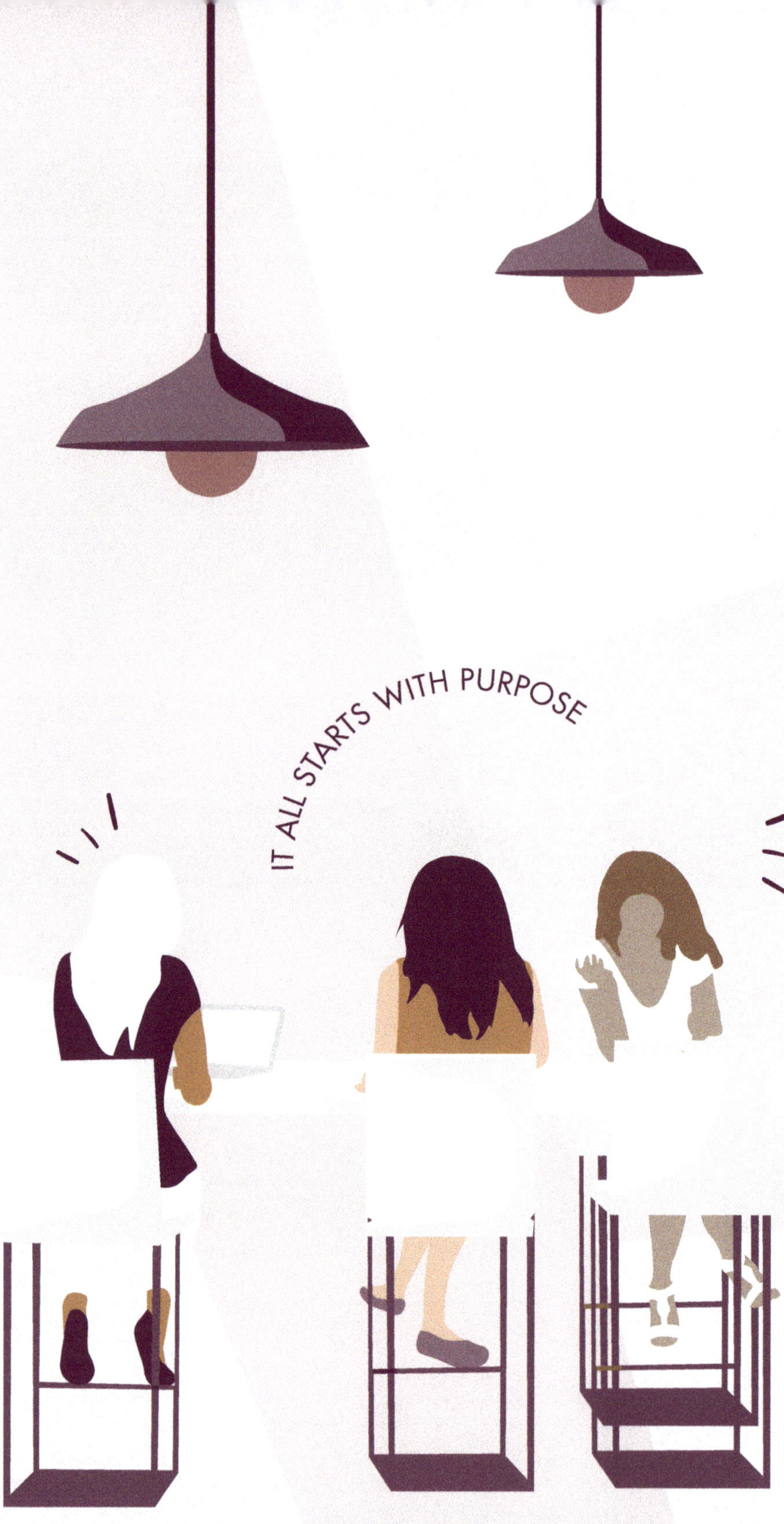
IT ALL STARTS WITH PURPOSE

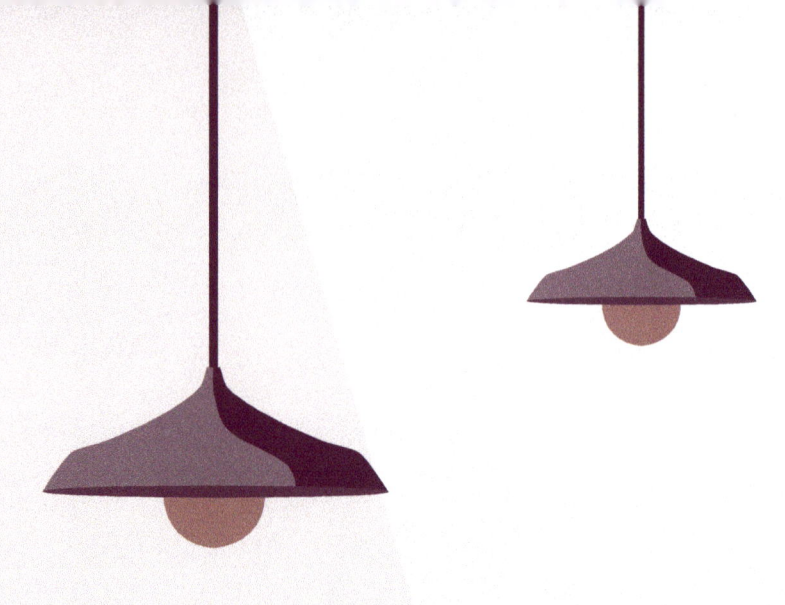

CHAPTER TWO

use your space to tell your story

The logo is an apple with a bite out of it. It's a simple icon, often white or silver, but Apple's excellent branding goes beyond its instantly recognisable logo. When we consider how an Apple product makes you feel, we experience the brand's personality. Apple's designs create an experience of inspiring imagination, of your liberty regained, innovation, passion, hopes, dreams, and aspirations. Through technology, Apple's late founder Steve Jobs aimed to return "the power to the people," and he wove that purpose throughout every facet of the company.

Apple's brand experience is also about simplicity. It uses intuitive design to eliminate complexity, create responsive and interconnective products, and provide seamless communication between devices. These products have rewritten how we think about technology and its capability, and they have positioned Apple as a product for the people, the choice of designers, and a supportive force for individuals and businesses as they strive to achieve their goals.

Now think about the experience of doing business with Apple. The store's design is open, bright and transparent, enabling customers to see front to back, one side to the other. The furniture is neatly ordered in rows, and the product display tables feel reassuringly familiar; they look like dining tables but with no chairs.

There is someone to greet me as I walk through the door and direct me toward what I want. However, this person's presence is more of a courtesy than a necessity as the products are laid out in groups, making it easy for me to navigate between the different models. And because of the transparency of the store, I can quickly identify where I need to go. I can interact with the products, try them out, play with them and see how they work together. It's a no-pressure environment where I can play as much as I like and for as long as I want without being hassled – and yet there is always someone "just there" to answer any of my questions.

Making a purchase is an easy transaction. It happens right there on the spot; it's mobile, with no centralised location and no queuing. My receipt is emailed to me, making it easy to file or forward for expense claims. Apple stores also offer the Genius Bar, where I can learn how to use my device or have someone help me set it up.

EACH OF THESE TOUCHPOINTS IS DELIBERATE AND DESIGNED TO COMMUNICATE APPLE'S PURPOSE:

to *challenge* the status quo and think *differently*

Now, compare that to other computer manufacturers. What other computer brand has a store in a shopping centre?

WHAT OTHER TECHNOLOGY COMPANY WILL TEACH YOU HOW TO USE ITS PRODUCTS FOR FREE?

Apple's brand is so much more than a logo. Similarly, your brand is more than your logo or suite of PMS colours. It is the experience you want people to have when doing business with you.

AND IT ALL STARTS WITH PURPOSE.

Purpose-led businesses are not a new concept; however, they are gaining traction in the current climate. In a shift from commercially oriented models that exist purely for profit and delivering stakeholder return, purpose-led organisations are leading a new era of work, connecting their employees to more meaningful work and positively impacting society.

The purpose of an organisation is the reason it exists beyond making money: who it exists to serve and the positive impact it wishes to make on the world. An organisation's purpose gives it meaning, an outcome that employees can feel fulfilled by and a sense that they are contributing to making the world a better place. Making this tangible for employees is about connecting what they do every day to the organisation's purpose, making it real and giving them a direct line of sight between their individual actions and that of the company as a whole.

When NASA was in the Space Race with the Soviet Union, President John F. Kennedy visited the facility and asked a janitor what he did there. The man's response? "I'm helping to put a man on the moon." The janitor didn't see his role in the organisation as simplistically as keeping the premises clean. He was deeply connected to the overarching purpose of putting a man on the moon and believed that he was an integral part of the team making this happen.

Purpose flows through an organisation, influencing each layer, informing, leading, defining and guiding the next. It is ultimately what is driving the decision making of the company. While the organisation's values guide our choices, our purpose is the "why" underpinning them. It is why we do what we do. As leaders of organisations, we have the opportunity to connect each and every employee to the company's overarching purpose and demonstrate how the daily tasks they perform impact the mission.

"Your why is a purpose, cause or belief," says Simon Sinek in his bestselling book *Start With Why*. "It's the very reason your organisation exists." That is why it helps to align and attract people who, as Sinek puts it, believe what you believe. As we all seek to find a more meaningful existence, our employer's organisational values and purpose become a significant factor in determining our career decisions – and that means your company's purpose can be an excellent employee attraction and retention tool.

In an employment market with numerous accounting firms, your purpose or "why" becomes the foundation of why a candidate chooses to work with your firm over the one across the road, even when there is a differential in pay.

And beyond making a positive impact on the world, a sound purpose can also be a solid commercial driver within your organisation. Research has shown that people with a strong sense of purpose tend to be more resilient and better recover from adverse events.

PURPOSEFUL PEOPLE ALSO LIVE LONGER AND HEALTHIER LIVES. THEY ARE:[1]

- 2.5 times more likely to be free of dementia
- 22 percent less likely to exhibit risk factors for stroke
- 52 percent less likely to have experienced a stroke

The impact that this can then have on an organisation, according to McKinsey, is that respondents who indicate they are "living their purpose" at work are much more likely than those not doing so to sustain or improve their levels of work effectiveness, demonstrating four times higher levels of engagement and five times higher levels of wellbeing.[2]

Sadly, however, I see companies make the same mistakes over and over again:

- They see their brand as little more than a logo and a suite of colours set by marketing
- The organisation's purpose isn't clearly defined or used in decision making
- The story and personality of the business aren't articulated clearly enough for the team to be connected to it
- The "feel" of the workplace doesn't align with the aspirations of the business

**Fortunately, these are all solvable problems.
Let's begin with purpose.**

CHAPTER 2 | USE YOUR SPACE TO TELL YOUR STORY

Discovering your organisation's *purpose*

An organisation's purpose is evident in its shared values and experiences and the stories that get retold like legends. These things give employees a collective sense of meaning, pride and belonging.

WHEN PURPOSE FLOWS THROUGH EVERY LAYER OF THE BUSINESS, IT DRIVES THE DECISION MAKING OF THE COMPANY.

And while the purpose of an organisation typically starts with the founder, with growth, time, acquisitions, mergers and generations of leadership, leaders may need to rediscover their organisation's purpose and reconnect "what we do" with "why we do it."

If you want to rediscover your purpose, you can download my worksheet at **melissamarsden.com.au/TheNextWorkplace_resources** to guide you in getting started; however, I strongly encourage you to spread the net a little wider.

Engage with your leadership team and ask them what they believe is the organisation's purpose, the "why" of what you do. While you are likely to find differing opinions and stances on priorities, you will also likely find an emerging story, a commonality that weaves itself through each person's perspective. Capture these words, phrases and thoughts and craft them into a statement that reflects the essence of the story.

Communicate this story back to your leadership team, invite feedback, and gauge how it lands and their body language as they receive it. Using this power of collective creation, iterate, evolve and improve until you have a statement that feels right for your organisation. Connecting with your organisation's purpose can solidify your identity.

You will likely find that this will uncover other aspirations for positive impact and social good, solidifying the organisation's identity. In essence, it is a story. *Your story*.

SO WHAT IS THE STORY THAT YOU WANT TO TELL?

Defining Your Brand

Your brand is more than your logo, colour palette and style guide. It is how people experience your business, both your clients and your employees. Your brand reflects elements that are as natural and inherent as they are deliberate and intentional. Your brand emerges from stories of why the business was established, what it intended to do, the people it intended to help and support, the motivations of the founders and the gap in the market it was trying to fill. Once established, it evolves to become more deliberate and intentional in the language used and the brand persona it is fulfilling.

Every organisation has its own unique personality. Its own way of expressing itself and its style. It may be young, fun, energetic and light or strong, stable and secure. It may be comforting, empathetic or compassionate. Each of these descriptions conjures up emotive images of how you would experience the organisation and its brand. Every organisation also has its own brand archetype.

Founded in the 20th Century and rooted in Greek mythology, the term "brand archetype" was coined by psychologist Carl Jung.

PS. My brand archetype is The Sage.

There are twelve archetypes:

- THE INNOCENT
- THE EVERYMAN
- THE HERO
- THE OUTLAW
- THE EXPLORER
- THE CREATOR
- THE RULER
- THE MAGICIAN
- THE LOVER
- THE CAREGIVER
- THE JESTER
- THE SAGE

and they represent the four quadrants of brand connections.

1. To leave a legacy
2. To pursue connection
3. To provide structure
4. To explore spirituality

These twelve Archetypes enable us to connect and build immediate understanding based on what Jung described as "an unconscious understanding of behavioral patterns." They allow organisations to make deeper connections that elevate them beyond the features, benefits and cost of their products and services, allowing them to create a point of difference and stand out in a market.

An organisation will typically strongly reflect one of these brand archetypes, supported by a further one or two, creating a unique mix of qualities, attributes and messaging.

Where does your organisation fit?

BRAND ARCHETYPES FORM A STRONG FOUNDATION OF THE STORY YOU WANT TO COMMUNICATE IN YOUR BUSINESS: WHO YOU SERVE, THE LEGACY YOU WISH TO LEAVE, AND WHO YOU WANT TO ATTRACT.

> When you can articulate your story, personality, and brand archetype, you are defining your brand.

– MELISSA MARSDEN

INFUSE YOUR SPACE WITH YOUR STORY

What is your brand story,

AND HOW IS IT SHOWING UP IN YOUR BUSINESS?

Every organisation has a unique story to tell: how the business started, the reason it started, the growth trajectory, and the hurdles that needed to be overcome.

These parts of the story are unique to your organisation and have moulded, guided and shaped your organisation into what it is today. By reflecting on this, you can begin to articulate your organisation's transformation. Here's an example.

case study
Plantation Homes

Plantation Homes is one of Queensland's most awarded builders, constructing quality designed homes to suit a variety of block sizes and shapes for everyone from first-time home buyers through to empty nesters looking to downsize.

Over a period of seven years, the COMUNiTI Crew and I completed four evolutions of their workplace to accommodate the expansion and elevation of the brand in Queensland. These projects saw the creation of a new workplace environment, a building services rejuvenation, a modular expansion of the building and the creation of a premium client showroom experience, the Design Studio.

the problem

When we first started working with Plantation Homes, their workplace environment did not reflect the beautiful homes they constructed for their clients. The drab work environment their employees experienced every day bore no resemblance to the stylish, well-designed, luxury, quality product they were providing for their clients.

The space was tired and run-down, with only minor improvements made over the previous fifteen to twenty years.

Departments were walled into individual cubicles, offices lined all the external glazing, and there were only three very distinct space typologies – meeting room, office and workstation – serviced by a simple tea point. The space reflected none of the qualities, values or aspirations of the organisation, leaving the employees with little relationship to the clientele and premium offering they were providing.

Due to the cellular nature of the office construction, there was no visible transparency across the floor of the office, creating a rabbit warren of nooks. The impact of this workplace was that the floor area was significantly under-utilised, departments were siloed, impacting the performance of operations throughout the business, and there was no visibility across the floor, affecting the availability of natural light.

As the business expanded, the space no longer supported the workforce requirements, for both office-based administrative employees and transient site-based employees. And the colour studio was tired and no longer represented the premium product delivered by Plantation Homes.

> WE NOW HAVE A PERFECT WORKPLACE WHERE OUR EMPLOYEES FEEL INSPIRED AND CONNECTED TO THE END PRODUCT WE DELIVER IN OUR AWARD WINNING HOMES. IT'S FABULOUS KNOWING EACH DEPARTMENT FEELS PROUD OF OUR BRAND, REFLECTING THE CARE AND QUALITY THAT WE PASS ONTO EACH OF OUR HOME OWNERS.
>
> – DI GAFFNEY, PLANTATION DESIGN STUDIO MANAGER.

the solution

BRING THE ESSENCE OF THE BUSINESS IN

The new workplace design was inspired by the style and sophistication of the buildings Plantation Homes was delivering to its clients. This alignment connected the office-based employees with the end user and the homeowner, and allowed both parties to experience a Plantations Homes space. We wanted the staff to feel proud of the product they were delivering and the quality and service they provided. Over the course of the four projects, this was achieved through:

The Colour and Material Palette
- Soft blue hues were introduced to the work environment, complemented by warm timbers
- Textural upholstery on the workstation screens
- Commercial-grade carpets that were plusher and more textural, with a residential essence to their aesthetic
- Residentially styled wallpapers and artwork
- Warm timber decking
- Stone benchtops and textural tiling

The Kitchen & Cafe
- Adapting the kitchen from a popular home design within the office environment
- An outdoor alfresco dining space, reminiscent of the indoor/outdoor dining spaces of their homes
- A collaborative cafe space supporting casual working, transient site-based employees and company gatherings in an alfresco styled space

Furniture and Fittings

- Introducing more residentially styled furniture to complement the space, from lounges to bar stools, internally and externally evoking the feeling of a residential home space
- Domestic-style light fittings to create a feeling of intimacy and domesticity
- Skylights to bring natural lighting into the heart of the space
- Upgraded lighting and mechanical systems throughout to enhance user experience and sustainability

The Design Studio

- A journey for the aspiring home owner to experience the quality and styles of key home features, from kitchens to bathrooms to fixtures and fittings
- A space that connected the client with the feeling of their future home, through tactile connection with materials, finishes and spaces
- Consultant workspaces to engage the client in the process, elevating the customer experience

These features were coupled with a modern workplace design that broke down the departmental barriers, opened up the floor for complete visibility and transparency, connected teams,

and introduced alternative work zones such as quiet rooms and collaborative spaces to support various task requirements.

Above: The reception space is warm and welcoming, like entering your own living room.

Right: The Design Studio takes the aspiring home owner on a journey to experience all the spaces of their future home and the quality of the product from Plantation Homes.

Below: The consultant workspaces engage with the home owner in a collaborative and intimate space.

CASE STUDY – PLANTATION HOMES

the result

REDUCED STAFF TURNOVER AND SICK LEAVE

From the initial project delivery, Plantation Homes observed immediate re-engagement from the team. The kitchen became a welcoming space for all team members and encouraged conversation between individuals and groups, increasing cross-departmental interaction. While employees were apprehensive about the shift to a modern work environment, they commented on how the desks were a nice size and that the new space felt "light, open and airy."

However, the true result that this workplace design created was the impact on employee retention. Staff turnover was reduced by 60 percent in the twelve months following occupancy of the new space, and sick leave was reduced by 45 percent. As a side note, the new workplace also reduced power consumption costs by 25 percent.

the mood board

The internal cafe is designed to bring the outside in, replicating the alfresco spaces of their homes.

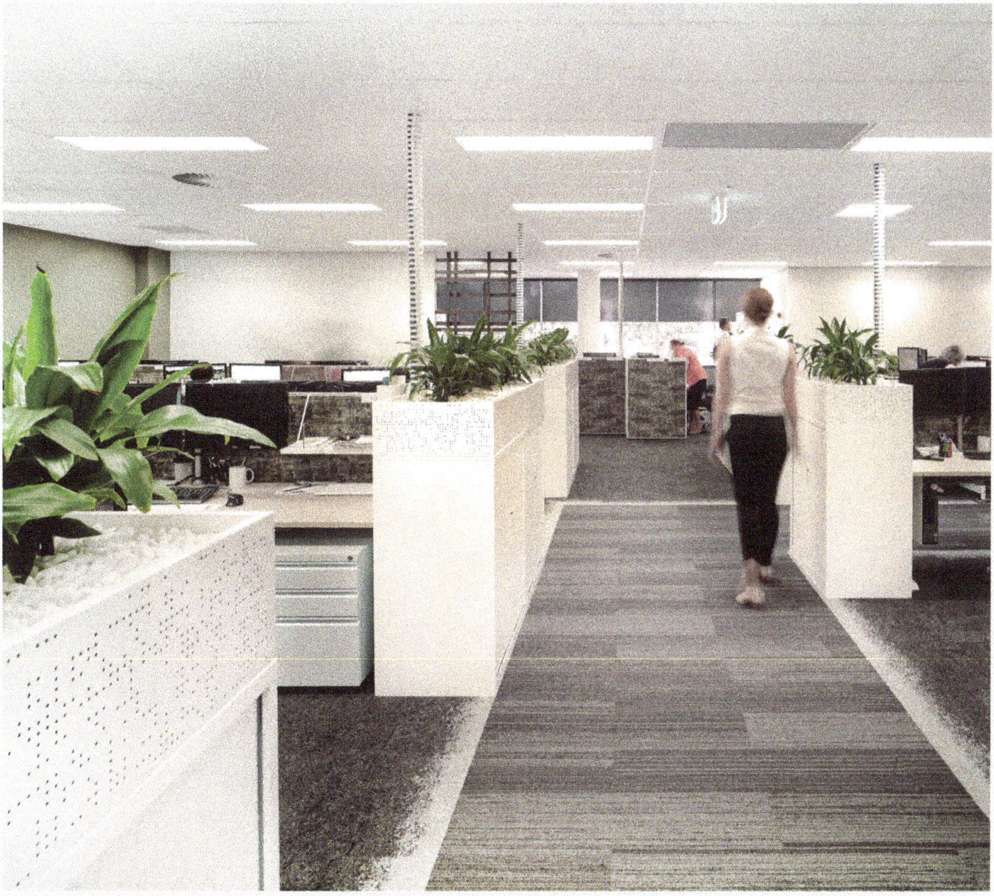

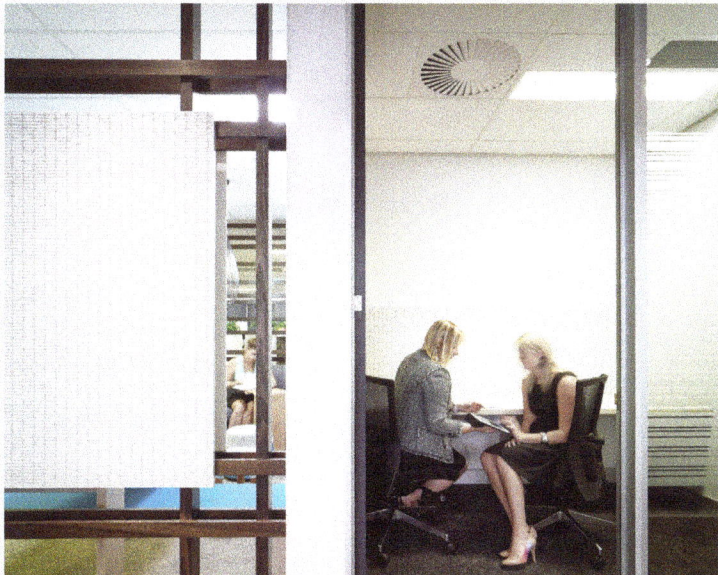

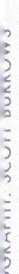

Above: The colour palette embraces a softer, more residential hue while still reflecting a corporate professionalism.

Left: Quiet rooms provide employees with alternative workspaces to support individual work and 1:1 conversations.

PHOTOGRAPHY: SCOTT BURROWS

Define Your Story

BEGIN TO COMMUNICATE YOUR **UNIQUE STORY** AND LAY THE FOUNDATION FOR YOUR **FUTURE WORKPLACE** BY ANSWERING THE FOLLOWING QUESTIONS.

- When did the business start?
- What were the frustrations about your industry that you thought you could solve by starting the business?
- Would you say you found a gap in the market, an emerging trend or even an emerging industry?
- How long have you been in business?
- Who were/are the founders?
- What did the early days look like? Was there struggle?
- How quickly did you grow? What did that look like?
- Who did you look up to/aspire to be like?
- What were/are your non-negotiables in business? The principles you operate by?
- What are the values of the organisation?

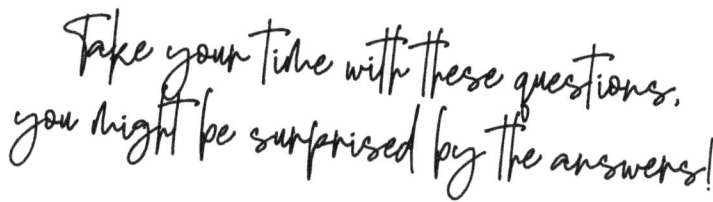
Take your time with these questions, you might be surprised by the answers!

- Who have been/are your key clients/markets?
- Why did you feel that your business is the best one to solve these problems?
- What does your business actually do? What are you in the business of?
- Did you experience any adversity in the beginning?
- How did you come up with the name of your business?
- What kind of growth are you experiencing, and how do you quantify that growth? Revenue? Profit? Employees? Locations?
- How many staff do you have?
- Do you have contractors/freelancers? What does this offer your business?
- What is the vision for the business? Where are you going?
- What have you learned from being in business?
- What do you wish you had done differently?
- What do you love most about being in business?
- What frustrates you the most about your industry? About the world? Environment? Politics? Society?

Discover your organisation's *personality*

JUST AS WE ARE **ATTRACTED** TO ANOTHER HUMAN'S TRAITS, QUALITIES, AND CHARACTERISTICS, WE ARE ATTRACTED TO THESE SAME PERSONALITY TRAITS IN **BRANDS.**

We look for qualities that seem familiar, that we aspire to or desire. By identifying and articulating your unique brand personality, you can communicate to your clients, customers, suppliers and employees what it's like to do business with you.

Perhaps you are fun, outgoing and energetic, or strong, staid and reserved. Whatever your personality, by articulating it you can begin to frame the context of what it is like to engage with you, which can be communicated by creating a feeling. We can then use these feelings to build out the aesthetic direction for your workplace to connect the senses, and guide how we want people to feel when they work with you.

Using the list of words on the next page, circle any that resonate with your business. Write a list of five to ten words that you feel most strongly communicate the unique personality of your business.

Tick the words

- Accountable
- Active
- Adaptable
- Adventurous
- Affable
- Affectionate
- Agreeable
- Alert
- Altruistic
- Ambitious
- Analytical
- Appropriate
- Articulate
- Artistic
- Aspiring
- Assertive
- Attentive
- Attractive
- Authoritative
- Balanced
- Bold
- Brainy
- Brave
- Bright
- Brilliant
- Bubbly
- Calm
- Captivating
- Careful
- Caring
- Charming
- Cheerful
- Clever
- Commanding
- Committed
- Compassionate
- Competitive
- Concise
- Confident
- Conscious
- Conservative
- Considerate
- Cooperative
- Coordinated
- Courageous
- Courteous
- Decisive
- Dedicated
- Dependable
- Determined
- Devoted
- Direct
- Disciplined
- Driven
- Dynamic
- Eager
- Edgy
- Educated
- Efficient
- Egalitarian
- Elegant
- Eloquent
- Empathetic
- Encouraging
- Energetic
- Engaged
- Enterprising
- Enthusiastic
- Entrepreneurial
- Even-handed
- Expressive
- Fair
- Faithful
- Feisty
- Feminine
- Flexible
- Fluent
- Focused
- Forgiving
- Friendly
- Fun
- Funny
- Generous
- Genius
- Gentle
- Giving
- Glamorous
- Glowing
- Good
- Graceful
- Grateful
- Gregarious
- Handsome
- Happy
- Hardworking
- Hardy
- Healthy
- Hearty
- Helpful
- Honest
- Humble
- Humorous
- Imaginative
- Independent
- Industrious
- Influential
- Informed
- Innovative
- Insightful
- Inspiring
- Intellectual
- Intelligent
- Interested
- Intuitive
- Involved
- Joyful
- Judicious
- Just
- Keen
- Kind
- Knowledgeable
- Leader
- Liberal
- Light-hearted
- Likable
- Logical
- Lovely
- Loving
- Loyal
- Lucky
- Luxurious
- Magnificent
- Mannered
- Masculine
- Mature
- Methodical
- Mindful
- Moderate
- Modest
- Motivated
- Mystical
- Natty
- Neat
- Neutral
- Nice
- Noble
- Nurturing
- Obedient
- Objective
- Observant
- Old-Fashioned
- Open
- Optimistic
- Orderly
- Organised
- Original
- Outgoing
- Passionate
- Patient
- Perceptive
- Poised
- Polite
- Positive
- Practical
- Precise
- Productive
- Professional
- Proper
- Punctual
- Qualified
- Questioning
- Quick
- Quiet
- Quirky
- Rational
- Realistic
- Rebellious
- Receptive
- Relaxed
- Reliable
- Resourceful
- Respected
- Responsible
- Romantic
- Rugged
- Secure
- Selfless
- Sensitive
- Serious
- Sexy
- Simple
- Sincere
- Skilled
- Sociable
- Spiritual
- Steady
- Stoic
- Striving
- Strong
- Sweet
- Talented
- Tenacious
- Thorough
- Tolerant
- Tough
- Trusting
- Trustworthy
- Understanding
- Unique
- Unpretentious
- Unselfish
- Unstoppable
- Uprising
- Versatile
- Vigorous
- Visionary
- Warm
- Whimsical
- Wise
- Witty
- Wonderful
- Worldly
- Xenodochial
- Xenophilic
- Young
- Youthful
- Zaftig
- Zappy
- Zazzy
- Zealous
- Zesty
- Zippy
- _ _ _ _

How your brand leads your *culture*

Tune into Episode 15 of the *Work Life By Design* podcast for the rest of our chat.

Your brand experience is your strategy. Your culture is how you will execute that strategy. Culture is, in essence, a collective view of how we engage, interact, behave and work together. It reflects what we believe, what we value and what we are working for, and it's fuelled by purpose and vision. Your organisation's culture should be led by the brand experience you want people to have, and it should define the actions and boundaries your people will operate with to deliver that experience.

You may well have heard the saying "culture eats strategy for breakfast," commonly attributed to Peter Drucker, dubbed the founder of modern management theory. Whatever its origin, the quote implies that the right culture in a business will always trump strategy. However, as pointed out by *Rules of Belonging* author Fiona Robertson, in Episode 15 of the *Work Life by Design* podcast, "culture and strategy need to eat at the table together." Aligning the organisation's strategic vision with its cultural ability to execute that vision will enable its successful fruition. Without this alignment, strategy is nothing more than words on paper. The two must be interwoven: purpose informs the brand strategy, and the culture supports and enables it.

YOUR BRAND IS THE EXPERIENCE THAT NEEDS TO BE ACHIEVED TO FULFIL THE ORGANISATION'S PURPOSE.

When we infuse the brand, both strategically and experientially, into the very fabric of the workplace, we lay the roadmap for employees to engage in a way that aligns with the brand experience and builds culture. When we have people engaged in our purpose, and living and breathing the brand experience, the culture will evolve and radiate beyond the business.

When designing a workplace, you must start with the end in mind. Organisational leaders view the service they want the organisation to provide, which in turn informs the work that the people will need to be performing. They have a preferred way they wish for people to interact, the type of communication they want to observe, and how employees collaborate with one another. In other words, they have a vision of the experience that people will have when working in this business, the brand. Yet the elements they envision are the cultural cues of "the way things are done around here," and are all guided and supported by the physical built environment they occupy.

By infusing the desired brand experience into the physical construction of your workplace, you can build an environment that leads your culture through its inherent subconscious cues. Every touchpoint, from the materiality and aesthetic to the type and style of furniture and how people move through a space, provides feedback and expectations of how individuals are engaged, essentially guiding behaviour.

case study
Hall Chadwick

Hall Chadwick is an accounting firm with a history that stretches back four decades, with strong ties to Longreach in Western Queensland. For years the organisation occupied an office that spread over two non-contiguous levels, a space that bore no relationship to who they were as a company nor their clients' experience of doing business with them.

Working closely with several of the directors, including Dugald Warby, we identified that Hall Chadwick needed to develop a strategic vision for its new workspace that embraced the company's heritage within the context of an exciting future. In 2016, with its lease expiry imminent, Hall Chadwick's existing workspace was problematic. Fifteen years of business growth had spread the staff across two separate and disparate floors, resulting in an unsuitable fitout and a siloed culture.

the task

Hall Chadwick's space did not signify anything unique or different about the business – nothing that would make it stand out from any other accounting practice.

The space was a rabbit warren of high-screened workstations. Offices hugged the perimeter windows, and mounds of files sat stacked on desks, in corridors, and in an extensive "filing" area.

The kitchen was a tiny, windowless room with limited seating space. The main reception area featured a free-standing desk, four single armchairs, and a logo hung on the wall; the floor was carpeted in standard-issue "landlord" carpet, and the chairs were upholstered in a red-maroon that reflected the branding colours. The office space was simple, traditional, and "did the job."

The brief was to reinforce Hall Chadwick's culture, provide a workspace that was flexible enough to support the company's evolving operational needs, and a space that clients felt comfortable visiting, which wasn't ostentatious.

the inspiration

We wanted to communicate the deep, rich history that Hall Chadwick has with Western Queensland, and tell the story of the large agricultural client base residing in this part of Australia that trusts them with their business, spanning generations. We also wanted to communicate the strong values that underpin the business operations of Hall Chadwick: mateship, welcoming hospitality, and that strong country essence that says:

We're in this together. And when times get tough, we've got your back.

before...

The reception was a standard landlord-issue carpet, with doctor's waiting room chairs and the logo mounted on the wall

The workstations were surrounded by high partitions, with filing piled high around them. Limited natural lighting penetrated the interior of the space, with offices lining the perimeter windows

5 reasons to clean up your workspace

There are plenty of benefits to adopting a clean desk policy – the more obvious being information security and, with the recent pandemic, hygiene and sanitisation purposes. But beyond that there are also other ways (perhaps less obvious) having a clean desk can enhance your workplace experience:[3]

1 **IT BOOSTS YOUR PRODUCTIVITY** The benefits to productivity are a major factor when it comes to a clean desk! Research has shown that immersing ourselves in disorganisation drains our cognitive resources and reduces our ability to focus, as our brains prefer order. An ordered environment makes decision-making easier, as there are fewer distractions enabling you to focus better and process information more easily. Plus, for many of us, having a clean and fresh desk can feel inspiring and motivating![3]

2 **IT'S BETTER FOR YOUR PHYSICAL HEALTH...** Have you ever thought that a neat space could help you make better food choices? Research shows that "Clutter is stressful for the brain, so [if you work in a messy environment] you're more likely to resort to coping mechanisms such as choosing comfort foods or overeating than if you spend time in neater surroundings."[4]

3 **...AND YOUR MENTAL HEALTH** From a mental health perspective, disorganisation and clutter has been shown to increase stress and can have an impact on your self-esteem. Often, if you feel disorganised, you can feel a lack of control; an organised space can help you feel much more focused and less stressed![3]

4 **IT CREATES A SENSE OF PRIDE** Think about your most valued client, or perhaps a manager or colleague you admire. Now think about showing them your desk space, your home at work. How would you feel? A clean desk not only makes the workplace look tidier, it also promotes a professional image – one that you should be proud of!

5 **IT BRINGS YOU AND YOUR TEAM CLOSER TOGETHER**
Clean desk policies in the workplace often go hand-in-hand with shared workspaces, and ideally this means there are designated areas (away from a workstation) where you can collaborate with others. Take a look at your workplace environment; look for ways and areas that you can "change your scenery" when working with others. Different spaces can also connect us to different work modalities and help you to transition both your mental focus and physical posture.

YOUR WORKSPACE CAN SAY A LOT ABOUT YOU AND YOUR BUSINESS! WHILE WE ALL WORK DIFFERENTLY AND CAN APPRECIATE INDIVIDUAL STYLES, THERE ARE CLEAR BENEFITS OF KEEPING YOUR WORKSPACE CLEAN AND ORGANISED.

the solution

Uncovering the story and the brand experience of Hall Chadwick enabled us to design the workplace to embrace the company's rich history and desire to establish long-term relationships with clients, where they are warmly welcomed and invited into the business. This brand experience translated through a complete sensory experience.

- You can **SEE** the red dirt: stained into the rustic pavers that tile the floor, the corrugated iron that lines the walls, the horse bits that adorn the banquet seating and the open-truss timber ceilings that define the spaces.

- You can **FEEL** the reclaimed timber posts, the coolness of the reception stone top, and the expansiveness of the space as it opens up and offers a warm welcome.

- You can **SMELL** the leather from the cowhide that upholsters the chairs, the coffee as it wafts from the kitchen cafe, and the freshness of the air.

- You can **HEAR** the receptionist's warm welcome and the chatter that lingers from the kitchen cafe, of both employees and clients alike as you enter the space.

You also experience the lack of division between client and staff areas on entering this space. It's purposely designed to invite clients into the heart of the workplace, the kitchen. Just as you would be invited in for a coffee and a yarn at a mate's farmhouse, the cafe is an informal space for business to take place and for clients to linger.

On exiting the lift you step into the foyer, immediately connecting you to the essence of the business: warm parquetry timber floors, charcoal Colorbond wall cladding, timber ceilings — and what country space would be complete without a cowhide rug!

Above: The client waiting area evokes the feeling of a communal business lounge, encouraging clients to relax while waiting and for informal meetings to occur.

Right: The timber-trussed ceiling leads you through the space, to enter the timber barn doors into the Boardroom.

The Boardroom embraces the timber-truss ceiling from the waiting area, as it carries through into the space, creating the atmosphere of a luxury barn. The walls and ceilings are lined with VJ panels, reflecting the materiality of the desired brand connection.

CASE STUDY – HALL CHADWICK

the detail

As you step out of the lift into the entry foyer, the Hall Chadwick story immediately starts to unfold. Considered materials and a warm colour palette are indeed reminiscent of Western Queensland, including reddish timbers, charcoal Colorbond vertical panels, warm greys, and rust. And what rural Queensland space would be complete without a cowhide rug? Moving from the foyer into the reception area, the desk is clad with eucalyptus-coloured tiles inspired by corrugated sheets.

The space opens up into a casual client waiting lounge with a 4.8m-high ceiling. Wrapping around the waiting lounge are client meeting rooms, a boardroom and a training room.

The 'red dirt' path traverses the waiting lounge to the boardroom and training room, with their heavy barn-style sliding doors. VJ boards nod to traditional Queenslander architectural vernacular, while the impressive timber truss ceiling extends out into the client waiting lounge, creating engaging interior views and continuity within the larger workspace.

Beyond the client waiting lounge, the staircase forms a transition point between the client space and the staff cafe.

The cafe's large perimeter windows offer views down Brisbane's bustling Queen Street, and flood the space with natural light. The space radiates a modern restaurant vibe suitable for a broad range of uses: a relaxing alternative workspace for staff, a casual meeting place with clients, a function space for events, and of course, Friday drinks.

Climbing the industrial-style staircase to level four, you are welcomed into the heart of the working floor. The playful placement of a breeze-block wall separates the main corridor from the utility space, simultaneously enabling visual connection across the office.

> A WORKPLACE THAT SETS HALL CHADWICK APART BY CAPTURING THE ESSENCE OF WHO THEY ARE AND INFUSING IT INTO THE PHYSICAL ENVIRONMENT.

It is hard not to love breeze blocks – their distinct Australian outdoor style gives them nostalgic, mid-century modern appeal. Widely used in Western Queensland, in turn they are used to great effect in Hall Chadwick's new workspace. Their positioning in public areas encourages knowledge sharing between departments and informal contributions from passing staff.

The workstations are fanned around the curved perimeter of the building, with offices stacked back off windows so natural light can penetrate deep into the floor plate without obstruction.

Finally, a quiet library space sits behind the stair void, its rustic tones and textures offering a peaceful alternative work environment. The triangulated timber ceiling echoes the entry foyer on level four, bringing the Hall Chadwick workplace story full circle.

Hall Chadwick's workplace embodies elements of rural life by incorporating earthy materials, rich, deep colours and textural finishes. Every aspect of the design, from the alfresco patio structure over the kitchen to the training room furnishings, subtly reflects the company's origins in Western Queensland.

By infusing the desired brand experience into the built environment, Hall Chadwick has created a space that reaffirms its culture. It elicits a feeling that draws in those it appeals to. It is a filter that attracts the right team members, clients and partners. Hall Chadwick is leading and enabling its culture by infusing its brand into every facet of its built environment.

The Cafe is a communal space where clients are welcome to make themselves at home, to linger after meetings and engage in informal conversation with the team.

Inspired by the patios of rural Queensland, the Cafe is an open space with a suspended timber structure defining the kitchen space. The materiality is reminiscent of the textures and tones of Western Queensland, with the stone benchtops reflective of an aerial view of the landscape during the wet season.

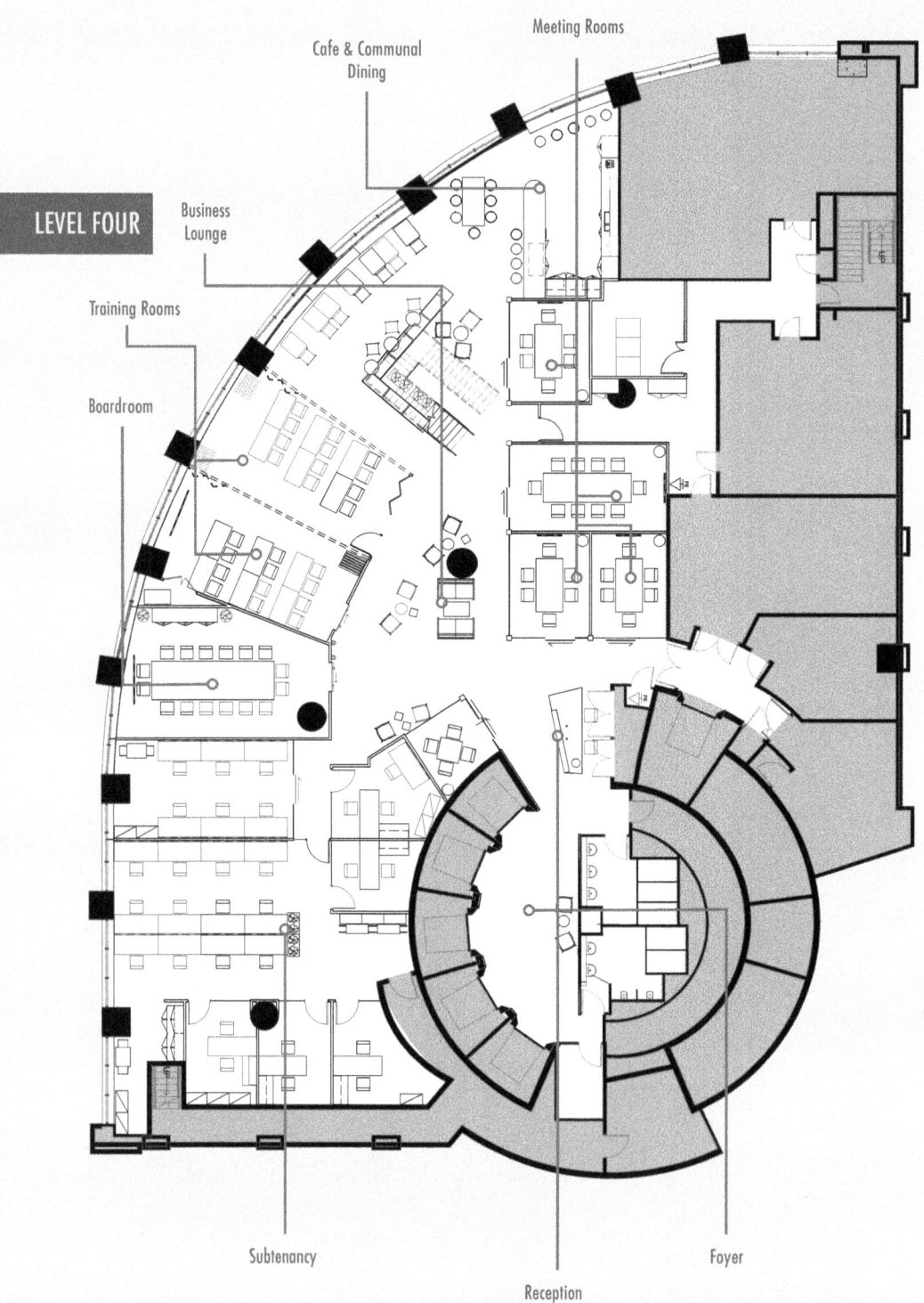

LEVEL FOUR

- Cafe & Communal Dining
- Meeting Rooms
- Business Lounge
- Training Rooms
- Boardroom
- Subtenancy
- Reception
- Foyer

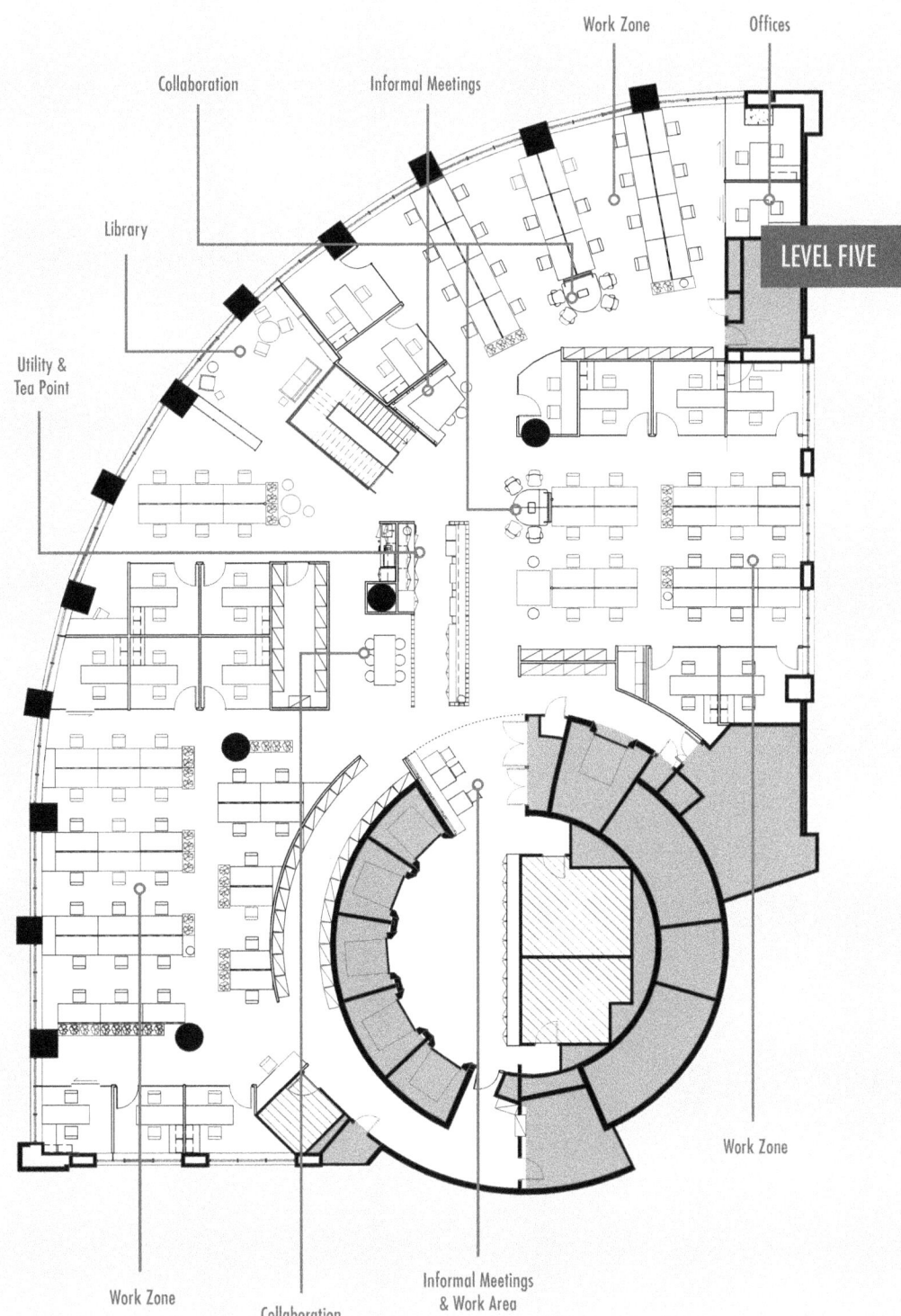

Left: Banquette seating in the Cafe wraps the curved facade of the building, optimising the prime location with views down Queen Street, and expansive natural light flooding the space.

Right: Horse bits adorn the banquette seating, providing subtle connections to the land, and the story of Hall Chadwick.

The stairs connecting the two levels were an integral part of the workplace strategy, enabling seamless connectivity between the two floors. The staircase provides a vertical street, encouraging movement through the space.

Breeze blocks were introduced to define spaces while maintaining open, visual transparency through the space, and reflecting the aesthetic of Western Queensland.

Above: The central area of the floor is designed to create a place of connection, bringing the various "wings" of the building together in a common zone, through the positioning of utility zones, tea points and collaborative meeting spaces.

Below: The Library gives employees a quiet place to work away from their work point, uninterrupted in a casual and relaxed environment, while taking in the external views.

CASE STUDY – HALL CHADWICK

> **You don't *often reflect* on who you are, but when we did we were happy with what it looked like in *design*.**

> **People can feel what the place is like before they've met someone.** *it starts a* **conversation about why it looks the way it does.** ”

— DUGALD WARBY, HALL CHADWICK

Culture is the system that shapes *the dynamics of the organisation*

Our brains are hardwired for belonging, the deep human need for social connection. We feel a deep-seated need to stay safe through connection and belonging to a group or a tribe, a culture. And when we look at the organisation as a "system," we can observe and consciously shape the systemic dynamics of our organisation; we can shape "how the group thinks." In that way, belonging is one of the most powerful principles shaping how our system functions.

Matthew Lieberman, Professor of Psychology, Psychiatry and Biobehavioral Sciences at the University of California Los Angeles, found that we feel physical pain when socially excluded. When we feel a sense of exclusion from a meeting, a water-cooler conversation, or even the fear that we don't quite fit in, that feeling of exclusion causes us physical pain. As such, we are perpetually trying to understand what's expected of us – we want to know the rules of belonging.

WHAT DOES IT TAKE FOR ME TO FIT IN HERE?

The stakes of belonging or not belonging feel exceptionally high at work. Recent studies have shown that employees feel a greater sense of belonging to their organisations than their peers, boss or industry, which makes this foundational principle of belonging increasingly essential as work evolves, with more project-based work, gig employees, part-time work, and remote and distributed teams becoming the norm. Never forget that your people want to belong.

WHEN YOU ARE CLEAR ON THE EXPERIENCE YOU WANT PEOPLE TO HAVE, AND KNOW WHAT IS IMPORTANT TO YOU, YOUR CULTURE WILL EVOLVE ACCORDINGLY.

Now, having said that, it's always a good idea to check your work. If you want to know whether your brand is steering your culture in the right direction, the best thing to do is: ask.

The insights of culture surveys

Transforming your workplace is the perfect opportunity to gather insights from your employees. Why? Because the creation of a new workplace is in itself a change project that your organisation is about to embark on, and is the perfect opportunity to support the implementation of cultural change initiatives in your organisation.

When businesses create a new workplace, it's the perfect time to do a deep assessment, one that enables a look at how we work, what works and what we can do differently. After all, the goals at the heart of any redesign are to leap forward and upgrade, wipe the slate clean and get a fresh start, and instil new behaviours, ways of working and cultural norms. So, starting with a deep knowledge of the current state can inform the new workplace's strategic goals and success measures.

Culture surveys offer direct insight into the employee psyche and show you how your business is performing from their viewpoint. While it can be a confronting situation to ask your employees how you're doing, without this knowledge you may be blissfully unaware of the water cooler chatter and where you have opportunities to improve. The good news is that these perspectives can be relatively easy to come by. A wide range of survey providers and styles are available to capture the data you need.

You may even prefer to develop a tailored survey specific to your organisation. However you choose to collect and collate the data, it is vital that you understand its patterns.

The data captured from these surveys can offer deep insights into a multitude of areas, ranging from relationships with peers to day-to-day roadblocks that employees are experiencing. It enables you to check the pulse of the inner workings of your organisation, so that you can celebrate where you are nailing it and take action to "right the ship" where you have veered off course.

THESE INSIGHTS BECOME ESPECIALLY VALUABLE IN THE DESIGN OF YOUR PHYSICAL WORK ENVIRONMENT.

They offer clues in reconfiguring and transforming the space to support existing activities and create places where new activities and interactions can form. Questions about an employee's personal development and their degree of satisfaction working in the business can offer insights into the individual's ability to perform their role due to environmental constraints.

For example, take the statement: "I have the materials and tools to do my job right." On the surface it may be considering stationery and technology, but the environment in which the work takes place is also a tool.

ARE THE SPACES OFFERED BY THE WORKPLACE CONDUCIVE TO THE TYPE AND STYLE OF WORK THE INDIVIDUAL NEEDS TO PERFORM?

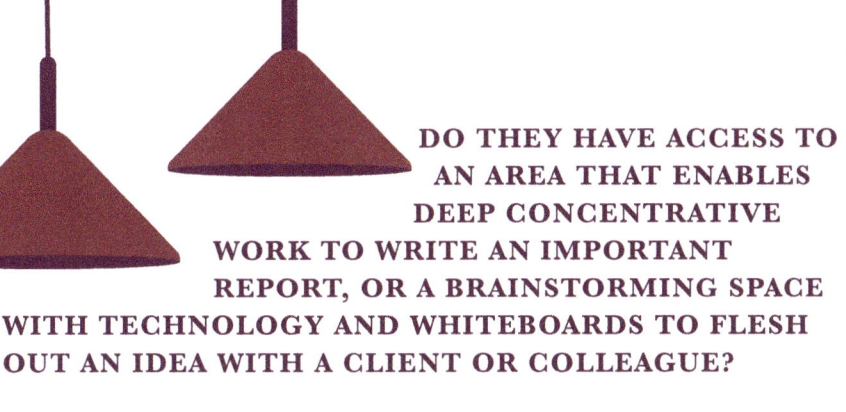

DO THEY HAVE ACCESS TO AN AREA THAT ENABLES DEEP CONCENTRATIVE WORK TO WRITE AN IMPORTANT REPORT, OR A BRAINSTORMING SPACE WITH TECHNOLOGY AND WHITEBOARDS TO FLESH OUT AN IDEA WITH A CLIENT OR COLLEAGUE?

Each of these "tools" is a physical element in the workplace and responds to an immediate need in how the employee is to perform the tasks of their role. Culture Amp, an employee engagement and performance analytics platform, has found that collaboration is one of the most commented-on employee survey questions. No matter the questions you choose to include, your employees' responses will offer opportunities that you can use to improve their work environment.[5]

Looking more objectively at the response and insights that the breadth of questions in the surveys offers, you are presented with a wealth of opportunities on how the environment may be working in opposition to the desired culture and, therefore, the desired brand experience. Your built environment is critical in establishing routines and rituals for your people's daily activities and interactions, and that opens up a huge opportunity to enable high performance.

The five words your team would use to describe your culture

The simple way to think of your culture is "the way things are done around here." It lays the foundation for the rules of belonging. So how would your team describe the culture in your organisation?

The quickest way to find out is to... ask them!

STEP ONE

Create a quick survey using an online app (we use Survey Monkey) and ask your team to list five words they would use to describe your organisation's culture.

STEP TWO

Once you have the results, you can upload them into another app to create a word cloud. We use wordclouds.com, a clever little app that consolidates all the words you enter into a punchy graphic. The more often a word gets repeated, the bigger it is presented in the picture. This is a super simple way to capture the thoughts of an entire organisation and deliver them back to the business in an easy-to-understand way. My clients love seeing these word clouds and have even printed them out and hung them on the wall.

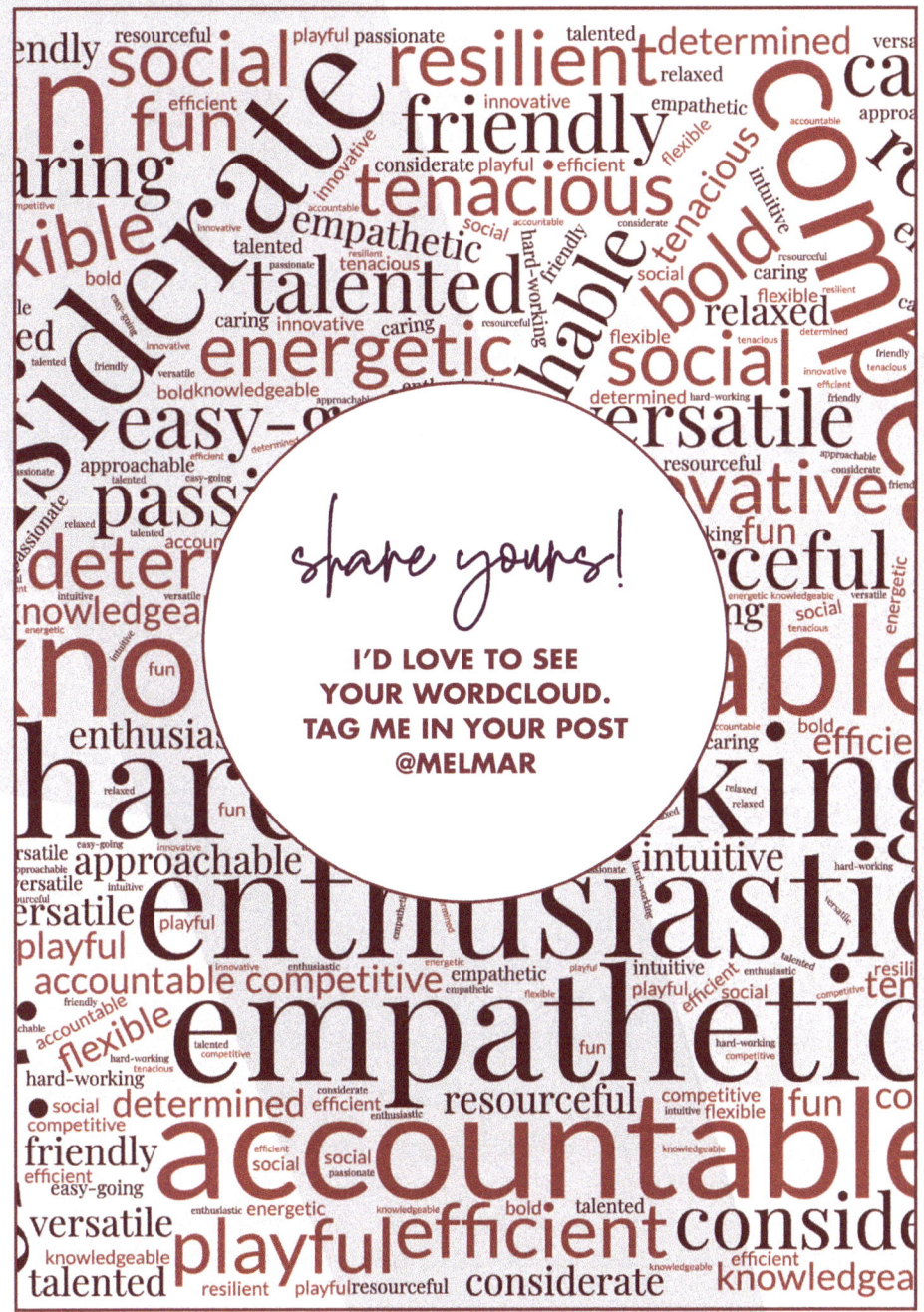

What your workplace design says about your *culture and values*

Organisational values are much more than the words that get stuck up on the wall, of course. Your workplace represents what your organisation believes, its values and its priorities.

DOES IT MATCH THE WORDS YOU USE?

Purpose-driven organisations understand how powerfully their workplace communicates their intentions and impact, and they make it a priority to embed their brand story throughout their design aesthetic so that employees, clients, suppliers and anyone who comes into contact with the space can "feel" what it's like to do business with them. The workplace design of Hall Chadwick illustrates this point well.

Infusing your brand into the built environment across all five senses provides subconscious cues that lead your culture by guiding behaviour. While the visual aspects of good workplace design can be seen, the strongest cues come from the elements that can be felt: the importance of relationships and mateship, that the door is always open and you are welcome to make yourself at home, and that the kitchen is a communal gathering space that draws everyone together are all values Hall Chadwick holds dear.

THE PLANNING AND FLOW OF THE SPACES ARE VITAL IN CONVEYING THOSE FEELINGS AND INVITING THOSE BEHAVIOURS TO COME NATURALLY. AND WHILE YOU MIGHT NOT BE ABLE TO PUT YOUR FINGER ON WHY YOU FEEL IT, YOU STILL FEEL IT.

Understanding your values and the behaviours that underpin them (and those you wish to create) enables your space to be intuitively designed to encourage these behaviours. The opposite is also true. One prospective client aptly described the disconnect we feel when our company says they value something, but the spaces we occupy do not support it. She explained how her organisation seeks to encourage collaboration, but their built environment makes collaborative work nearly impossible. They are not speaking the same language.

An organisation's business strategy also plays a significant role in the execution of the design. The strategic vision the organisation has for its future is critical to defining the parameters of the future space.

WHAT IMPACT ARE YOU LOOKING TO MAKE? DO YOU PLAN TO GROW OR DOWNSIZE? WHAT IS THE ORGANISATION'S CULTURE, AND HOW IS THIS LINKED TO THE WORK ENVIRONMENT? HOW MIGHT YOU NEED TO EVOLVE OVER THE NEXT DECADE?

Multiple factors are applying external pressure to our organisations, ranging from job titles that didn't exist five years ago to rapid technological shifts, changing how our organisations are required to operate. This pace of change means workplaces need to evolve and adapt to these changing requirements. The type and style of work conducted is changing and requires workplaces to respond to the personalities of the people there. In planning the workplace, it's critical that the environment meets the organisation's needs and leads to stronger connections.

The organisation's purpose defines the strategic direction and enables the space to support these goals.

YOUR WORKPLACE PLAYS A SIGNIFICANT ROLE IN SUCCESSFULLY CREATING A HIGH-PERFORMING TEAM – BUT IT RELIES ON THE INHERENT COMMUNICATION OF YOUR VALUES AND BUSINESS STRATEGY.

> **Knowing what your *business stands for* and having a vision for the future is key to *defining* an effective workplace that embodies a sense of *belonging* and connects your *community*.**

– MELISSA MARSDEN

Why your story is the foundation *and reflection point for all decisions*

When I start working with a client, a large proportion of my time goes to engaging with them and getting to know their business. Who they are, where they came from, and the milestones along the journey to who they are today. I want to know the clients they work with, the people that work for them and those they want to work with in the future. In essence, capturing all the elements that we have just traversed in this chapter.

When the answers to these questions are distilled down, they reflect a story unique to that business. And it's that story that we can then transform into the underlying reference point for our workplace design decisions.

YOU MAY BE SITTING HERE THINKING: *HOW ON EARTH DOES THAT WORK?!* **WELL, LET ME WALK YOU THROUGH IT.**

As someone who thinks in visuals, when I understand a client's story, I associate words and phrases with images, colours and textures. I visualise ways that their story can be communicated through their environment. We examine different business functions – such as what the first experience is for a client or employee – through a design lens, like whether the space is dark or light, neutral or colourful, noisy or quiet.

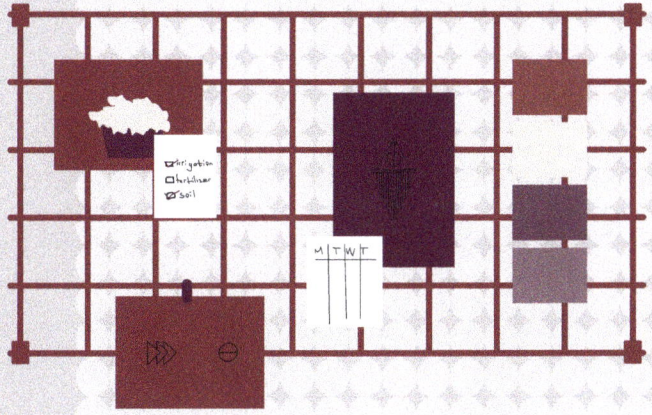

You might see this take the form of a vision board, mood board or other image-driven form of communication (hello, Pinterest!) to capture the essence of that story After all: "a picture paints a thousand words."

We refer to this story as our Design Metaphor. A visual communication tool that captures the essence of your organisation's unique story. We then use this tool as a reflection point for ALL our decisions throughout the development of a project. Are our decisions about materiality, colour, texture and flow all consistent with the Design Metaphor, your unique story? If not they are evaluated, ensuring that the project doesn't evolve into what's on-trend, an individual stakeholder's personal aesthetic or the designer's unique style preference.

So, to capture the unique story of your business, reflect back over the chapter, take note of what stands out, capture your story, analyse your brand archetype and then think about how that might feel to you.

DOES IT HAVE A SENSE OF COLOUR? IS IT MASCULINE OR FEMININE? DARK OR LIGHT? WARM OR COOL? SMOOTH OR ROUGH? NEW OR OLD?

These contrasts help you define how that story translates into a physical environment. A feeling. This is how you ensure that your space's decisions stay true to your business and that you don't get distracted by the new, bright, shiny object. •

Chapter Huddle

BRING YOUR BRAND AND CULTURE TO LIFE THROUGH YOUR ENVIRONMENT

AN ORGANISATION'S BRAND IS FAR MORE THAN A LOGO, WEBSITE OR A SUITE OF COLOURS.

It is the experience you want people to have when they do business with you. And it all starts with purpose.

EVERY BUSINESS HAS A UNIQUE BRAND PERSONALITY, A STORY OF WHERE IT CAME FROM AND WHERE IT'S GOING.

When infused into the very fabric of the environment, it elicits emotion so that employees, clients, suppliers and anyone who comes into contact with the space can "feel" what it's like to do business there.

AN ORGANISATION'S PURPOSE IS WHY YOU DO WHAT YOU DO.

It goes beyond making money. It helps you to align and attract those who "believe what you believe."

YOUR STORY CAN BE COMMUNICATED THROUGH EACH OF THE FIVE SENSES.

This informs the functional planning and aesthetics of your workplace environment, influencing behaviour and reinforcing your purpose.

WHEN YOU ARE CLEAR ON YOUR PURPOSE, IT INFORMS YOUR BRAND.

When you infuse your brand into the physical construct of your workplace, it will lead your culture. That culture, in turn, defines the values that guide the behaviours. Your workplace can influence every step of that experience.

**HOW DO YOU WANT PEOPLE TO FEEL?
WHAT IS THE EXPERIENCE YOU WANT THEM TO HAVE?**

> "People will forget what you said, people will forget what you did, but people will never forget how you made them feel."
>
> – MAYA ANGELOU

CHAPTER THREE

bringing your values to life in the workplace

Think about your commute to work this morning (if and when you commute). Was it stressful? Punctuated by car horns, a broken heater and your car's dirty interior? Or was it peaceful, with soothing music playing on your radio, a comfortable car seat cushioning your body, and that perfect latte you made sitting in the cup holder?

We've established how the design of our physical environment influences how we interact within that space. Now I want to take that conversation a step further. Our surroundings can also elicit a behavioural change through subtle, subconscious cues. A peaceful driving environment can lead to a calm, easygoing driver; a stressful one can make a driver agitated. And changing the environment can change the behaviour.

IF WE'RE GOING TO INFLUENCE HOW PEOPLE BEHAVE IN AN ENVIRONMENT, WE SIMPLY NEED TO ADJUST THE CUES THAT ARE GENERATED BY THAT ENVIRONMENT.

Casinos are masters of this concept. The early design model felt like a maze, winding and claustrophobic, leaving patrons feeling trapped – but today's casinos are modern-day adult playgrounds. This revolutionary shift was first seen in early 2010, with the rise of the Bellagio and the Wynn in Las Vegas. The playground design concept transformed casinos from a place of confusion and apprehension to a palace where players could feel comfortable and excited, a space that encourages the belief that anything is possible. "Players who are more at ease are happier when they win," says Christopher Null of 888Casino. "And they're more understanding when they lose – all of which convinces them to bet more." So what can we learn from the Bellagios and Wynns of the world?

Whether you're a hotel guest casually passing through, a high roller wanting to get to the real action or a casual gamer passing by looking for the comfort of the slot machines, casinos need to appeal to you and attract you, so that you don't take your business elsewhere.

To that end, casinos employ a range of visual cues to influence your mood and behaviour. High ceilings elicit the "cathedral effect," the perception that anything is possible and encouraging people to stay longer. There are no natural lighting sources, windows or clocks, which removes any association with time; the wild, swirling carpet designs and colourful flashing lights keep you awake and alert, and a cacophony of bells and whistles goes off every time someone hits the jackpot. *Play one more hand, stay a bit longer, and you might be next* is the implicit promise.

Every successful business model comes with a defined strategy for how the business operates. This includes the vision for the future, goals and how they are to be achieved, and the values the company lives by. These are unwavering concepts, regardless of the nature of the business. For casinos, the strategy is simple: get you to spend your money! And what behaviour contributes most to that goal? Spending time in the casino. The longer guests are seated at the table, exploring the labyrinthine floor, or stopping to see what everyone at the roulette table is so excited about, the more money they will spend. So casinos pull out all the stops to create an environment where guests feel comfortable and want to keep playing.

THESE SAME OPPORTUNITIES ARE AVAILABLE TO YOUR ORGANISATION, TOO.

By shaping your environment to elicit behaviours that will contribute to the success of your business model, and by describing the behaviours that demonstrate how success is lived, you create a social economy for people to participate in. Repetition of these behaviours leads to the establishment of culture.

LET'S LOOK AT THE CREATION OF A RETAIL PRECINCT AS AN EXAMPLE: A PLACE THAT WE CHOOSE TO TRAVEL TO, SPEND TIME IN, AND WHERE WE EXCHANGE OUR MONEY FOR PRODUCTS AND SERVICES.

Key metrics that are considered markers of a successful development include: foot traffic counts, tenant sales figures, the longevity of tenants, and the number of regular customers. By transferring these metrics into identifiable behaviours, we can wrap environments around them that intuitively guide people.

If we want our space to attract regular customers, we need to develop an environment that appeals to them, where they enjoy being and, more importantly, encourages their repeated return. We want them to feel comfortable, welcome, and part of the community. So what are some real-world design ideas for encouraging these desired behaviours?

One way of achieving this may be the introduction of identifiable communal seating and perch spaces (aka spaces that are not tenant-owned). These spaces provide visual cues that encourage people to stop and linger without necessarily engaging in transactions. This creates an environment where there is no pressure to buy, and the irony of this is that without the pressure, the customer then has the time and space to assess their needs and make an informed decision about how they would like to

spend their money. They are intrinsically happier due to this no-pressure environment, are more satisfied with their choice, and are more likely to return to an environment that elicits these behaviours. A win for all!

Other sensory experiences often support these visual cues, such as the selection and volume of the music playing, the smells wafting from the restaurant kitchens, the plant type, placement, and their biophilia effect. These elements are designed into the physical environment to influence behaviour and ultimately support the set business model objectives. In the case of the casino, it's encouraging customers to spend more time and, eventually, money. In the case of the retail precinct, it's about fostering a sense of joy so that shoppers want to continuously return. Again, more time and money spent equals business success.

These same principles apply to the design of your workplace environment. In an age where employees can choose whether to come to the office or not, we need to create an environment that attracts them, connects with them, and one that they feel they want to belong to.

Regardless of the nature of your business, tailoring your environment can directly affect the behaviour of the people who engage with it, be it your customer or your employees.

SO NOW ONLY ONE QUESTION REMAINS… RED OR BLACK?

Nudge Theory:
What is it and how to use it

Nudge theory is a behavioural economics concept that proposes we can influence the behaviours and decision-making of groups and individuals through indirect suggestions and positive reinforcement. It was popularised in 2008 in *Nudge: Improving Decisions About Health, Wealth, and Happiness*[1] by authors Richard Thaler and Cass Sunstein.

THALER AND SUNSTEIN DEFINED THEIR CONCEPT AS THE FOLLOWING[2]:

> A nudge, as we will use the term, is any aspect of the choice architecture that alters people's behavior in a predictable way without forbidding any options or significantly changing their economic incentives. To count as a mere nudge, the intervention must be easy and cheap to avoid. Nudges are not mandates. Putting fruit at eye level counts as a nudge. Banning junk food does not.

Nudges are described as small changes to an environment.[3] These small changes could take the form of:[1]

1 A default behaviour – this form of nudge requires the individual to do nothing, as the "default" option requires no effort on the behalf of the user. An example of this is our Netflix subscription. Each month the service automatically renews without any action from us, thus activating another human behavioural concept: the "status-quo bias." This is our natural preference for the current state of affairs, which results in inertia and resistance to change.[4]

2 Social-proof heuristics – this is when we look to the behaviour of others to guide our own behaviour. These behavioural "shortcuts" enable us to make quick decisions in relation to behaviour norms by observing and mimicking the behaviours of those around us, reducing our own cognitive load. For example, when we enter a library and observe others speaking in hushed tones or not at all, we are less likely to speak loudly or behave outlandishly.

3 Increasing the salience of a desired option – by making the desired option more visible and appealing, an individual is more likely to choose that option. The use of internal stairs vs the lift is a perfect example of this in our workplaces. Positioning a staircase centrally ensures visibility and quick and easy use. The lift is still there, but the stairs are a more visible connection to my destination and therefore more appealing, also ticking that incidental movement box.

We are often unaware that we are being nudged, as these subtle suggestions are simply appealing to our internal norms and beliefs. Take, for example, the sign in a hotel bathroom with the simple request: "By reusing your towel, you are doing your part for the planet." This simple nudge appeals to the inner beliefs of the hotel guest and their desire to be environmentally friendly.

Of course, nudging cannot make people do something they don't wish to do. It merely reminds them of their options and makes the preferred choice an easy one; take the stairs rather than the lift, have a conversation with your colleague rather than send an email, get up and move during the day rather than sitting, eat lunch in the cafe rather than at your desk. Our environments can make it easy for us to align with desired behaviours.

Take as an example **A HIGH-BACKED LOUNGE CHAIR** that wraps around you, with a perfectly sized laptop table. It enables you to feel relaxed yet offers enough privacy to productively work your way through emails and dive into that report you've been meaning to review. It encourages productive, focused work. The very shape and design of the chair – a single seat with high sides – implies that this is a space for one, and discourages sparking up a conversation with the person beside you due to the cocoon-like nature of the space and its narrow line of sight.

Similarly, **A LARGE CIRCULAR LOUNGE** allows a team to hold a meeting, sharing thoughts and ideas on a screen while brainstorming on an adjacent wall and having other parties join the discussion. This deliberate use of space encourages openness, contribution and collaboration by providing spaces and tools that enable these behaviours.

EACH OF THESE IS AN OPPORTUNITY TO NUDGE PEOPLE IN A WAY THAT ENCOURAGES THEIR BEHAVIOUR TO ALIGN WITH THE BUSINESS' DESIRED OUTCOMES. THESE BEHAVIOURS ARE THE RESULT OF YOUR VALUES.

HOW MIGHT YOUR SPACE FACILITATE YOUR VALUES?

INDIVIDUAL FOCUSED SPACE

COLLABORATION SPACE

Spaces designed to influence value-aligned *behaviours*

A few years ago, I began reflecting on my own unique personality and personal values, the things that light my fire and drag me down. That *aha* moment for me involved looking at my personal values and our organisational values at COMUNiTI, and then digging deeper to understand the behaviours underpinning these values.

This small change in thinking opened up a whole new world of opportunity. I started to think more pointedly about how the environments we surround ourselves with influence our behaviour – or, more correctly, how our spaces are designed to influence our behaviour. This new perspective has flowed through to my work, how I look at an organisation and its particular values, and how we support those values through the environments we create for them. I have begun to ask my clients and their teams what their vision and values look like in practice. This is where I have found the gold. Understanding the behaviours the organisation wants to encourage arms us with much more information about the types of spaces required to support these behaviours.

In discussion with one client, she aptly described how her company's workspace had a detrimental impact, not supporting the behaviours staff were told to have. She explained how her organisation sought to encourage collaboration, but the built environment's spatial cues said the opposite.

There were no collaborative spaces and the office was so heavily segmented, it was difficult to strike up a conversation with a colleague without a meeting invite. This kind of mixed messaging is confusing and works directly against the collaborative culture the organisation says it wants to see. To create clarity, there needs to be a significant shift in thinking, from "all about me" to "we" – and the design of the work environment needs to reflect that shift in mindset.

IF AN ORGANISATION SEEKS TO CREATE CHANGE, THE FIRST STEP IS TO CLEARLY ARTICULATE THE BEHAVIOURS THAT DEMONSTRATE HOW THE CHANGE IS TO BE LIVED.

Then the space that supports the organisation needs to be created, beating to that same drum. Changing a culture is not easy – and I'm not suggesting you can change a culture by simply changing the environment – but when all the pieces are facing in the same direction, it certainly makes it easier.

How your values define the behaviours of *your people*

What are values? Values are the ideals that we care about, the things that are important to us. We each personally have values that define how we live our lives based on what we believe to be right and essential. Organisations also have values, centred on what they believe to be important in doing business. Values can often be abstract and idealised, failing to communicate the behaviours the organisation expects of its people. Words can often have varying degrees of interpretation depending on your upbringing, culture and personal experiences. So how do we articulate what it looks like to be living a company's values?

The answer is clarity. By simply changing our language from one of abstract context to one that is tangible and definitive in its expectations, we can clearly communicate the expected manner in which someone is to conduct themselves in the workplace. We are simply reframing the value in the context of an action.

Take the importance of "collaboration" and consider how this might look as a behaviour. It might sound like "engage in active problem solving" or "invite feedback". An observable behaviour, an action, is far easier to communicate than a value, so reframing your values in actionable terms will make it easier for your people to understand and align with them.

So, the question is:

- **WHAT ARE THE BEHAVIOURS YOU WANT TO SEE FROM YOUR TEAM?**

- **WHAT DO YOU WANT TO SEE YOUR TEAM DOING?**

- **HOW WOULD YOU DESCRIBE THE BEHAVIOURS YOU WISH TO SEE IN YOUR ORGANISATION?**

BY UNDERSTANDING YOUR ORGANISATION'S DESIRED BEHAVIOURS, YOU CAN INFLUENCE HOW THEY ARE ADOPTED, IN HOW THE WORK ENVIRONMENT IS CONSTRUCTED.

There are three ways behaviours are influenced *by design*

1. FLOW
How your space is laid out, guiding a sequence of activities

2. ZONING
The arrangement and proximity of spaces

3. SPACES
The variety of furniture types and styles

FLOW

The sequencing of spaces guides our days and influences what we do and when we do it. It can also reinforce (or inspire) workplace rituals and routines, which are essential to establishing a rhythm and pattern throughout the day. For example, if we want our employees to socialise and connect on entering the workplace before diving into their work, having people enter via the cafe will ensure that they connect, communicate and engage with other employees as they move through the space.

SPACES

Our spaces are defined by the type and style of the work settings within them, predominantly the furniture. They influence our posture, work modalities and even the mental and physical energy we bring to a task.

ZONING

The collocation of spaces is critical in guiding behaviours. By clustering activities of similar energy intensities – individual, quiet work versus collaborative, loud work – we are visually communicating the intended behaviour of the space and discouraging alternative behaviours. Through careful consideration in the planning of spaces, a wide variety of work behaviours can be catered to, influencing the style of work that employees engage in. By altering the ratios of quiet versus collaborative spaces in a workplace, we can guide how employees work. A higher proportion of collaborative spaces over individual ones indicates to employees that the organisation values time spent in group work, collaboration and brainstorming, more than isolated individual work.

THE RELATIONSHIP OF ACTIVITIES TO SPACES AND ZONES

OPEN SPACE — **NOISY**

SPACES (Open / Individual)
- Workstations
- Touchdown desks
- Focus pods
- Library

SPACES (Open / Group)
- Collaboration tables + lounges with screens and whiteboards
- General workspaces
- Cafe and breakout

ACTIVITIES (Open / Individual)
- General individual work zones (activities)
- Reading

ACTIVITIES (Open / Group)
- Brainstorming
- Group work
- Active meetings with whiteboards and screens
- Coffee chats
- Informal meetings/conversations
- Lunch breaks
- Spontaneous conversations

INDIVIDUAL SPACE — **GROUP SPACE**

ACTIVITIES (Enclosed / Individual)
- Phone calls
- Teams/Zoom chats
- Webinars
- Data analysis
- Deep work
- Report writing
- Meditation/yoga

ACTIVITIES (Enclosed / Group)
- Video conferencing
- Meetings
- Training sessions
- Small private meetings

QUIET — **ENCLOSED SPACE**

SPACES (Enclosed / Individual)
- Quiet rooms
- Shared offices
- Phone booths
- Wellness rooms
- Work booths

SPACES (Enclosed / Group)
- Meeting rooms
- Boardrooms
- Training rooms
- Enclosed booths

THE NEXT WORKPLACE

OUR SPACES SIT ON A CONTINUUM FROM NOISY TO QUIET ZONES, EACH INFLUENCING BEHAVIOURS

NOISY o─ ENTRY SPACES ─ CAFE/KITCHEN HUB ─ COLLABORATION SPACE ─ COMMUNAL WORKSPACES ─ GENERAL WORK AREAS ─ OPEN QUIET WORK AREAS ─ FOCUS PODS ─ QUIET ROOMS ─o QUIET

Environment influences behaviour

These elements influence the perception of how a room is to be used, the energy to be brought to the environment, and how we are to engage with others. Spaces meant to invoke a feeling of quiet and concentration would utilise furniture suitable for individual use. Instead of having multiple seats it may be softer in its appearance, indicating a higher level of acoustic properties, higher barriers, and more enclosed spaces. The area may have books or screening, creating the feeling of a library and similarly intimate spaces.

In contrast, a zone intended for active and robust conversation may have high tables, stools or no chairs; it may be supported by whiteboards and other tools to promote brainstorming and communication. Standing and moving quickly energises us, and the ability to physically contribute to a conversation by drawing out ideas creates more engaged behaviour and encourages lively communication with colleagues.

WHEN YOU UNDERSTAND THE BEHAVIOURS YOU WISH TO SEE IN YOUR ORGANISATION, YOU CAN HELP THEM TO BE BROUGHT TO LIFE.

When Steve Jobs was at Pixar, he was adamant that collaboration was crucial for success, which meant that people needed to communicate from all different business departments. Jobs identified that we humans share a basic need: we all need to use the bathroom. So when designing the Pixar headquarters, he determined that to create this cross-collaboration across the business – or "serendipitous personal encounters," as he called them – the bathrooms needed to be in the centre of the building, ensuring that the paths of various employees were bound to cross.

When Marissa Mayer was CEO of Yahoo, she notoriously ended a work from home policy and called everyone back into the office, pointing out: "people are more collaborative and innovative when they're together."

Cisco designed its office with corridors wide enough to support a few casual couches, and lined the walls with whiteboards. This arrangement enables colleagues to meet in passing, actively explore a conversation by mapping it out, and other colleagues to join the discussion in passing.

SPACES TO ENCOURAGE COLLABORATION

EACH OF THESE ORGANISATIONS IS WORKING TOWARDS THE OPPORTUNITY FOR PEOPLE TO CONNECT FACE-TO-FACE AND BUILD DEEPER RELATIONSHIPS BETWEEN COLLEAGUES, TO INCREASE THE QUALITY OF CONVERSATIONS AND COLLABORATIONS.

And while the pandemic challenged many organisations on the need for an "office", what has become evident is the workplace's role in enabling collaboration and communication, and supporting our fundamental desire as human beings to feel a sense of belonging.

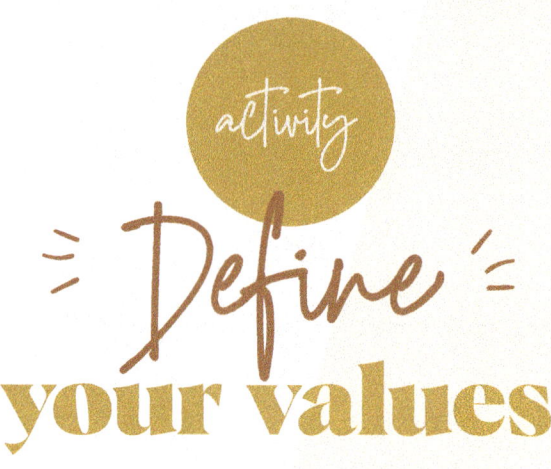

activity
Define your values

Values are often communicated as words that illustrate the expected standards within an organisation. They communicate the culture of an organisation and are the guideposts the company can operate between, providing a moral compass that helps employees understand what the organisation stands for and against; the non-negotiables of how we conduct ourselves in business.

Values create alignment in organisations, directing employees towards a common goal, by underpinning the expected behaviours, the rules of engagement and belonging at work.

In this exercise reflect on what is important to your organisation, what the expectations are and the non-negotiables in how you do business.

If you need some more inspiration, check out **Atlassian's** values

ATLASSIAN.COM/COMPANY/VALUES
link

1 Let's begin!

It's recommended that this exercise is carried out by a group of the organisation's leaders – those who understand and uphold the expectations of the organisation.

Read through the list of words and tick any that really stand out to you, and strikethrough any that don't resonate. You might need to do this a few times to get to your long-list.

Tick the words

- Above and beyond
- Acceptance
- Accessibility
- Accomplishment
- Accountability
- Accuracy
- Accurate
- Achievement
- Activity
- Adaptability
- Adventure
- Adventurous
- Affection
- Affective
- Aggressive
- Agility
- Aggressiveness
- Alert
- Alertness
- Altruism
- Ambition
- Amusement
- Anti-bureaucratic
- Anticipate
- Anticipation
- Anti-corporate
- Appreciation
- Approachability
- Approachable
- Assertive
- Assertiveness
- Attention to detail
- Attentive
- Attentiveness
- Availability
- Available
- Awareness
- Balance
- Beauty
- Being the best
- Belonging
- Best
- Best people
- Bold
- Boldness
- Bravery
- Brilliance
- Brilliant
- Calm
- Calmness
- Candour
- Capability
- Capable
- Careful
- Carefulness
- Caring
- Certainty
- Challenge
- Change
- Character
- Charity
- Cheerful
- Citizenship
- Clean
- Cleanliness
- Clear
- Clear-minded
- Clever
- Clients
- Collaboration
- Comfort
- Commitment
- Common sense
- Communication
- Community
- Compassion
- Competence
- Competency
- Competition
- Competitive
- Completion
- Composure
- Comprehensive
- Concentration
- Concern for others
- Confidence
- Confidential
- Confidentiality
- Conformity
- Connection
- Consciousness
- Consistency
- Content
- Contentment
- Continuity
- Continuous improvement
- Contribution
- Control
- Conviction
- Cooperation
- Coordination
- Cordiality
- Correct
- Courage
- Courtesy
- Craftiness
- Craftsmanship
- Creation
- Creative
- Creativity
- Credibility
- Cunning
- Curiosity
- Customer focus
- Customer satisfaction
- Customer service
- Customers
- Daring
- Decency
- Decisive
- Decisiveness
- Dedication
- Delight
- Democratic
- Dependability
- Depth
- Determination
- Determined
- Development
- Devotion
- Devout
- Different
- Differentiation
- Dignity
- Diligence
- Direct
- Directness
- Discipline
- Discovery
- Discretion
- Diversity
- Dominance
- Down-to-earth
- Dreaming
- Drive
- Duty
- Eagerness
- Ease of use
- Economy
- Education
- Effective
- Effectiveness
- Efficiency
- Efficient
- Elegance
- Empathy
- Employees
- Empower
- Empowering
- Encouragement
- Endurance
- Energy
- Engagement
- Enjoyment
- Entertainment
- Enthusiasm
- Entrepreneurship
- Environment
- Equality
- Equitable
- Ethical
- Exceed expectations
- Excellence
- Excitement
- Exciting
- Exhilarating
- Exuberance
- Experience
- Expertise
- Exploration
- Explore
- Expressive
- Extrovert
- Fairness
- Faith
- Faithfulness
- Family
- Family atmosphere
- Famous
- Fashion
- Fast
- Fearless
- Ferocious
- Fidelity
- Fierce
- Firm
- Fitness
- Flair
- Flexibility
- Flexible
- Fluency
- Focus
- Focus on future
- Foresight
- Formal
- Fortitude
- Freedom
- Fresh
- Fresh ideas
- Friendly
- Friendship
- Frugality
- Fun
- Generosity
- Genius
- Giving
- Global
- Goodness
- Goodwill
- Gratitude
- Great
- Greatness
- Growth
- Guidance
- Happiness
- Hard work
- Harmony

- Health
- Heart
- Helpful
- Heroism
- History
- Holiness
- Honesty
- Honour
- Hope
- Hopeful
- Hospitality
- Humble
- Humility
- Humour
- Hygiene
- Imagination
- Impact
- Impartial
- Impious
- Improvement
- Independence
- Individuality
- Industry
- Informal
- Innovation
- Innovative
- Inquisitive
- Insight
- Insightful
- Inspiration
- Integrity
- Intelligence
- Intensity
- International
- Intuition
- Intuitive
- Invention
- Investing
- Investment
- Inviting
- Irreverence
- Irreverent
- Joy
- Justice
- Kindness
- Knowledge
- Leadership
- Learning
- Legal
- Level-headed
- Liberty
- Listening
- Lively
- Local
- Logic
- Longevity
- Love
- Loyalty
- Mastery
- Maturity
- Maximising
- Maximum Utilisation
- Meaning
- Meekness
- Mellow
- Members
- Merit
- Meritocracy
- Meticulous
- Mindful
- Moderation
- Modesty
- Motivation
- Mystery
- Neatness
- Nerve
- No bureaucracy
- Obedience
- Open
- Open-minded
- Openness
- Optimism
- Order
- Organisation
- Original
- Originality
- Outrageous
- Partnership
- Passion
- Patience
- Patient-centred
- Patient-focused
- Patients
- Patient-satisfaction
- Patriotism
- Peace
- People
- Perception
- Perceptive
- Perfection
- Performance
- Perseverance
- Persistence
- Personal development
- Personal growth
- Persuasive
- Philanthropy
- Play
- Playfulness
- Pleasantness
- Poise
- Polish
- Popularity
- Positive
- Potency
- Potential
- Power
- Powerful
- Practical
- Pragmatic
- Precise
- Precision
- Prepared
- Preservation
- Pride
- Privacy
- Proactive
- Proactively
- Productivity
- Profane
- Professionalism
- Profitability
- Profits
- Progress
- Prosperity
- Prudence
- Punctuality
- Purity
- Pursue
- Pursuit
- Quality
- Quality of work
- Rational
- Real
- Realistic
- Reason
- Recognition
- Recreation
- Refined
- Reflection
- Relationships
- Relaxation
- Reliability
- Reliable
- Resilience
- Resolute
- Resolution
- Resolve
- Resourceful
- Respect
- Responsibility
- Responsiveness
- Rest
- Restraint
- Results
- Results-oriented
- Reverence
- Rigour
- Risk taking
- Rule of law
- Sacrifice
- Safety
- Sanitary
- Satisfaction
- Security
- Self-awareness
- Self-motivation
- Self-responsibility
- Self-control
- Self-directed
- Selfless
- Self-reliance
- Sense of humour
- Sensitivity
- Serenity
- Serious
- Service
- Shared prosperity
- Sharing
- Shrewd
- Significance
- Silence
- Silliness
- Simplicity
- Sincerity
- Skill
- Skilfulness
- Smart
- Solitude
- Speed
- Spirit
- Spirituality
- Spontaneous
- Stability
- Standardisation
- Status
- Stealth
- Stewardship
- Strength
- Structure
- Succeed
- Success
- Support
- Surprise
- Sustainability
- Sympathy
- Synergy
- Systemisation
- Talent
- Teamwork
- Temperance
- Thankful
- Thorough
- Thoughtful
- Timeliness
- Timely
- Tolerance
- Tough
- Toughness
- Traditional
- Training
- Tranquility
- Transparency
- Trustworthy
- Truth
- Understanding
- Unflappable
- Unique
- Unity
- Universal
- Useful
- Utility
- Valour
- Value
- Value creation
- Variety
- Victorious
- Victory
- Vigour
- Virtue
- Vision
- Vital
- Vitality
- Warmth
- Watchful
- Wealth
- Welcoming
- Willfulness
- Winning
- Wisdom
- Wonder
- Worldwide
- Work/life balance
- _ _ _ _ _ _ _
- _ _ _ _ _ _ _
- _ _ _ _ _ _ _
- _ _ _ _ _ _ _

2 Consolidate into five groups

Write down the values you highlighted, grouping them together into five categories. Each category is to represent the essence of the words you've captured describing your values.

3 Five words to describe your groups

Now select one word from each category that you feel best represents that group of words. That word is your value.

4 Top five values

Now it's time to bring them to life. For each value, add an actionable statement. This takes your values beyond a single word into something that is rich, meaningful, and inspiring, guiding behaviour.

For example… One of our values at COMUNiTI is communication. Our value statement is: *"It's a dialogue not a monologue,"* emphasising the importance of two-way communication, listening, learning and exchanging stories.

Translating values into behaviour

When I start working with clients they often share their values, whether written down, printed on the wall, or described as a general feeling of what they believe is essential to them. What is also interesting is how these values then align with the organisation's culture. By engaging the broader organisation in completing the Five Words Culture Survey from chapter two, we can identify what the organisation's people believe necessary. This exercise in itself can create a transformational conversation. Still, the objective is to uncover how the organisation's people think they need to behave to align with its culture and values.

Our next step is to translate how this culture comes to life. What do I "see" when someone behaves in alignment with the values? That's where the magic happens. By talking through their values, and digging into how their people need to show up, the actions they need to take, and the behaviours they need to demonstrate, we can begin to describe what it "looks" like to live the values and align with the culture.

When we can understand what it looks like to live the values, we can then influence others to align with them by manufacturing opportunities for them to do so. We can create spaces, zones and environments that guide people to act in a particular way that aligns with the organisation's desired outcomes.

FOR EXAMPLE, WHAT WOULD YOU EXPECT TO SEE IF YOUR ORGANISATION VALUES THE HEALTH AND WELLBEING OF ITS EMPLOYEES?

- You might see people wearing their gym clothes at lunch or arriving in their cycling gear in the morning.

- You might see people engaging in conversation in the breakout space.

- You might see people standing at their workstations or having standing meetings.

Each of these "actions" is a behaviour that can be influenced by how the environment is constructed.

- Going to the gym at lunch or before work requires provision of adequate showers and change facilities for employees to engage in such activities and then freshen up for the rest of the day.

- Conversations in the breakout space require it to be suitably positioned and provisioned to encourage employees to interact, communicate and build relationships with colleagues, supporting their emotional wellness.

- Employees standing at their workstations or in meetings requires the provision of stand-up workstations or high meeting tables to encourage the active movement of people throughout the day.

Each of these actions is driven by the value of health and wellbeing, and the spaces and furniture provided create opportunities for employees to engage in aligned behaviours.

Another way of considering this could be around another value of "One Team". As organisations are transitioning to new ways of working and the need to increase communication amongst teams grows, previously existing silos need to be dissolved.

THE CHALLENGE IS THAT MANY OF THESE SILOS ARE A PRODUCT OF THE ENVIRONMENT AND THE CONSTRUCTION OF BARRIERS.

Offices, densely built areas, walled-off departments and multiple floors and amenities contribute to the division and separation of departments, teams and people. While some of these requirements are unavoidable due to team sizes requiring multiple floors and buildings, measures can be taken to limit the impact of these factors.

By creating large singular communal spaces, such as cafes, we can encourage movement throughout the building, consolidating employees into a distinct space, moving them off their individual floors and engaging in an unstructured way with people from other floors and departments. While a lift provides the same technical function as stairs, to move people from one floor to another, the visible connection gets lost when you step into that rectangular box. Introducing voids, atriums and internal staircases creates visibility and connectivity through a building, enabling people to move between spaces and improving their awareness of teams on other floors.

Your organisation's values can guide every behaviour within your workplace, so it pays to take the time to consider what it looks like when your people act in alignment with your desired values.

The result for Mapien...

case study
Mapien

Mapien is an organisation with a strong foundation of family and inclusivity that translates into its value set: integrity, flexibility, leadership, courage, excellence and fairness. But Mapien struggled to live its desired culture due to the constraints of the physical environment. As a specialist people consultancy offering bespoke workplace people solutions, creating a workplace that enabled its vision was core to its business objectives.

As Nadia Taylor, CEO at Mapien, explained in Episode 1 of the *Work Life by Design Podcast*, The Value of Designing for Business Values, this foundation of family showed up in a number of ways:

> In working with COMUNiTI, one of the things we discovered was that very strong family orientation that sits within the organisation. That comes through our values, but probably most strongly in fairness and flexibility.
>
> And that's because we know flexibility is essential to family. But it's really essential to anyone being able to be their best self at work, whether it's because they have young children or they have a parent to care for.

Nadia noted that these considerations extended beyond familial responsibilities, explaining that Mapien wanted its employees to have the flexibility to do what they love and value most. She highlighted one employee who is passionate about surfing and able to restructure his day when the surf's up. "That's what it's all about," she continued. "We take family in its broader meaning. It's everything you want to achieve out of life, and having the flexibility to do that is core to our values."

However, Mapien's previously occupied space prevented its staff from interacting and behaving in a conducive way.

the task

Tune into Episode 1 of the *Work Life By Design* podcast for the rest of our chat.

Even though Mapien wanted employees to collaborate, the office space was a physical barrier preventing that happening. The space consisted of 36 individual offices for 36 employees, a small kitchen space, and formal reception and meeting room areas. Its structure offered little to no flexibility, an issue highlighted most prominently when Nadia, a new mum, put her baby to sleep in the server room, as it was the only available space.

> "The brief was to encourage team collaboration and enrich workplace relationships. Through the creation of communal spaces, the workplace brings together the three key business units to drive high performance."

> "CHANGING THE PHYSICAL ENVIRONMENT HELPED CHANGE THE PSYCHOLOGY OF OUR PEOPLE. NOT LONG AFTER MOVING INTO THE SPACE WE MERGED WITH ANOTHER BUSINESS, WHICH WOULD'VE BEEN FAR MORE DIFFICULT AND NOT AS SUCCESSFUL IF WE HADN'T BEEN THROUGH THE PROCESS OF MOVING INTO THAT SPACE. WE WERE A 35-YEAR-OLD BUSINESS, NOW WE ARE AN AGILE, FLEXIBLE BUSINESS READY TO EMBRACE OPPORTUNITY."
>
> – NADIA TAYLOR, CEO

the inspiration

In understanding Mapien's desired behaviours and observing what wasn't working in the current environment, we could workshop a vision for the organisation's future state.

It involved encouraging social interaction and informal communication, active collaboration spaces and lounges for social conversations, contrasted by intimate work zones for deep concentrative work, casual lounging areas, flexible spaces easily reconfigured to support wellbeing activities, and the inclusion of a parents' lounge.

Formerly known as Livingstone's, the organisation underwent a significant merger, rebranding to Mapien shortly after occupying the premises. The original Livingstone's logo, was a sextant, a nautical navigation device with sub-branding depicting stylised constellations. Upon their rebrand to Mapien, this nautical theme was retained, connecting to the business's core philosophy of "guiding clients through rough seas with rocks underneath, whilst looking to the stars for guidance."

This nautical narrative inspired a conceptual metaphor of a luxury Scandinavian boat deck, expressed through blended materials and a tonal palette featuring limewashed timber, VJ panelling, navy blues and crisp whites.

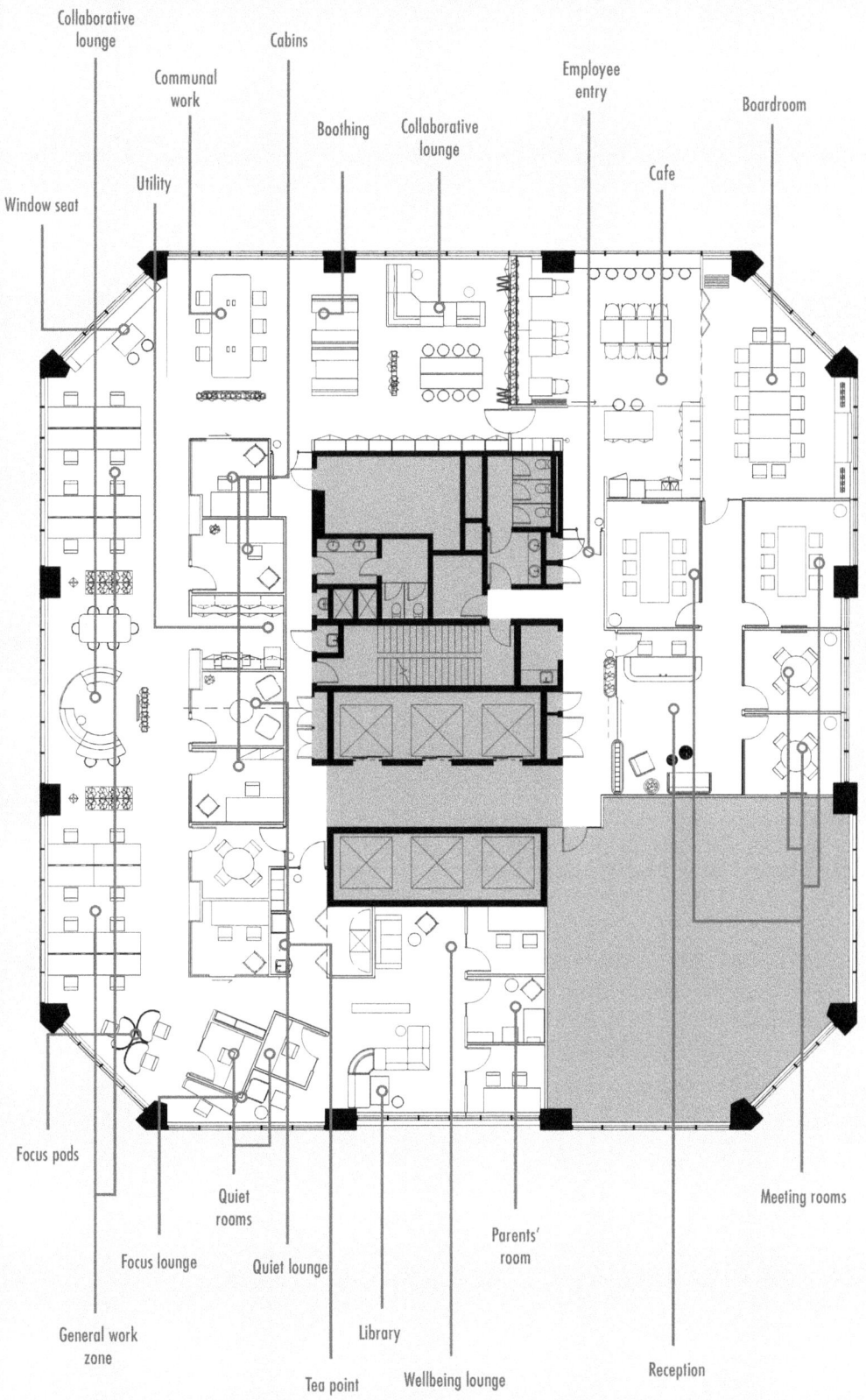

the solution

This vision was then overlaid into the workplace planning through carefully considered flow, zoning and furniture typologies. With a largely transient workforce, creating an agile approach enabled flexible use of and movement through the space to enhance team dynamics and connectivity, reinforcing the desired collaboration and connection and ensuring inclusivity for all employees.

Embracing a residential feel to reflect the family values of the business, so visitors feel welcome while staff feel at home, furniture and joinery are used imaginatively to encourage a range of new behaviours. These behaviours underpin the values of Mapien and the desired shift in mindset required for the next horizon for the business.

the detail

The employee journey starts on entering the tenancy. This first interaction is through the cafe, where you can grab your morning coffee, greet your colleagues and start your day by catching up. A large world map covers one wall and pinpoints recent staff travel destinations, offering a talking point and ice-breaker for employees. Hanging proudly on this same wall is the 'HMAS Success bell' – a playful element that's rung as a calling bell for social gatherings and to mark the appointment of new projects.

As the conversation turns to work and the need to nut out a problem, you can quickly move to the adjacent collaboration space, complete with whiteboards to enable visual problem solving and multiple inputs.

The furniture encourages active participation through stand-up tables and invites passers-by to share their opinions by sitting alongside the main office thoroughfare.

As the solution becomes apparent, it's time to turn our attention to putting the ideas into context. So we move to a workstation, where we can continue to sit alongside our colleagues yet begin to document our thoughts and formalise them. If a more concentrative space is required, we move deeper into the floor plate to occupy a more intimate work setting, a quiet room, or make ourselves comfortable in the library.

Throughout, the changing furniture types provide employees with behaviour cues regarding the appropriate work style: standing desks, whiteboards and open working tables to imply collaboration and conversation, while contained lounge spaces and workstations suggest a quieter, focused environment.

Mapien is also a proactive advocate for parents returning to the workplace and encourages employees to consider alternative and flexible work structures to support their life aspirations, from parenthood to climbing the career ladder. Bringing your children into the office is an everyday occurrence at Mapien. Whether balancing a new baby and a career or providing occasional care for your child, the workplace is a comfortable space. The parents' lounge has a changing table, toys and independently controlled lighting.

All these spaces, zones and furniture have been carefully considered and planned out to provide a holistic and supportive experience that reflects the values of what Mapien is and how the business wishes to create a collaborative and family-orientated workplace.

In our podcast, Nadia also reflected on how the physical environment supported the attraction and retention of employees, and how they aligned with the business:

I think our physical environment has strengthened our culture, and therefore those who perhaps didn't fit as cleanly have moved on.

And I absolutely believe that due to us being able to more visibly connect and sense and feel those expected values and behaviours, people have either become more aligned or self-selected.

Even as part of our recruitment process, we always walk people through the space, and you can see their reaction; people are either energised and excited about the workspace, or they start to look a bit uncomfortable. And those are just not going to be the right fit. I think people go: "oh well, that's because it's the workspace." But the workspace is reflective of our values and our culture, so by them reacting in that way, they're reacting to our culture overall.

– NADIA TAYLOR, CEO

Welcoming guests into the workplace, the reception area is a warm space embracing the nautical aesthetic. Limed timber floors, panelled walls and soft curtains adorn the glazing to the meeting rooms.

Shortly after occupying the space, Livingstones underwent a significant merger with another business, rebranding to Mapien. The environment was a significant factor in the success of the merger, having transformed the mindset of their people to become agile and adaptable to change.

CASE STUDY – MAPIEN

the result

12 months after moving into the new workplace, we asked Mapien's people what they thought of their new environment. Here's what they had to say...

100%
COMMUNICATION
100 percent felt that the new office has increased communication among staff in the new environment

84%
PRODUCTIVITY
84 percent of staff felt they were more productive in the new environment

91%
JOB SATISFACTION
91 percent felt that their job satisfaction had increased in the new environment

100%
COLLABORATION
100 percent of staff felt that they were more collaborative in the new environment

92%
RELATIONSHIPS
92 percent of staff felt the new office environment "greatly" to "significantly" enhanced personal relationships between individuals and departments

Plus, Mapien has been certified as one of the Best Places to Work in 2022

HAPPIER WORKPLACE

Employees rated their average level of happiness in the new environment at 8.92/10

CULTURE REPRESENTATION

100 percent felt the new work environment represents the culture of the company

BRAND ALIGNMENT

100 percent felt that the design represented the brand and what it stands for

We had the highest financial performance on record in our 35 years in business in the first six months after we moved into our new premises.

It's really driven another component of our culture, too: we're flexible, agile, and ready to face the new world.

We attribute that to the way our newly designed workspace enabled our different teams to engage and come up with multi-disciplinary solutions for our clients.

Our teams are able to interact better than ever before.

– NADIA TAYLOR, CEO

The cafe is intentionally the first touch point for staff on entering the workplace, positioned to encourage social connection as people grab a coffee to start their day. The world map is a conversation starter — each employee is given a tag to pin on their last holiday destination, providing an ice-breaker to get to know each other.

Above: The cafe is a multi-functional space that can be reconfigured to support various needs, from the usual dining space to an informal work area, informal meeting space and a training area. The bi-fold windows above the banquet can remain open to create connectivity through to the general work area, or can be closed to create privacy and separation as needed.

Below: The boardroom adjoins the cafe, facilitating the creation of a function space for larger gatherings. The boardroom and meeting rooms take on a more residential dining feel, reflecting the family values of the business.

Below: Varying furniture configurations influence the behaviour of people within the space. High tables, bar stools and whiteboards encourage active brainstorming, while a casual lounge encourages conversation over a coffee.

Above: Booth seating provides semi-enclosed spaces for people to work collaboratively or individually in a more relaxed, casual space.

Above: A variety of different work settings support a range of work styles and modalities throughout the space. Large communal lounges encourage informal conversation, working and collaborative activities, while shared offices support deep concentrative work, webinars and video conferencing.

Left: Fun fact! Each of the individual work zones, called cabins, has a light outside to signal to team members when the room is in use — making it easy to scan the workspace to find a vacant room.

Left: The cabins have been furnished to support different work styles. This cabin has been fitted with casual armchairs to encourage conversation between employees. It's a space dedicated to the company's late director, Laurie, whose door was always open for a chat.

Above and left: A relaxed lounge area supports individual work in a quiet setting, while adjacent spaces encourage employees to relax and rejuvenate with meditation, reading or yoga in the wellness area.

Designing for
deep work

Cal Newport's book *Deep Work: Rules for Focused Success in a Distracted World* offers a range of work practices to reduce distraction and enhance your ability to engage in deep work, and makes a case for why intently focused work is so vital to our modern economy.

I often speak about the need for all employees to be able to perform "deep work", and with the recent redesign of our work practices (courtesy of the pandemic) leading to more employees working remotely, this conversation has become even more important.

However, an increasingly remote workforce doesn't negate the need for us to consider the provision of spaces to support deep work in our corporate workplaces. While we may have the ability to perform more of this uninterrupted, individual and concentrative work in the isolation of our homes, it remains a critical requirement of our workplaces for several reasons.

INDIVIDUAL WORK STYLE PREFERENCES VARY, AS DOES THE DESIRE TO BE SOCIALLY CONNECTED.

EMPLOYEES' PERSONAL HOUSING SITUATIONS ARE DIFFERENT, AND PERHAPS NOT CONDUCIVE TO WORK FROM HOME ARRANGEMENTS DUE TO:

1. Small children, constant interruption and distraction
2. Shared living arrangements, no dedicated office space
3. Poor internet connection

Newport described the ideal workplace layout as a "hub and spoke" model in which there are communal spaces for serendipitous encounters or collaboration, and private, isolated spaces for uninterrupted focus. This hub and spoke model responds to the continued backlash that open-plan offices have received due to their failure to appropriately support individual deep-focus work, and the constant distraction many people experience working in these spaces.

Newport also presents the concept of the Eudaimonia Machine, developed by architectural professor David Dewane. Eudaimonia comes from Ancient Greek philosophy, specifically Aristotelian ethics, and is described as the condition *of human flourishing or of living well.* The Eudaimonia Machine seeks to create this sense of flourishing through a linear series of spaces or rooms that move the individual through increasingly deeper levels of cognitive work, culminating in deep-work spaces. In essence, enabling employees to flourish in the performance of their work.

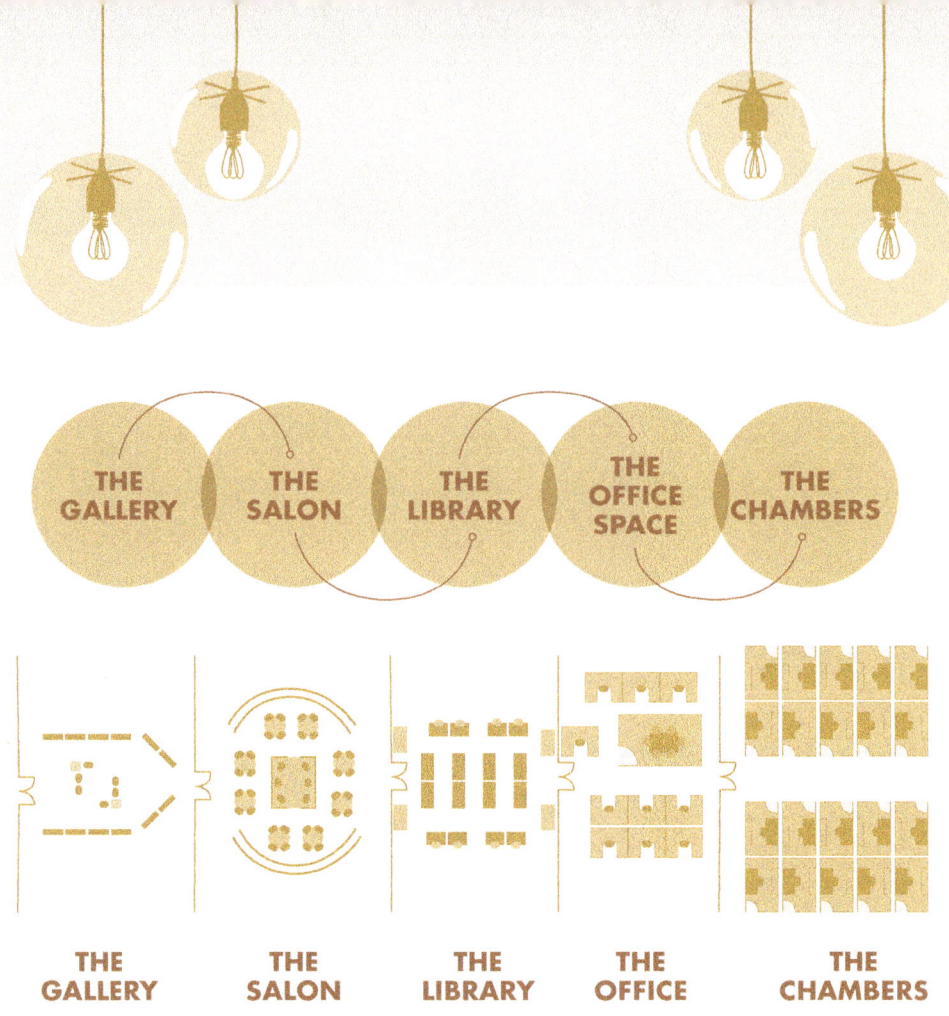

Before being aware of the Eudaimonia Machine[5] model, I had applied a similar conceptual approach in the Mapien workplace layout design. Our goal was to transition employees through a series of spaces supporting deeper and deeper cognitive and individual work levels, guiding them in their flow through workplace zoning.

This foundational design for Mapien's agile and subsequently hybrid work model has since gone on to guide the design principles of my work. By transitioning employees through a series of behaviourally cued spaces, we can shape their work experience in a way that responds to the organisation's value-driven behaviours and employees' individual work preferences.

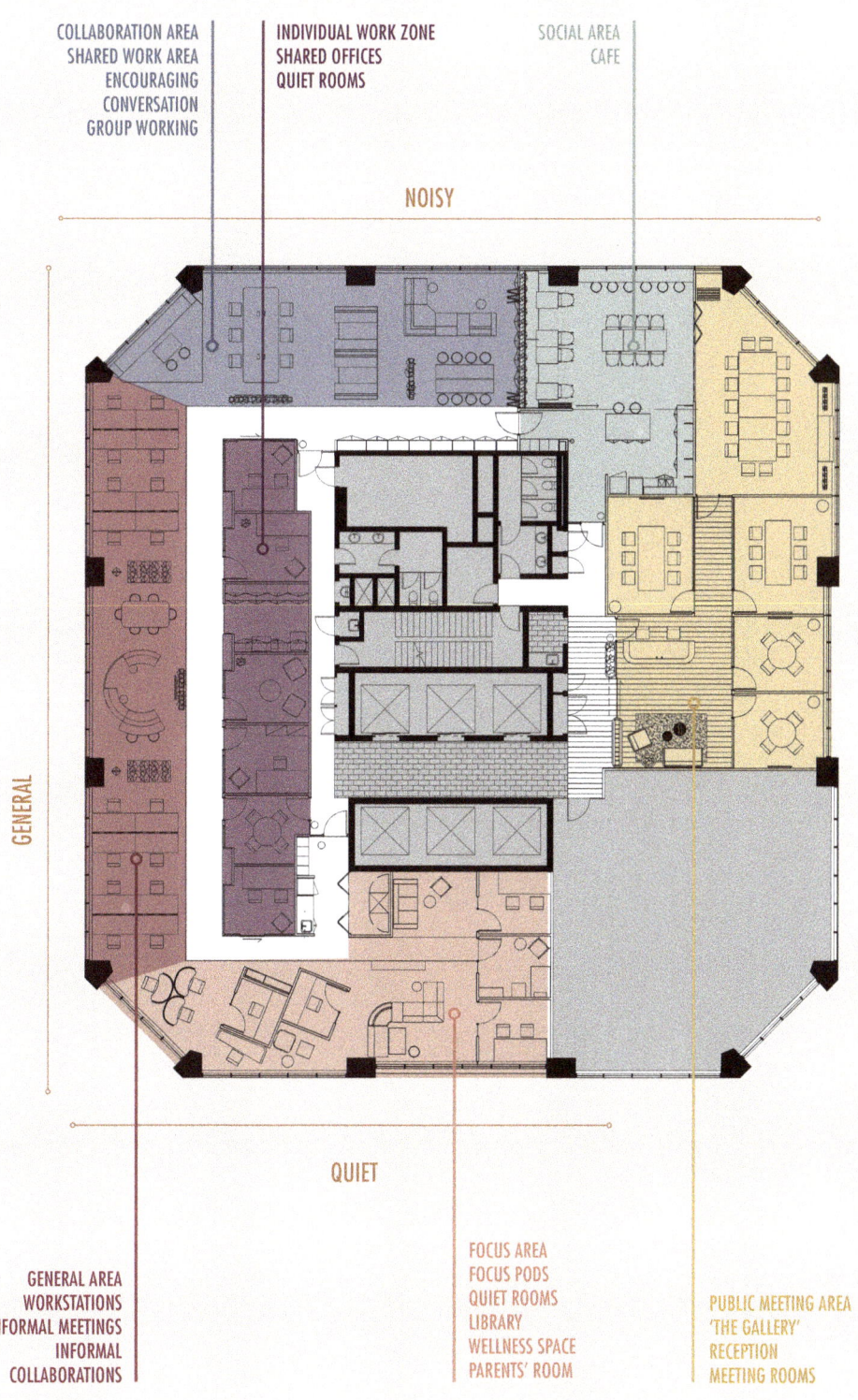

This workplace planning style supports employees to work in a way that suits the task and activity they are required to perform and their individual work preferences; social and meeting activities happen in collaboration spaces while focused report writing, data analysis, and other complex cognitive tasks occur in individual spaces.

Extroverts preferring more vibrant, active and noisy spaces will gather in the collaborative zones, while introverts will tend to gravitate towards the library and quiet rooms to satisfy their need for personal space.

As more and more organisations transition to hybrid work models, they will need to foster social capital, prioritise culture and connectivity as the primary purpose for visiting the workplace, and transition employees through layers of cognitive work. These strategies can all be achieved through intelligent workplace design. •

Chapter Huddle

TRANSFORM YOUR WORKPLACE AND INSPIRE THE BEHAVIOUR OF YOUR PEOPLE.

VALUES GUIDE BEHAVIOUR.

Your organisation's values are expressed through the behaviours you want your employees to engage in: how you want them to show up, act and communicate. It's your people living in alignment with the values through their actions.

OUR ENVIRONMENT INFLUENCES OUR BEHAVIOUR.

When you can articulate the behaviours you want to see, you can then influence them through the environment's design, guiding the work type, tasks and activities your people perform. There are three key ways:

FLOW — How your space is laid out, guiding a sequence of activities

ZONING — The arrangement and proximity of spaces

SPACES — The variety of furniture types and styles

BEHAVIOUR DETERMINES PERFORMANCE.

Your environment doesn't just transform external behaviours. It also influences mindsets – not just those of the individuals but the whole organisation. Mapien was a 35-year-old traditional, staid business. Now it is an agile, flexible business ready to embrace opportunity.

Shift the mindset of your oganistion

WHAT BEHAVIOURS DO YOU WANT TO SEE IN YOUR WORKPLACE?

DESIGNING SPACES FOR THRIVING PEOPLE

CHAPTER FOUR

wellbeing at work

The concept of being healthy and safe at work is not new, however, the context in which it is presently evolving is unprecedented. Formerly, organisations operated Organisational Health and Safety (OH&S) departments to ensure a physically safe work environment that adhered to regulatory standards. But today, a physically safe workplace is the baseline, and employees are looking for more significant consideration of their overall wellbeing.

In the last decade, we have seen the rise of workplace initiatives aimed at supporting the physical wellness of our employees, however, providing a truly "well" environment requires a holistic approach. Fostering a wellness culture is the key to employees adopting and maintaining healthy behaviours, and creating an environment in which your employees will flourish is essential.

The pandemic has started a broader conversation on the role that organisations play in keeping us healthy and safe, and this is not just in the realm of good hygiene practices but also in the mental wellbeing of employees through extended periods of isolation, unusual work practices and the significant shifts that have occurred in our personal work routines.

WELLBEING IS NO LONGER JUST ABOUT BEING HAPPY OR PHYSICALLY FIT. IT'S ABOUT EVERYTHING THAT TRULY MATTERS TO US AND HOW WE EXPERIENCE OUR LIVES – AND A "LIFE WELL-LIVED" MEANS SOMETHING DIFFERENT TO EVERY PERSON.

A fruit box is not wellness

Workplace initiatives aimed at supporting the physical wellness of employees are common these days – from programs like the Global Step Challenge, where you compete against other organisations to virtually circle the earth with your daily step count, to a weekly fruit box that offers up a healthy snack alternative to the cookie jar. While these are great steps to encourage a healthier workforce, they are hardly a holistic solution. And because they are rarely monitored or measured, these programs risk being scrapped in any budget cuts when the organisation fails to see a return on the investment.

While most people consider employee wellbeing important, some leaders may not see it as a business concern. *"Surely wellbeing is an individual concern and not the organisation's responsibility to manage?"* they assume. *"Leaders are responsible for business performance, not managing an employee's personal wellbeing and social life."* And to some extent, fair point. However, this thinking overlooks the impact that an individual's wellbeing has on the organisation's performance. Thriving employees positively influence an organisation's bottom line.

SO, MUCH SO THAT WELLBEING SHOULD BE A CORE ASPECT OF ORGANISATIONAL STRATEGY.

GALLUP FOUND THAT EMPLOYEES WITH THRIVING WELLBEING:[1]

- are 36% more likely to report a full recovery after an illness, injury or hardship

- are more than twice as likely to say they always adapt well to change

- miss 41% less work as a result of poor health

- are 81% less likely to seek out a new employer in the next year

The data tells us that employees want employers to be partners in their wellbeing. Employees desire to be seen and understood as a "whole person." It's a topic that has been a focus of organisational leadership discussions for over a decade now: we need to be able to bring our "whole selves" to work, to be authentic and genuine. Companies that have built a reputation for supporting this conversation and are known to care for the whole person have become talent magnets. It's a critical advantage that will serve them well as employers of choice in the future.

When employees have a stronger sense of connection to the company, their engagement skyrockets. This translates to productivity improvements, profitability increases, and enhanced levels of loyalty. As the Gallup study noted:[1]

People with *thriving* wellbeing simply do better in life. And companies with thriving *employees* do better business.

The elements of wellbeing *at work*

OUR OVERALL WELLBEING AT WORK CENTRES AROUND THREE KEY AREAS: MENTAL, EMOTIONAL, AND PHYSICAL.

Let's explore each in turn.

MENTAL WELLBEING

Our mental wellness is challenged more than ever in today's hyper-connected world in which we are always "on," always available. Technology has also enabled us to have a window into others' seemingly perfect lives as they share their highlights reel while we sit and compare our less-than-exciting night sitting on the couch, watching reruns of Suits and eating chocolate ice cream . . . or is that just me?

As a society, we face higher levels of burnout, working long hours and under increasing pressure to achieve more with less. Employees may not only be caring for children but also for ageing parents. Our workforce comprises the largest generational mix, ranging from Gen Z through to Baby Boomers, each with vastly different work styles and expectations of their work environment.

While office sleep pods may have taken things a step too far, the need to introduce spaces that enable employees to retreat, recharge and recover is increasingly valuable in today's workplace. Wellness spaces cater to yoga and Pilates classes. Meditation spaces allow employees time and space to just sit and recharge. Multipurpose rooms provide privacy for breastfeeding mothers, employees to pray, and those needing a quiet moment. These spaces all enable employees to feel empowered to consider their mental wellbeing, and communicate that it is an essential focus of the organisation.

EMOTIONAL WELLBEING

Our emotional wellbeing is directly linked to our mental wellbeing and is the internalisation of feelings that set our thoughts in motion. Our sense of belonging and our ability to build relationships and connect with others also feed into our emotional wellness at work. When we don't feel like we belong, we feel outcast and isolated, which feeds into a deepening sense of loneliness. It's also increasingly important that employees feel they are doing meaningful work. Connecting our own personal values and ambitions to those of the company and our colleagues strengthens our sense of belonging and reinforces our emotional wellbeing.

PHYSICAL WELLBEING

Our physical wellbeing affects our energy levels, ability to concentrate and overall sense of wellness. Studies have shown that an uncomfortable chair can have a negative impact on our productivity, equating to lost revenue for an organisation.

The mainstream adoption of sit-to-stand desks addresses the concern that "sitting is the new smoking." Research completed by Dr David Dunstan of ODI Baker in

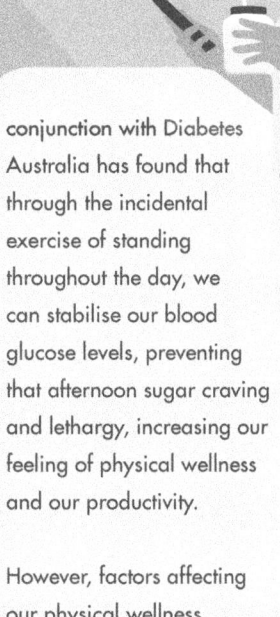

conjunction with Diabetes Australia has found that through the incidental exercise of standing throughout the day, we can stabilise our blood glucose levels, preventing that afternoon sugar craving and lethargy, increasing our feeling of physical wellness and our productivity.

However, factors affecting our physical wellness also go beyond the ergonomic setup of our work points. The quality of the air, lighting, and temperature control systems contribute significantly to our overall experience of physical wellness in the workplace.

I encourage companies to consider wellness in this holistic way – mental, emotional, and physical – and consider how they might design their space to make it more wellness-centric.

The impact of socialisation *at work*

I've had many conversations with key people in professional services firms confused about the need to have social spaces at work, believing that if you're socialising at work, you're not working. Often, I'm met with a look of bewilderment as to why their employees would want to establish friendships with their coworkers and why I would even be suggesting that this should be a factor for their consideration in the design of their new workplace. The truth is that, as humans, we are hard-wired with a desire for connection and a need to belong.

Healthy relationships at work have many advantages for both the employee and the employer. They lead to effective collaboration and increase employee engagement, wellbeing, and retention. That's why socialisation is a critical factor in the design of a workplace. When we shape spaces, we think about how they can spark conversations and enable the community to thrive, encouraging people to interact and connect at a personal level.

By creating workplaces that encourage socialisation, we enable cross-collaboration, which in turn can support us to develop more meaningful connections with those we work with. These connections help us establish trust and lay the foundations for building high-performing teams. And the more an industry is disrupted by digital technologies, the more it values "social competencies" such as collaboration, empathy and entrepreneurial skills.

SOCIALISATION BEFORE WORK COLLABORATION.

Collaboration spaces are great for bringing people together to brainstorm, ideate and contribute to a more extensive discussion, but what good are they if they're not creating successful outcomes? Before collaboration can happen, people in your organisation need to know their colleagues – who they are and their skills and abilities. When you know the people you work with, you know who you can bring to the table. Who can help you come up with solutions? Who are the key people for your project? Without socialising, there is no opportunity for effective collaboration. It's also easier to ask for help and guidance from someone you regularly talk to.

Research from MIT[2] supports this approach, recommending that managers promote socialising in the office by encouraging morning teas, lunch meetings, and coffee dates to create social, warm, open environments in which employees feel comfortable connecting with coworkers and sharing work experiences.

fika

[fee-kah] *noun*

a lovely swedish word meaning to slow down, take a break with friends or on your own and have a coffee and sweet treat such as a cake or a pastry.

KNOWING YOUR COLLEAGUES ON A PERSONAL LEVEL INCREASES EMPLOYEE ENGAGEMENT, WELLBEING, AND RETENTION.

In some organisations, this kind of workplace relationship is discouraged and possibly even frowned upon due to a belief that it lowers productivity by wasting time on idle chit-chat. However, you can increase employee engagement and retention through these social connections.

Research by Gallup[3] shows that having a best friend at work increases employee engagement, with these employees putting more effort into their work than those who don't have a best friend in the office. The same report found:

> *"When employees possess a deep sense of affiliation with their team members they feel driven to take positive actions that benefit the business—steps they may not even consider if they did not have strong relationships with their coworkers."*

Aside from increasing performance, strong social connections and friendships make a person happier and healthier. These genuine relationships satisfy the fundamental human need to belong, and help reduce stress, loneliness, and other mental health issues, all of which are becoming more and more prevalent in today's society. And to top all that off, people think twice about leaving a company where they have built friendships and established a solid support system within the organisation.

WHY LOSE THAT?

Employees today place greater importance on company culture, and one that stimulates solid social relationships would be hard to leave. Creating such a culture is a massive win for your people and your business, as happy, healthy employees are more productive and engaged.

SO HOW DO WE DO IT?

Designing workplaces for connection

Spaces that influence social behaviours are not new. Once, the water cooler was where people gathered to connect and share informal banter; today, the coffee machine has taken its position within the broader café/kitchen environment. These communal spaces draw people together and create opportunities for informal communication that crosses departmental boundaries, breaking down invisible divides.

As organisations explore new horizons in workplace design, we must consider the workplace environment's role in attracting employees back into the office. As hybrid working continues to become the norm and mandated office attendance becomes a thing of the past, we must ask, "What is the purpose of the workplace? What is the space required to do? What must it offer and provide for employees to want to come in?" In this context, we assess how the workplace encourages connectivity, socialisation and belonging.

When designing a space, I always consider the flow: how the workplace layout brings people together, creates chance encounters, and positively influences behaviour. I design distinct socialisation points throughout the office – entry areas, café spaces, stairways, print zones, tea points, bathrooms and breakout areas.

THESE SPACES ENABLE SPONTANEOUS INTERACTIONS THAT OPEN UP OPPORTUNITIES FOR PEOPLE TO MEET AND CONNECT WITHOUT AN AGENDA.

I'll often employ a technique to channel people from various departments together by having a singular kitchen or café space. People from different teams and across several floors come together at this social spot and start conversations whilst preparing and sharing a meal, breaking down barriers and silos often unintentionally created by departmental structures or multiple floor tenancies. Singular print zones are also perfect for "bumping" into colleagues as work-related tasks encourage people to move around and engage in spontaneous conversations. These social areas bring people together and promote deeper work relationships.

At COMUNiTI, we believe that a community is formed wherever people meet and interact. The shared values, experiences, and stories are what give these communities a collective sense of meaning, pride, and belonging.

According to Jenny Sauer-Klein[4], an experience designer focused on increasing connection, building community happens through a sense of connection – and that sense of connection comes from our experiences. If we want to enhance belonging and improve culture or team dynamics, we first need to change our people's experiences. And those experiences are most remembered at the beginning and end, our onboarding and offboarding, our entry and exit from a space, and the start and end of our days. If our intention is to create connection, then we need to shape those experiences accordingly.

AND THAT SENSE OF CONNECTION OCCURS IN THREE WAYS...

1 BODY - PHYSICAL TOUCH.

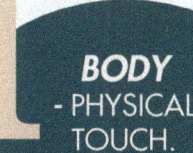

Physical connection and contact in a professionally acceptable way; high fives and handshakes.

2 HEART – VULNERABILITY.

Taking a relationship from a closed door to an open one, finding common ground, a relatable or shared experience that establishes a sense of connection. As Brené Brown says, " vulnerability is the key to connection."

3 MIND – PLAYFULNESS.

A state of mind that is not focused on what you do but on how you do it. It's a mindset that embraces the joy of the journey, creating a state of flow. And when we are in flow, our brain begins to create new neural pathways, essentially making us smarter. Play is vulnerable and revealing, so we need to feel safe by removing any risks and lowering the stakes. Stress is the opposite of play.

OUR WORKPLACES HAVE THE OPPORTUNITY TO ENHANCE THESE EXPERIENCES AND BUILD COMMUNITY BY ENABLING BEHAVIOURS CONDUCIVE TO CONNECTION.

Connecting in person supports our wellbeing on many levels.

1 The overwhelming increase in digital information and the urgency of virtual work has led to increased levels of exhaustion. Having in-person conversations allows our brains to assess tone, social cues, and body language to make meaning, whereas technology can create digital static. "*The gap between what you try to communicate online and what the person receiving the message understands*", according to Dr. Mary Donohoe, Founder of the Digital Wellness Centre. As this digital static increases, so does employee fatigue, anxiety, and burnout rates, while motivation and engagement decline.[5]

2 Establishing relationships with our fellow humans requires a face-to-face connection. When we meet people face to face, and our eyes meet, a neurological synchronisation occurs called a Retinal Eye Lock. According to Dr. Fiona Kerr, the founder of the NeuroTech institute, this synchronisation sets off a neurological process in the brain, creating a chemical reaction in the body. Your body then remembers this feeling and recreates it when meeting virtually, enabling the continuation of that relationship bond. However, it's important to note that this process cannot be activated virtually over a Zoom call. It must first be established in person.

3 You may also be familiar with Albert Mehrabian's Communication Model. The message behind this model is that our verbal (words), non-verbal (voice), and visual (body language) communication methods must be consistent.[6] Failing this, we will revert to the words spoken to understand the message's content. The issue with communicating in a virtual environment is that in seeking out these non-verbal cues over a screen, we have to concentrate harder to see them, further contributing to increased fatigue. When we meet in person, these subtle cues are easier to identify.

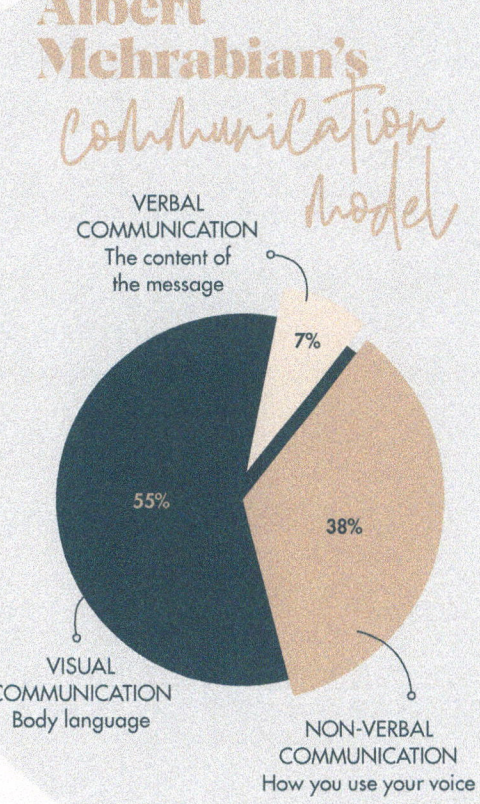

Albert Mehrabian's communication model

- VERBAL COMMUNICATION — The content of the message — 7%
- NON-VERBAL COMMUNICATION — How you use your voice — 38%
- VISUAL COMMUNICATION — Body language — 55%

As an employer, you have an *opportunity to* create a workplace environment that cares for your people's health *and wellbeing.*

One avenue to achieving this is making the office a hub for building solid relationships and a place where people want to come to and connect. Socialisation will lead to strong outcomes and creative solutions through collaboration, whilst physical proximity will lessen the burden of digital fatigue and burnout.

SO, DOES YOUR WORKPLACE ENCOURAGE CONNECTION?

Create an environment where interactions naturally happen and enable friendships in the workplace, and see how this works for your business.

EVERYONE WINS!

BUILD COMMUNITY THROUGH CONNECTION

CHAPTER 4 | WELLBEING AT WORK

DESIGNING A WELLNESS STRATEGY

Tune into Episode 7 of the *Work Life By Design* podcast for the rest of the chat.

Katrina Johnson is a Workplace Wellness Strategist and the Director of Wellness Designs, a boutique workplace wellness business supporting Australasian organisations to create healthy, safe, engaged and high-performing workplaces. In Episode 7 of the Work Life by Design[6] podcast, I spoke with Katrina about why every organisation needs a wellness strategy, and her case is compelling.

A wellness strategy is a blueprint that aligns to and integrates with the business' goals, vision, and culture and includes a clear set of goals, objectives, and strategy—whether at an individual, policy, culture or environmental level—to address employees' health and wellness needs. This includes the key parties responsible, the resources required, and measures of success and evaluation methods. This strategic approach often makes the difference between a successful workplace wellness program and one that outspends what it delivers.

Too often, we see organisations adopting a scattergun or 'tick-the-box' approach to workplace wellness. Free flu shots, lunchtime boot camps, and health checks are all nice things, but how are they tied to your business goals? It's common for organisations to not know why they have implemented initiatives; they only know they should 'do wellness.' You need a targeted and results-oriented strategy.

The key to measurable success is a systematic approach to well-being. It all comes down to how your strategy is designed and executed. We take our clients through our proven six-step Wellness Blueprint™ framework, designed to support and protect your greatest asset—your people—over the long term.

The framework looks like this

1. The first step is to **explore** the actual cost of poor health and wellness to the organisation and how this aligns with and supports your organisation's goals.

2. The second step is to **assess** the needs of individuals and organisations. If you don't undertake this critical step, you will be unable to get to the real heart of the issues and potentially waste time and money on the 'wrong' initiatives.

3. Third is to **design** a wellness strategy tailored to your unique business to ensure you stay on track, minimise risk and engage and secure commitment.

4. The fourth step is to **engage** in getting senior leaders, employees and other stakeholders to embrace it because, ultimately, nothing happens until people participate.

5. Fifth is to **monitor** and evaluate your strategy, which is critical to getting and demonstrating results. Yet only 12 percent of Australian workplaces measure the overall value of their investment. You need to show the value back to the business, linked to the key drivers and measures of success for your business.

6. The final step is to **sustain** how to deeply embed your strategy into your organisation so it continues to yield results. Agility will be key. You will need to be able to evolve and adapt to the needs of the business.

Ultimately meaningful results will come back to the key drivers for investing in the first place (being an employer of choice, boosting employee engagement) and consist of a mix of process, impact, and outcome measures using quantitative and qualitative methods. As the saying goes, tell the numbers to the CFO and the stories to the CEO.

How hybrid work contributes to wellbeing

Just as encouraging employees to physically connect in the workplace contributes to wellbeing, so does the flexibility to determine when and where an employee works. I know this may sound contradictory, *"You want people to come to the workplace, but you also want them to stay at home?"* However, it's about understanding what is right for your organisation and establishing the working rhythms that enable your people to perform by empowering their work environment choices.

The case for hybrid working from a wellbeing perspective extends far beyond the physical environment. Research has shown that schedule flexibility dramatically impacts employee experience compared to moderate schedule flexibility.

CHANGING WORK RHYTHMS, REQUIRES A CHANGE IN WORK ENVIRONMENT

KNOWLEDGE WORKERS WHO HAVE LIMITED ABILITY TO SET THEIR OWN HOURS REPORT;[7]

- 3.4x worse work-related stress and anxiety
- 2.2x worse work-life balance
- Employees with rigid work schedules also say they are 3x more likely to "definitely" look for a new job in the next year.

Engaging employees in a conversation around their preferred work rhythms is crucial to understanding how the work environment will be used and, therefore, support their preferred work choices. However, it is essential to note that this is a multi-layered conversation that requires us to consider what is needed by the business, the team, and the individuals to achieve the company's objectives. We must understand each group's requirements and design the workplace to support their interaction and objectives.

Tune into Episode 72 of the *Work Life By Design* podcast for the rest of our chat.

The pandemic left many of us questioning our priorities, with 36% of workers reporting that the pandemic has decreased the importance they place on their careers.[8] Add to that the global phenomenon of the Great Resignation, the rising rates of burnout, and the increasing levels of poor work-life balance plaguing our workplaces, it is clear we need to look at more sustainable ways of working. However, we also know that for any business to invest in a solution, they need to see a return on that investment.

> **EMPLOYEES WHO POSITIVELY RATED THEIR BUSINESS' COMMITMENT TO WELLNESS WERE 63% MORE LIKELY TO BE LOYAL.**[8]

A significant impact on organisations as we all compete in the war for talent and one that Mars Inc. has observed firsthand. In Episode 72 of the *Work Life by Design* podcast, Dr. Gary Webb, Regional Health and Wellbeing Manager at Mars Inc Global Health & Wellbeing Centre of Excellence, explained the ROI of the organisation's global wellbeing initiatives:

I remember doing some return on investment analysis and presenting it to the leadership team, I got about 30 seconds into it, and they said, "Gary, we don't need to hear this. We feel it. We see it. We don't need you to show us numbers to justify what we're doing".

AND THAT REALLY TALKS TO THE STRENGTH OF THE CULTURE AND HOW THEY UNDERSTAND THAT WELLBEING IS A MUST-DO. IT'S NOT A NICE-TO-DO.

As Gary explained in our chat, wellbeing is not a stand-alone concept.

To be successfully executed, it must be embedded in the systems and operations of the entire organisation. Our physical environments and workplaces form a large part of the solution. By creating an environment that enables the wellbeing objectives of the organisation, it will attract employees into the workplace, act as a magnet for aligned talent, and deliver an inclusive experience for all.

But a word of *Caution*

As we embrace increased remote work practices, we need to remain mindful of the social impacts that come with a hybrid workforce, ensuring the right mix of time in the office vs our time at home.

Working from home is making us lonely

Loneliness has been a subject of societal discussion well before the pandemic, with the Australian Government announcing a $46 million investment to combat it back in 2018.[9] According to research by the Australian Institute of Health & Welfare, over half of respondents have felt lonelier since the pandemic's onset.[10]

FORTUNATELY, THIS LONELINESS CAN BE COUNTERACTED BY EMPLOYEES WORKING TOGETHER IN A PHYSICAL WORKPLACE DUE TO THE DYNAMIC SOCIAL INTERACTIONS THAT SPONTANEOUSLY OCCUR THERE.

It has also been reported that support from our colleagues in the office can protect against loneliness.[2] Likely a result of our ability to physically connect (remember that retinal eye lock), creating more meaningful neurological and chemical connections and enhancing our sense of belonging.

> "You have to recognise that **loneliness is** actually a structural problem. It's the fact that my **environment** doesn't give me what I need."

– MARK MORTENSEN
Associate Professor for Organisational Behaviour at INSEAD Business School

Work-life balance is a fine line we walk

While we have all experienced the joy of having a few extra hours in our day due to the lack of commute time, working from home has also introduced new challenges for us to navigate. How to establish new routines and rituals to bookend our work day has been one of the questions I have encountered the most, along with "How do I shut down at the end of the day?" and "How do I separate 'work' from 'home' when there is no longer a physical separation between the two?" This lack of routine, structure, and ability to disconnect is contributing to a sense of poor work-life balance and burnout, which is directly tied to our ability to be productive.

- Employees who stated that they had poor work-life balance over the last three months were 76% more likely to also have felt burnt out. [8]

- Those who felt burnout were 35% more likely to feel that their productivity was low. [8]

- Employees with poor productivity were 280% more likely to feel a poor sense of work-life balance. [8]

IT'S A VICIOUS CYCLE OF WORKPLACE STRESS THAT CONTINUES TO DETERIORATE OUR WELLBEING.

> When we work in alignment with our neurobiology we optimise our performance and wellbeing.

— DR KRISTY GOODWIN
Digital Wellbeing & Neuro-Productivity Speaker, Author And Researcher.

Digital Wellbeing expert Dr Kristy Goodwin refers to our ability to create boundaries and disconnect in this technologically driven work environment as "Digital Guardrails":

"As we redefine new ways of working, we need to consider how we can start to use digital technologies in ways that are congruent with our human operating system (hOS)- our brains and bodies."

She encourages organisations to establish guiding principles on how they can communicate, collaborate and work efficiently in a distributed, asynchronous environment that empowers employees to protect both their focused work time and personal time without the feeling of "always being on and available". These Digital Guardrails range from education around technology management, such as silencing notifications between set hours to social contracts on acceptable response times.[11]

Locational divides introduce a new dynamic

Physical visibility, access to mentoring, and the opportunity to have spontaneous conversations with a manager are minimised when working from home, which can impact career progression and development. According to McKinsey, working from home also comes with a risk of losing our sense of belonging, common purpose and shared identity due to the emergence of two cultures; those "in the office" and those "at home".[12]

This impact can range from a graduate's ability to absorb work practices and industry knowledge organically through overhearing conversations or tacit learning while working remotely to a widening gender gap with women typically taking on more of the family caring role. And 46 percent of employees agreed mental health conversations are harder to have remotely.[8]

case study
Entain Aus.

THE NINE DAY FORTNIGHT AND A WORKPLACE FOR THE FUTURE

Reimagining the workplace for Entain Aus. began with a similar catalyst to many; they wanted to know how to utilise their space more effectively. Working closely with Entain Aus.'s Chief People Officer, Jessica Sharpe, we started by looking at their current state.

the task

Occupying 4,400 square metres over two floors, the sports betting and gaming group were exploring options to maximise the utilisation of their space. A series of business mergers and space acquisitions of adjacent tenancies had created a range of mismatched and segregated areas that did not bring the business together in a cohesive way. Large, outdated workpoint settings, limited collaboration spaces that didn't support the way they worked, and poor layout planning all contributed to an underutilised and impersonal space.

Adding to this, as they emerged from the lockdowns of the pandemic, the business adopted new ways of working that no longer saw them occupying the workplace the way they had before, leaving the space feeling empty and lacking the buzz and vibrancy that was and is a large part of their culture.

The first step in unravelling this problem was to understand the layers of the business, including the various business units, teams, relationships and work activities. The different work styles and working rhythms were highly varied, with groups ranging from analysts to product development and marketing to trading. Working closely with Jess, and team representatives, we developed working personas for each team that captured their work style preferences covering everything from:

- How they worked and collaborated
- Team size
- Workflow rituals throughout the day
- The spatial tools and equipment required
- Cross-team collaboration
- The amount of time they were likely to spend in the office and when

> " WE'VE SEEN WHAT OUR PEOPLE ARE CAPABLE OF WHEN THEY'VE BEEN TRUSTED AND EMPOWERED TO DO WHAT THEY NEED TO DO, WITHOUT BOUNDARIES ABOUT WHEN AND WHERE THAT TAKES PLACE. SO WE WERE A VERY COOL CASE STUDY IN THAT WAY THAT SHOWED WHAT HUMANS ARE CAPABLE OF WITHOUT BEING SAT DOWN AT A DESK IN FOUR-WALLED CUBICLES. "
>
> – JESSICA SHARPE, CHIEF PEOPLE OFFICER

the solution

The outcome of this data analysis was a map of the workplace ebb and flow across a week, customised to each team's needs, enabling us to capture the minimum work setting requirements and the supporting spaces necessary to facilitate employee performance. It responded to the product team's need for large groups to colocate in the office multiple days a week, engage in daily huddles, brainstorm and communicate new product developments, and be collaborative yet focused in their work delivery. Conversely, it also responded to the analysts' need for quiet, focused space, with limited requirements for group collaboration. These varying business unit needs were addressed by considering each team's flow, zoning and spaces, positioning them into neighbourhoods according to their unique requirements.

Maximising the capital investment in the project saw us repurposing the structure of the existing fitout, reallocating owned spaces to shared spaces such as meeting rooms and quiet zones, and reconfiguring workstation layouts and existing cafe facilities.

To achieve the desired workplace outcomes, we introduced a variety of collaboration spaces, quiet areas, training facilities, and more space-efficient workstations by consolidating work zones, overlaying the occupancy data and swapping out "owned" spaces such as workstations for "we" spaces such as communal work tables, open meeting areas and lounging. This enabled us to achieve the data-led requirements identified through the strategy whilst leveraging the capital investment to achieve the highest return for the client.

Throughout this process, the client has been on a high growth trajectory, which the fitout now enables them to accommodate without leasing additional space. An area that could previously accommodate 475 people on any given day now provides workpoint settings for 594 people, with a further 230 seats across meeting rooms, the cafe, and lounge spaces. With new workplace rhythms of hybrid working, the environment comfortably supports the ebb and flow of the 620-person workforce, with room for their continued expansion.

Whilst the initial catalyst for this project was of a financial nature, the subsequent decisions were anchored in ensuring that each team was provided with the necessary tools and empowered with the choice of how and where they would work to best support their individual and team's work objectives.

First impressions count. Connecting Entain Aus.'s employer brand to their corporate brand, the entry is a vibrant, fun, social space, with strong colours and geometric patterning.

CASE STUDY – ENTAIN AUS.

Tune into Episode 70 of the Work Life By Design podcast for the rest of our chat.

ENTAIN DAY

Throughout this process, Entain Aus. also introduced their nine-day fortnight, with every second Monday gazetted as "Entain Day", a compulsory, all company, no work day, along with "Meeting-Free Wednesday".

As Jessica Sharpe, Entain Aus.'s Chief People Officer, explained in Episode 70 of the *Work Life by Design* podcast.

> I'd been conferring on the seriousness of burnout with our leaders to identify what it looks like, how prevalent it is, and why. But more importantly, in thinking about how, as a tech business, our objectives are to be bold and innovative and to create solutions for our customers. How is what we're doing with our BAU and very busy schedules supporting our ability to do that? I'd suggest that along with the very competitive war for talent, it's no longer enough to say, *wellbeing is important and productivity is important.* We really needed to walk the talk.

What research have you done to support this concept and how are you encouraging people to use their Monday off?

> There's a book by John Fitch and Max Frenzel, *Time Off: A Practical Guide to Building Your Rest Ethic and Finding Success Without the Stress*, about building your rest ethic. That book inspired my thinking around changing my paradigm about rest, from just getting enough sleep or finishing the workday so that you can get to bed at a reasonable hour to being intentional about how we rest and recover.
>
> Your rest can be very active and still be beneficial. The book points out that even learning can be restful and rejuvenating. And I realized that this point was true to my experience. When I go away and learn about a topic that I'm really interested in, even if it's related to my work, it's energizing. So the idea of a nine-day

fortnight was about giving that one day to go, *"We've always said we're serious about learning and development. We give all the opportunities. We've got subscriptions online for Udemy and LinkedIn learn. But what you really need is time and space to do that."* Your learning doesn't even need to be work-related. Maybe you want to learn guitar and express some creativity in a different way. That's great. We're really promoting what active rest looks like. And using that tenth day of the fortnight to give back to yourself.

How have you supported employees to build the self-awareness to know what's right for them?

I think, like anything, it's about the example set. We're lucky to have a leadership team who are really behind this initiative. The executive team will be there and taking the day for themselves. We are sharing success stories on LinkedIn to show what's possible – and to remind everyone that they have permission to use the day freely. And so, I think seeing examples of how people are using the time to recharge themselves will hopefully be a powerful catalyst.

Developing a program around ongoing awareness in that space might buy people back a little bit more of their productive time too. So there's a range of ways we can make better use of our time, with self-awareness and knowing what we need to give themselves back just being one of them.

And Meeting Free Wednesday is another way to support productive time?

Absolutely. Meeting free Wednesday has been a critical piece in this initiative. By introducing that meeting-free day, we transformed a day that is quite often spent between various meetings, interruptions, and distractions and cleared a path for people to do their focus work and, hopefully, achieve a lot more.

How will you measure success?

It's definitely the most challenging piece. Rather than extensive surveys at the end of the period, we want to ask people how they're feeling and what their productivity is like along the way. There will be a lot that comes down to the listening sessions with leaders. We also plan to partner with our various department groups to help them articulate what productivity looks like in their teams. We can't always quantify it the way we can in our customer service team, where we can track and log the calls in the live chats. We know what's happening there. But in our knowledge worker space, it's very challenging to be able to put a measure on productivity. So we want to talk about what that looks like.

And we have spent a lot of time in the last two years building an understanding of our methodology for goal-setting and performance reviews based on the OKR model or methodology. So we've, again, inadvertently prepared ourselves for this in some way where we've shifted our idea of performance, and our performance conversations have been centred around the goals that we set each quarter and talking to those specifically when it comes to our team. So we're already in more of an outcomes-focused performance mindset than we have been sitting at the desk. So that will certainly help.

> **OUR BRAINS HAVE NOT ADAPTED TO THE PACE AND THE TECHNOLOGY THAT NOW IS ESSENTIALLY WHAT RUNS OUR LIVES**
>
> – JESSICA SHARPE, CHIEF PEOPLE OFFICER

This commissioned artwork connects employees and guests to the core values and essense of Entain Aus., guiding them from the Entry through to Café Sigma.

Café Sigma is the heart of the workplace. With barista coffee service, games area and lounge, the café encourages social interactions and restoration.

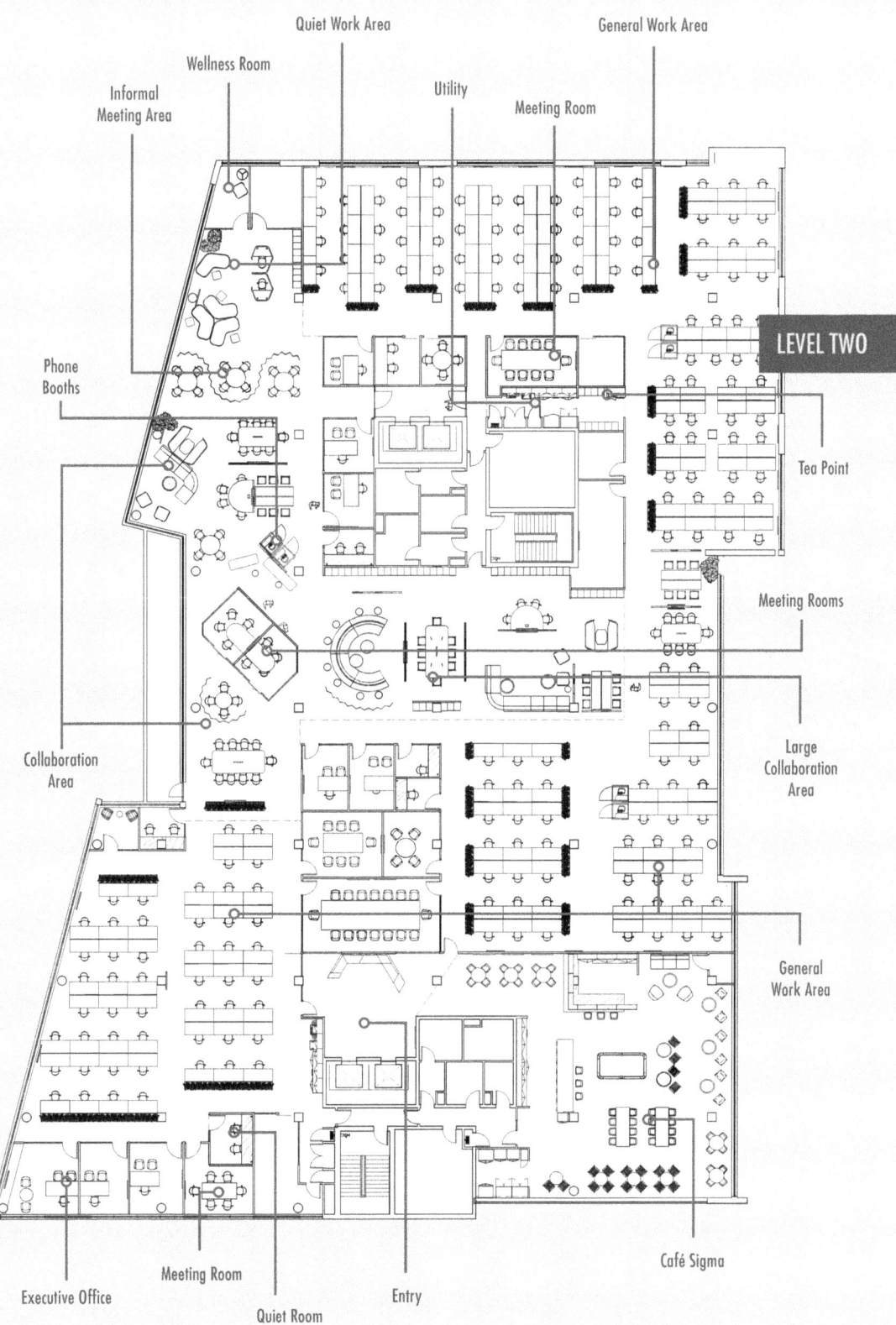

Large collaborative spaces with multiple communication tools, both digital screens and analogue whiteboards, support the 12 person strong teams to come together and actively solve complex problems.

A variety of furniture styles, enable employees choice, supporting varying individual work styles away from the typical 'workstation'.

THE NEXT WORKPLACE

The collaboration spaces transition from large active spaces to more intimate areas as they move to the extremities of the floor plate. Lightweight functional screens separate these spaces into a series of 'rooms' providing a sense of privacy whilst maintaining the openness of the space. The colour palette also reduces in its intensity shifting from vibrant colours in the active spaces to more subdued tones in the quieter zones.

As the floor plate transitions to quieter spaces, the furniture transitions to smaller, more intimate setting.

The workplace is divided into zones supporting a variety of work activities. The library promotes quiet, individual and reflective work.

Flexible, movable screens divide the open space creating pockets of space for smaller informal meetings.

The general work area balances the vibrant colours in the collaboration area, employing a subdued monochrome palette.

The Recording Studio supports the creation of multi-media across a variety of platforms.

Balancing shared space with individual work space, numerous quiet rooms are scattered throughout the workplace.

THE NEXT WORKPLACE

A variety of enclosed spaces support the needs of the business, ranging from four person spaces through to a large divisible training room.

CASE STUDY – ENTAIN AUS.

The financial case of designing *for wellbeing*

As business leaders, we are entrusted with a fiduciary duty to ensure our business' successful and profitable operation. So when it comes to wellbeing, it is often met with hesitancy, usually because we have been uncertain as to what we require to measure and how we measure it to demonstrate the impact of our buildings on our people.

As we've already heard from Dr Gary Webb and Wellness Designs, there are financial benefits in investing in the health and wellbeing of our people, but what about the health and performance of our buildings? Often the financial incentives of creating high-performance buildings are related to a reduction in energy savings and increased asset valuations.

HOWEVER, ANOTHER SIGNIFICANT INCENTIVE IS THE IMPROVED HEALTH, WELLBEING, AND PERFORMANCE OF THE OCCUPANTS, ENHANCING A COMPANY'S BOTTOM LINE.

43% of the total value of a High Performance Building, [HPB] comes from enhanced employee productivity, 41% from increased employee retention, 7% from improved employee wellness, 7% from utility savings and 2% from maintenance savings. Given this breakdown, human-centred design should be a critical consideration when creating a HPB.[13]

THE DESIGN OF OUR BUILDINGS AND THE QUALITY OF THE BUILD ARE OFTEN DRIVEN BY COST, RESULTING IN ENVIRONMENTS THAT, WHILE DESIGNED TO ACCOMMODATE PEOPLE, FAIL TO SUPPORT THE HEALTH AND WELLBEING OF THOSE PEOPLE.

However, when looking at the distribution of costs associated with the lifecycle of a building, the impact of our investments becomes clear. The 1-10-100-1000 phenomenon emerges, communicating the financial investment and effects of the decisions we make when designing and building spaces for people.

TYPICAL COMPANY LIFECYCLE EXPENDITURE COMPARISON[16]

EMPLOYEES $1000 | OPERATIONS $100 | CONSTRUCTION $10 | DESIGN $1

Legend:
- 80% Remaining OpEx
- 20% Energy, water & waste

Typical company spend breakdown throughout real estate / space / lifecycle, referred to as the 1-10-100-1000 phenomenon

CHAPTER 4 | WELLBEING AT WORK

And whilst there is no prescriptive solution to designing a high performance building, according to Stok, a global team of interdisciplinary experts in the built environment:

"Each building must be designed specifically for the needs of the occupant. These needs may include the tenant's business model, company culture, brand, and products or services."

Ken Yi Fong, WELL Building Accredited Professional and Global Advisory Board member, describes the value of investing in our wellbeing and that of our environments using the 90/90/90 principle. The principle being that there are three spheres that influence the wellbeing of our lives and contribution to work.

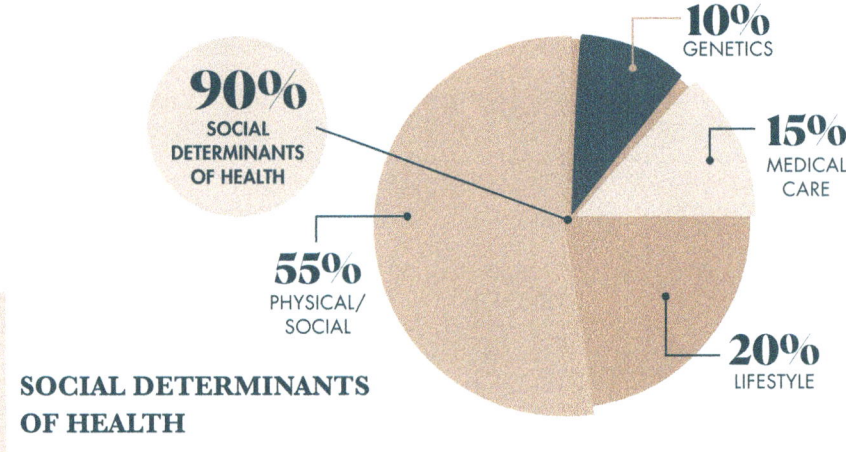

1. SOCIAL DETERMINANTS OF HEALTH

The social determinants of health are the economic and social conditions that influence individual and group differences in health status.[14] And 90 percent of those social determinants of health are influenced by our environment, our physical and social activity, our access to medical care and the lifestyle that we lead. It is only our genetics, which makes up 10 percent of these social determinants, that we cannot influence. Demonstrating the impact the design of our buildings and cities have on our health, which is within our ability to improve with conscious decision making.

THE AMOUNT OF TIME WE SPEND INDOORS[15]

- **90%** TIME SPENT INDOORS
- **7.6%** OUTDOORS
- **5.5%** IN A VEHICLE
- **11%** OTHER INDOOR LOCATION
- **1.8%** BAR/RESTAURANT
- **5.4%** OFFICE/FACTORY
- **68.7%** IN A RESIDENCE

We spend almost 90 percent of our day indoors, 86.9% to be exact. Think about your day; you wake up in your house, you travel to work in your car, or on the bus/train, you arrive at the office and head inside, where you spend the majority of your day, popping out to have lunch with friends or colleagues in a cafe or restaurant, before reversing the trip back to your home. Very little of our day is spent outside, usually the short commute between buildings or, if you are fortunate enough, spending your lunch break in the park. So it goes without saying that the health of the spaces we inhabit influences our personal health.

3. THE COST OF PEOPLE TO A BUSINESS[16]

This one is probably the most compelling for businesses looking to demonstrate a financial return! With employee wages and benefits typically accounting for 90 percent of a business's operating costs, the productivity of those employees should be a clear focus for the organisation.

Weighing heavily on a business' operating costs, even the smallest incremental improvements in employee productivity can have a far more significant impact on organisations' finances compared to other business costs. A 10 percent improvement in employee productivity yields a far more impactful result than saving 10 percent on rent, given the sheer cost associated with employees.

What may be considered only a slight improvement in employee health and productivity can have a significant financial return for employers. According to the World Green Building Council, it should be at the heart of any business case for healthy, productive offices.

90% OF WORKPLACE COSTS ARE PEOPLE

1% ENERGY

9% RENT

90% STAFF WAGES & BENEFITS

Tune into the full interview with **Ken Yi-Fong** in Eps 85. of the *Work Life by Design* podcast.

When designing our buildings and the spaces within them for their occupants, these factors should contribute to business leaders' decision-making. With the ability to tangibly measure the impact of these small incremental changes on the health and performance of our people, this is now a compelling business case worthy of serious consideration.

> **"There is overwhelming evidence which demonstrates that the design of an office impacts the health, wellbeing and productivity of its occupants."**
>
> – WORLD GREEN BUILDING COUNCIL

To measure these incremental changes, we need to be collating, analysing and unlocking the data that already exists in our organisation, demonstrating our environments' impact on our people's productivity and performance.

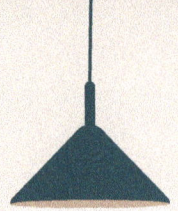

THIS DATA IS COLLECTED ACROSS THREE KEY METRICS;

1 FINANCIAL METRICS

- Absenteeism
- Staff turnover
- Revenue analysis; by employee, team, department and building
- Reported workplace medical incidents & injuries
- Physical complaints; glare, hot/cold, noise
- Operational costs; energy, maintenance

2 CULTURAL METRICS

Whilst not as tangible as the financial or operational metrics, the attitudes and perceptions of your people impact their performance. Gathering insights via engagement surveys or other feedback mechanisms can provide great insights into how your people view the work environment and any underlying contribution due to the physical workplace. For example, siloed teams resulting from physical barriers [walls] or lack of camaraderie due to a lack of facilities to encourage this connectivity.

3 PHYSICAL METRICS

Gathered via a mix of both observed and measured data collection, the physical metrics of your workplace provide an insight into how the built environment impacts your people's health, wellbeing and performance. Observed; layout, positioning of support spaces, quality of the environment, views, access to natural light, quality of facilities and amenities, provision and range of spaces. Measured; noise levels, reverberation, air quality, temperature, lux levels.

Gathering and analysing this data provides a baseline from which to make incremental improvements, some easier than others. This data can guide the prioritisation of projects to improve the health & wellbeing of your people via the environment and also measure the ROI of your efforts upon completion through continued evaluation post-implementation.

WELL building *standard*

A product of the International WELL Building Institute, The WELL Building Standard is:

A COMPREHENSIVE APPROACH TO WELL-BEING SPANNING 108 FEATURES AND 10 CONCEPTS, WELL IS A ROADMAP FOR IMPROVING THE QUALITY OF OUR AIR, WATER AND LIGHT WITH INSPIRED DESIGN DECISIONS THAT NOT ONLY KEEP US CONNECTED BUT FACILITATE A GOOD NIGHT'S SLEEP, SUPPORT OUR MENTAL HEALTH AND HELP US DO OUR BEST WORK EVERYDAY.[17]

Traditionally sustainable building standards have focused on the environmental impact of materiality, operations and construction methods that go into designing a new building.

The WELL Building Standard takes the concept of sustainability to another level, beyond the baseline of environmental sustainability and the use of "green" materials and concepts, to introduce more human-centred elements, ensuring the sustainability of its occupants.

THE WELL BUILDING STANDARD ADDRESSES TEN CONCEPTS;[17]

1. AIR
2. WATER
3. NOURISHMENT
4. LIGHT
5. MOVEMENT
6. THERMAL COMFORT
7. SOUND
8. MATERIALS
9. MIND
10. COMMUNITY

Whilst several of these concepts have objectives consistent with other sustainability standards, the WELL Building Standard also introduces human-centred principles relating to the creation of community, access to nourishment, encouragement of movement and design strategies that support the mind. A more human-focused and holistic approach centres on enhancing the wellbeing of the people occupying the building.

These concepts can be utilised whether you're looking to lease new premises, build a new fitout or refurbish an existing fitout. Utilising these ten concepts as a guide, you can make more informed choices in the selection of your tenancy and the design of your workplace, supporting the health and wellbeing of your people and, ultimately their performance at work.

So what does this mean for workplaces?

Thanks to the enablement of technology and our ability to physically work from anywhere, I firmly believe that our work environments' role has forever changed. We no longer need to come to the office to work, as our technology enables us to work from anywhere. Our workplaces will instead continue to evolve and transform into central hubs that facilitate organisational socialisation, where we establish deeper connections with our colleagues, break open those challenging problems by seeking out alternative viewpoints, and remind ourselves why we work here and not for the competitor down the road.

It means that wellbeing is a far broader conversation. It's about questioning the business' working rhythms and strategic focus to ensure we provide suitable spaces for people, no matter their location.

It's about understanding what your workplace needs to offer to attract employees into your workplace environment and supporting the productive and efficient work they're doing when they're there.

IT'S ABOUT CONSIDERING ALL OF THE ELEMENTS THAT ENABLE OUR WELLBEING AND HOW THE WORKPLACE ENVIRONMENT CAN THEN CONTINUE TO SUPPORT AND COMMUNICATE THE ORGANISATION'S COMMITMENT TO THE WELLBEING OF ITS EMPLOYEES AT ALL LAYERS; CULTURALLY, STRUCTURALLY AND PHYSICALLY.

Spaces for *wellbeing*

The health and wellbeing of your employees has a direct impact on the operational performance of your organisation. Whilst there is a wide range of activities that we can implement to enhance the wellbeing of our employees, in the form of policies, procedures and initiatives, your physical workplace environment can also take steps to support your employees. Use the space below to brainstorm areas that your organisation could incorporate into the physical environment to begin to support the physical, mental and emotional wellbeing of your employees.

WHAT SPACES CAN YOU PROVIDE TO SUPPORT EMPLOYEE WELLBEING?

WELLBEING	SPACE
PHYSICAL	
MENTAL	
EMOTIONAL	

Is your workplace suffering from *presenteeism?*

As work has evolved we have become increasingly sedentary due to the impact that machines and technology have had on our ability to do our jobs. We often spend a large proportion of our day sitting, and I don't need to tell you about the research that has been done on the impacts of physical inactivity at work! Presenteeism is the loss of productivity in workplaces due to employees being "present" but not fully functioning due to illness or injury. Its estimated that this is costing $26 billion per year. The largest contributors being; depression, allergies, hypertension and type 2 diabetes.[18]

Physical activity is a proven treatment for three of the four contributors and therefore, can have a significant impact on peoples performance at work.

HERE ARE THREE EASY WAYS THAT YOU CAN ENCOURAGE PHYSICAL ACTIVITY IN YOUR WORKPLACE:

ONE
Provide standing desks in some meeting spaces so that people can stand up when meeting [they also make the meetings shorter. BONUS!] Sit to stand desks are a great idea too!

TWO
Consolidate [get rid of!] the number of photocopiers that you have across your floor. By encouraging people to walk that few extra steps you are supporting their daily movement goal.

THREE
Provide bluetooth headsets so that employees can stand up and walk around when they are on the phone, so they aren't tethered to their desk. Soft phones and mobile diversions are another way to support this.

Chapter Huddle

CHAPTER FOUR recap

ENABLE YOUR PEOPLE TO THRIVE AT WORK, NOT JUST SURVIVE.

WELLBEING IS NOT A DEPARTMENT, AN INITIATIVE, OR A PROGRAM.

It is an integral part of the systems, processes, and organisational structures. It's required to be embedded into the operations and the culture at every level. It's not a product it's a philosophy.

A FRUIT BOX IS NOT WELLNESS.

Adhoc and scatter gun approaches to wellbeing do not provide the long term returns organisations desire.

WELLBEING IS A BUSINESS CONCERN.

The health and wellbeing of your people directly impacts their productivity and performance, and shows on a businesses bottom line.

WELLBEING AT WORK CENTRES AROUND THREE KEY AREAS:

Mental. Emotional. Physical

ENABLING SOCIALISATION AT WORK IS GOOD FOR PEOPLE AND FOR BUSINESS

Fostering strong relationships between colleagues supports employee engagement, wellbeing and retention and enables more effective collaboration and communication

HYBRID WORK ARRANGEMENTS ENHANCE WORK LIFE BALANCE AND IN TURN OUR WELLBEING.
Empowering employees to work flexibly between the office and other spaces enables more sustainable ways of working, catering to all parts of their lives, provided the appropriate structures are in place to support flexible working.

ENVIRONMENTS DESIGNED FOR WELLBEING HAVE BETTER BOTTOM LINES.
At 90% of business costs, employees far outweigh any other business expense. Even a marginal improvement in the health, wellbeing, and productivity of your people, can have a significant impact to the bottom line. And the design of your workplace directly impacts the health, wellbeing, and productivity of your people.

ELEVATING THE HEALTH AND WELLBEING OF YOUR PEOPLE IS A BUSINESS IMPERATIVE. WHAT ACTION CAN YOU TAKE TODAY TO MAKE A POSITIVE IMPACT?

CHAPTER FIVE

designing the employee experience

The art of placemaking
creating an experience

How often have you gone somewhere and felt good the instant you walked through the door? Is there a particular coffee shop that you're drawn to? What about it appeals to you? Is it the smell of the brewing coffee, the friendly smile that welcomes you as the barista asks, "the usual?" Is it the gentle hum of the surrounding conversations, ambient lighting and interior detailing? Chances are, the combination of all these factors working in perfect harmony makes this place feel so good. Placemaking is the art of forming spaces that generate experiences and create fond memories, and environments that establish a connection and make you want to experience more.

Placemaking is not a new concept, first gaining traction in the 1960s with William H Whyte, an American sociologist with the abstract idea of designing cities for people, not just cars and shopping centres. *Who would have thought?!*

Today, the company Whyte inspired, Project for Public Spaces (PPS), works to create communities with placemaking activities, adhering to the motto: *"It takes a place to create a community and a community to create a place."*

But what makes a place that creates a community? Where we live, work, and play are all communities. They differ from one location to another, bringing their unique blend of people, cultures, activities and traditions. The office tower where you work is as much a community as your local street. And the strength of your connection with the community is strongly influenced by the place itself, how it facilitates connections, supports the activities of its community and brings together its tribe and people united by a shared vision.

BUT WHAT DOES IT TAKE TO MAKE A PLACE GREAT?

I believe the answer lies in many different elements balanced harmoniously together. When looking at the development of our public areas, a few key features contribute to the appeal of a "place".

A "place" that draws you in and keeps you coming back can take many forms. It could be as simple as your local coffee shop or the restaurant where you are a regular, through to the thoughtfully constructed community where you live. These spaces have adopted their own personality through the architecture and styling they employ.

THESE ELEMENTS CREATE A SENSE OF COMMUNITY AND COHESION, INSTILLING A SENSE OF BELONGING AND ACCEPTANCE.

Layered onto these building blocks are engaging and welcoming customer services, well-considered signage and wayfinding, green spaces brimming with life and colour, lighting that creates atmosphere, and prominent pedestrian paths that navigate you through a space and designate areas for congregating and public seating. These elements engage your senses through colour, texture, sound and smell, creating an emotional connection with the environment and instilling a sense of belonging. The buildings, precincts and suburbs our workplaces occupy all contribute to our experience of place. Everton Plaza, in Brisbane's inner north, is a prime example of this art in practice.

Reds Group, the developer for Everton Plaza, wanted to leverage COMUNiTI's ability to strategically blend business objectives with human experience. They engaged us to revitalise a tired suburban shopping centre, turning it into a thriving local hub. Our brief was to create an innovative new retail and dining precinct to support local businesses and facilitate human connection. Embracing the centre's authentic 1970s red brick character, we aimed to create a place for the local community that brought people together and offered a unique experience.

Utilising our robust process and applying it at a grander scale, we crafted the development's strategic brief and brand experience. Instead of analysing employee data, we looked at the demographics of the surrounding suburbs, who lived there, their age, family makeup and employment statistics. We mapped surrounding precincts, considered the existing amenity, retailers and service providers and their offerings and analysed the gaps. Before developing a vision for the plaza, the experience visitors would have, the journey they would take, and what they would see, touch, hear and smell.

EVERTON PLAZA WON GOLD IN THE GOOD DESIGN AWARDS 2020

EVERTON PLAZA HAS BECOME A HUB FOR THE LOCAL COMMUNITY.

The development offers a wide range of service options across several precincts, including a large grocery retailer, medical facilities, hair and beauty, a gym, a variety of specialty food retailers and dining cuisines. Add to this a program of community engagement activities through weekend markets to an outdoor cinema, and the precinct addresses the qualities that underpin the art of placemaking. Everton Plaza is a shining example of what is possible when place and community are at the heart of a vision. You create a place people want to be part of, drawing them in.

case study
Fathom

Attracted to the revitalised Everton Plaza precinct by its intimate community atmosphere and extensive offering of food, beverage and retail amenities, along with its suburban location in Brisbane's inner north, Fathom – a financial analysis and forecasting software developer – decided to call Everton Plaza home for its rapidly expanding global workforce.

While Everton Plaza was the preferred choice for the expansion, Fathom's Directors, David Watson, Geoff Cook and Daniel Walls, partnered with COMUNiTI to ensure that it was also the smart choice. By engaging in a robust process of strategic analysis, unpacking everything from employee sentiments and value propositions, through to operational growth, amenities and commercials, Fathom ensured that its leasing decision was not purely an emotional one based on affinity to the precinct, but a solid commercial decision as well.

> "MEL FACILITATED A COMPREHENSIVE PROCESS WHERE EVERY VOICE AND EVERY NEED WITHIN OUR ORGANISATION WAS CONSIDERED BEFORE MAPPING OUT THE OPPORTUNITIES BEFORE US. THIS PROCESS NOT ONLY GAVE US, AS DIRECTORS, CONFIDENCE IN OUR DECISION, BUT ALSO OUR PEOPLE, KNOWING THAT WE HAD CONSIDERED EVERYONE IN HOW OUR FUTURE WORKPLACE WOULD WORK."
>
> – DAVID WATSON

the task

The growth of the organisation and its impact on the desired tenancy size was a significant consideration in Fathom's leasing decision. Together we mapped out three horizons of expected growth over eight years, along with the required workplace tools, spaces and amenities, to establish the footprint at each horizon. As a result of our efforts, Fathom could move forward on its final leasing commitment with clarity and confidence. This detailed modelling also enabled foresight into the possible workforce split that would be required to accommodate the business over two floors

With Fathom's commitment to the precinct ahead of the building's finalisation, we were able to massage the design of the building to accommodate the unique needs of the business. Altering floor plate sizes and orientation, internal stairs, external balcony sizes and access locations, lift core and amenity positioning enabled workplace design optimisation. Fathom was even able to introduce a rooftop basketball half-court!

the inspiration

As a technology solutions company focused on delivering beautiful accounting insights, Fathom's external brand presence is one of sophistication, elegance and simplicity. However, due to the nature of its online work, establishing a client-focused space was not a priority, so our attention was turned to the internal employee brand experience.

Fathom's robust culture and youthful, vibrant, collegiate workforce guided the creation of an environment for its people that was fun and connected yet with a level of sophistication.

The team shared stories of bonding over morning barista sessions at the coffee machine and lunchtime basketball games. Even Fathom's origin story is a modest one. The company was established in a suburban garage by the three directors, bootstrapped, self-funded, and driven by the belief that building a world-class software company is a marathon not a sprint. They approached their business's growth with resourcefulness and creativity, taking five years to grow the team to five before moving into their first workplace in 2015. As of 2022, Fathom employs more than 80 people, with offices in Australia, the UK, the US and the Philippines. Fathom's humble origins are still ever-present in the business' culture and operations; a quality that was to be protected as it grew.

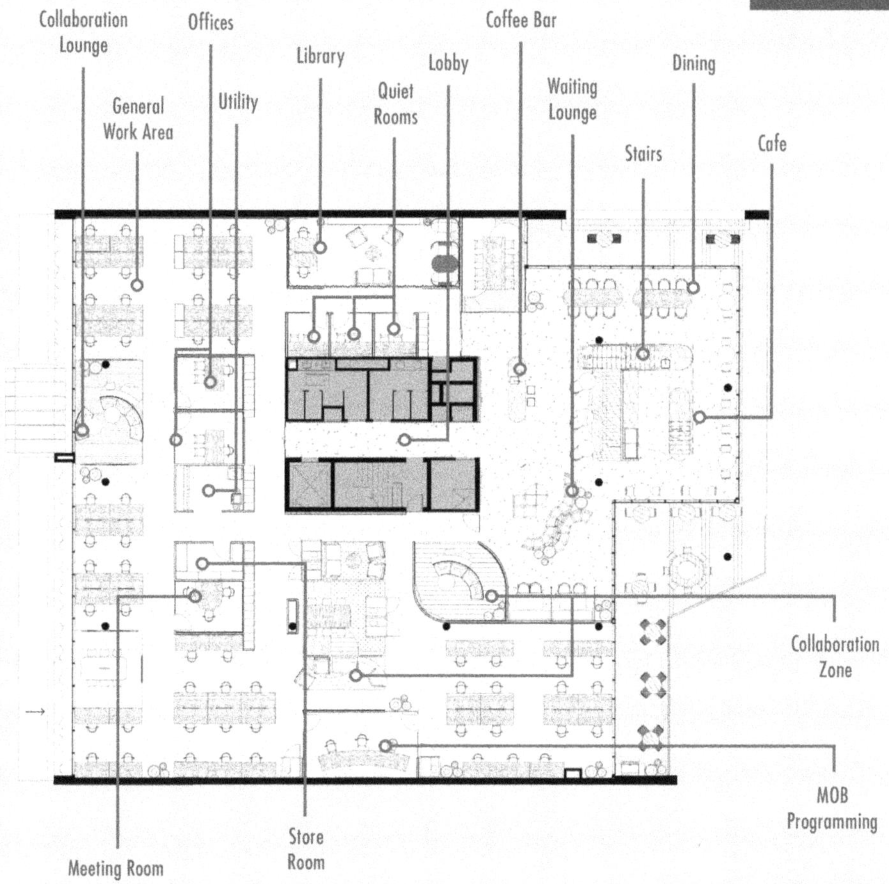

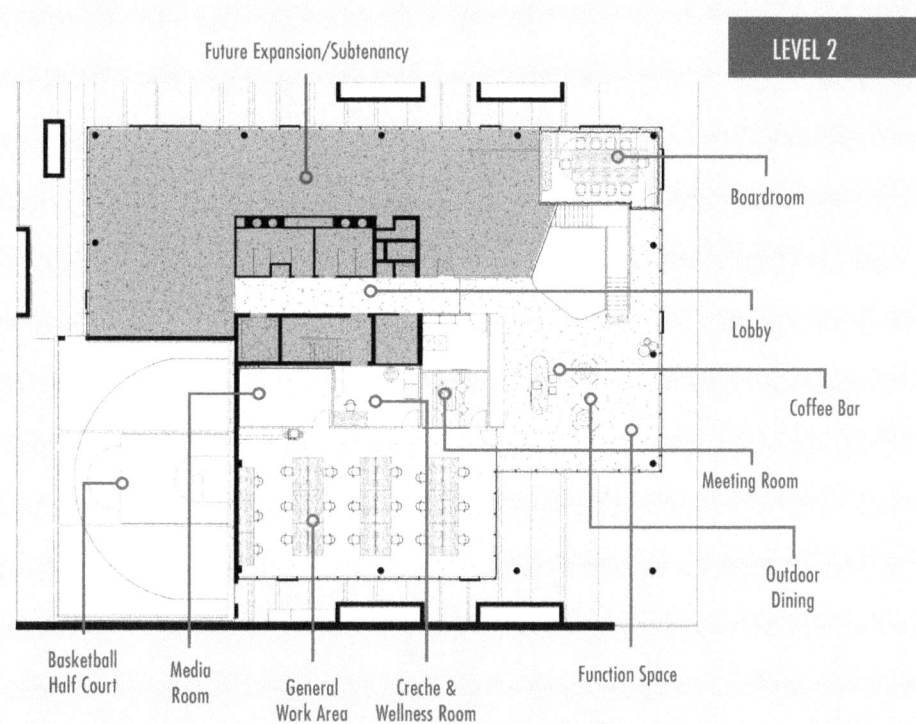

the solution

Engagement with the core team early in the process unearthed exciting opportunities to encourage collaboration in an environment that requires uninterrupted, focused work for coding and group collaboration. One of these solutions was introducing a "mob programming" room – an enclosed quiet space where three programmers can simultaneously code a single program.

Split across the two levels, the workplace is planned into three distinct work zones, catering to the incremental growth horizons predicted by the business. With two of these work zones occupied from day one, the third has been let as a short-term sublease to meet the company's commercial objectives, while securing its longer-term workplace requirements – a direct result of the early strategic accommodation planning.

Connected by internal stairs that form a sculptural element in the front-of-house space, the two floors enable ease of movement through the tenancy, ensuring seamless access to all the workplace amenities.

the detail

Upon entering the first level, you step into an expansive space with direct views out over the balcony and down into the laneways of Everton Plaza. This space has been created to enable all-hands meetings, welcome employees and visitors, and provide a hub of socialisation.

Fathom's strong coffee culture forms the core of its in-office socialisation, so we introduced a barista station as the pride of place as you enter the space. This coffee station sits within this expansive space, facing the interconnecting stairs, which are wrapped with tiered seating creating an informal congregation zone for town hall meetings inspired by college bleachers. Behind this seating is the staff cafe, connected to the expansive outdoor dining deck with bifold doors, overlooking Everton Plaza's Park Lane, optimising the view of the community outdoor theatre.

The shapes and colours of Fathom's brand palette have inspired the creation of dividing screens, along with the selection of fabrics, carpets and other materials employed in the space, creating a subtle thread of connectivity through the space. Blended with the building's unadorned raw and industrial form, the space also pays its respects to the iconic red brick of the plaza itself, bringing it up into the workspace through the wall forming the tiered seating, the first thing you see on entering the space.

The work area is laid out in pockets of work zones, interjected with a range of collaborative work settings, to support the variety of group communication and brainstorming methods within the business, punctuated by private phone booths to support team and personal calls, reducing disruptive communication with the designated work areas. A library space encourages quiet work and reflection time, complemented by private booths for quiet conversation.

A workplace with diverse spaces and furniture settings creates a truly dynamic and engaging space that will continue to evolve and support the business' operational needs as they expand.

Fathom's workplace is a testament to approaching design strategically, with ample consideration of its core requirements, culture, and vision for the future. While many businesses needed to realign their workplace to accommodate disruptive pandemic-related changes, Fathom's design commenced in 2018 and finished construction in 2023 completely unchanged. This example demonstrates the future proofing and the adaptability possible when workplace design is infused with strategy.

Above: Upon entering the space you are welcomed by the barista coffee bar [to the left] and immersed in the buzz of the workplace. It's a space designed to welcome visitors, for employees to engage in casual conversations and to host all hands meetings.

Below: The employee cafe sits beneath the stairs, visually connected to the upper level, while taking in views out into the busy plaza.

CASE STUDY – FATHOM

Above: Collaboration spaces punctuate the work area, supporting spontaneous conversations and informal work sessions, accentuated with bold tonal colours to elicit energy from participants.

Left: The work areas embody softer, more muted tones, with sculptural, acoustic panels suspended overhead. Walls are lined with whiteboards to encourage visual communication and brainstorming.

Below: The Library is tucked into a secluded space to the side of the core, facilitating quiet concentrative work in an open environment. The colour palette shifts to blue tones, encouraging feelings of serenity and orderliness, enabling concentration and focus.

Left: The half court on the roof is a popular lunchtime destination, bringing the team together over common interests and strengthening relationships

The layers of *employee experience*

Attracting employees back into the office is no easy task in a post-pandemic world. Still, with the right environment, your workplace can be one of your greatest assets, enticing your people back, drawing in new talent, encouraging loyalty and helping everyone fulfil their potential. Employee experience has many layers in your organisation and in the context of creating a new "work" environment.

- **IT'S AN EMPLOYEE'S EXPERIENCE WORKING WITH YOUR COMPANY,** the lifecycle of attraction, retention and departure, and often in the purview of People and Culture or the HR Department. What experience do we want to create for each employee in this organisation?

- **IT'S AN EMPLOYEE'S EXPERIENCE OF THE PHYSICAL WORKPLACE ENVIRONMENT,** what they see, hear, touch, smell and feel. It's the journey they take and the connections they make as they move through space. Why do I come here every day? What is this place offering me that I can't get anywhere else?

- **IT'S AN EMPLOYEE'S EXPERIENCE OF CHANGE,** how they're consulted, prepared and informed of the what, why and how of a new workplace. As we transition from one environment to another with the creation of a new workplace fitout, what is my experience of that change?

The reality is we are all in the business of curating employee experiences. A clearly defined strategy for your employees to experience your purpose, brand and culture is the foundation. I will stick to my knitting here and not begin to tell you how to do your job or run your business – but I will say that Gallup's framework for designing an employee experience dovetails nicely into how we curate the design of your space.

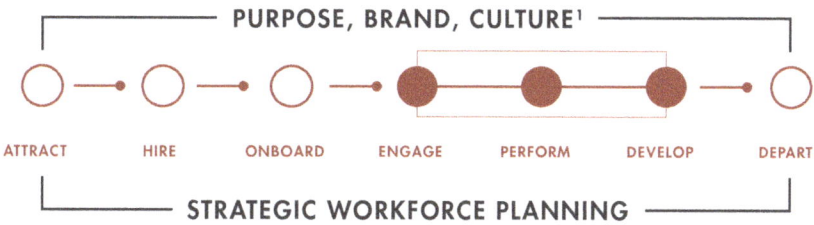

GALLUP EMPLOYEE EXPERIENCE FRAMEWORK

As workplace strategists, our role is to translate your objectives and contribute to your strategic workforce planning. Together, we can create an aligned environment, enabling your people and curating the spaces to encourage the moments that matter.

The foundations of your workplace strategy are laid by having a top-down approach, employing our earlier chapters of Purpose, Brand and Culture, across an employee's lifecycle, with a bottom-up approach that addresses your strategic workforce planning.

The three environments of *employee experience*

ALL EMPLOYEE EXPERIENCES ARE COMPRISED OF THREE ENVIRONMENTS

Designers work at the intersection of people, place and technology to create human experiences. In the context of workplace strategy, the confluence of the cultural (people), physical (place), and technological (tech) environments delivers employee experience.

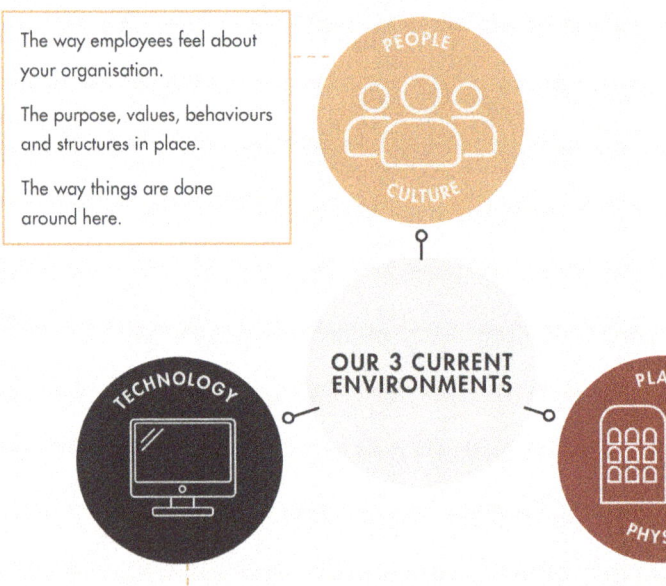

The way employees feel about your organisation.

The purpose, values, behaviours and structures in place.

The way things are done around here.

OUR 3 CURRENT ENVIRONMENTS

The virtual environment and tools that employees use to do their work.

Laptops, devices, software, systems and apps.

The built space in which employees actually work.

What they see, touch, hear and smell.

ABSTRACTED FROM JACOB MORGAN[2]

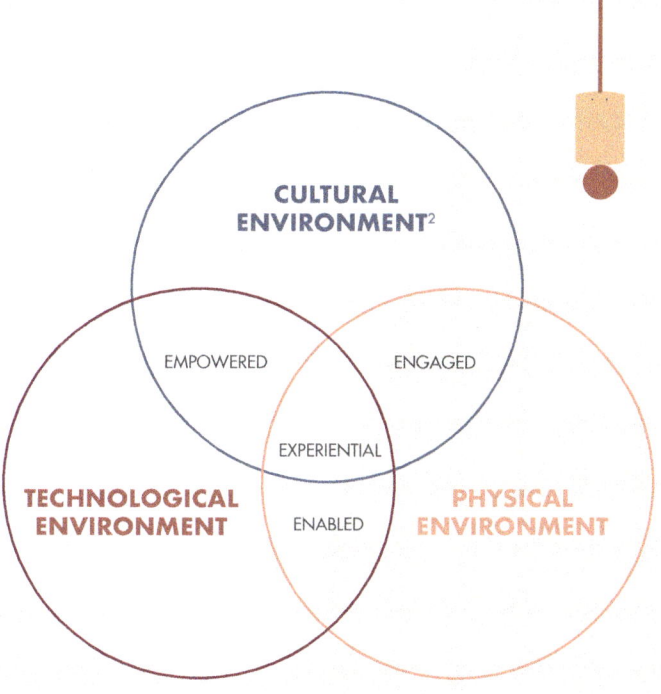

As work futurist Jacob Morgan[2] describes, when we can deliver these three environments holistically, infusing the organisation's purpose, we can provide an experiential environment instead of simply an empowered, enabled or engaged one – a place that appeals to all of our senses and emotions. This holistic delivery of the experience engages employees and drives a range of positive outcomes for the business, from increased innovation and productivity to employee attraction and retention.

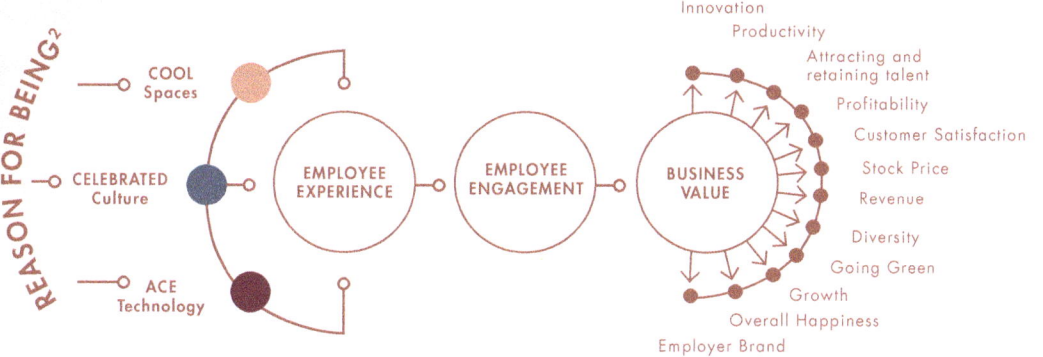

JACOB MORGAN EMPLOYEE EXPERIENCE BUSINESS OUTCOMES

Each of these three environments demands equal weighting in the delivery of your organisation's employee experience. A well-intentioned culture program will fall short when the environment physically undermines the desired behaviours or the technology is so clunky that it fuels frustration among your people. Similarly, a workplace crafted to enhance your employees' experience cannot succeed alone. While it is another tool in delivering on your employee experience, it requires the active participation of aligned culture programs and the implementation of enabling technology.

With studies showing that 41 percent[3] of people still prefer to work virtually, how can we use our environments to curate an employee experience that attracts them back to the office?

What is the difference between a workplace where attendance is mandated and a workplace where people choose to go, because it brings out the best in them and their teams?

What we are really talking about is connecting to the hearts, bodies and minds of our people, bringing together all the earlier concepts within the pages of this book. By showcasing and celebrating what's unique to your organisation, your workplace can become the conduit for employees to tangibly experience that uniqueness.

> **OUR HEART** is the collective emotion of a space, how we feel and connect – otherwise known as an organisation's brand and culture.
>
> **THE BODY** is the physical environment, how it looks and feels. And just like a body, is it a place that is put together for flexibility, agility and performance, or is it slow, rigid and fixed?
>
> **AND OUR MIND** is the technology that brings together the organisation's collective intelligence, making it easily accessible and reducing friction.

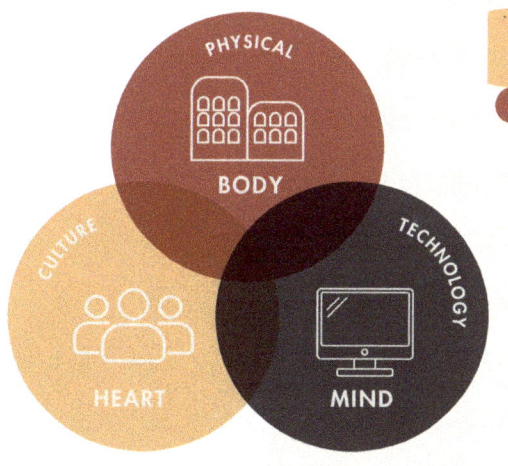

When these three pillars are aligned, you create a dynamic workplace that energises the people within it. Your space becomes self-energising, alive, buzzing and vibrant.

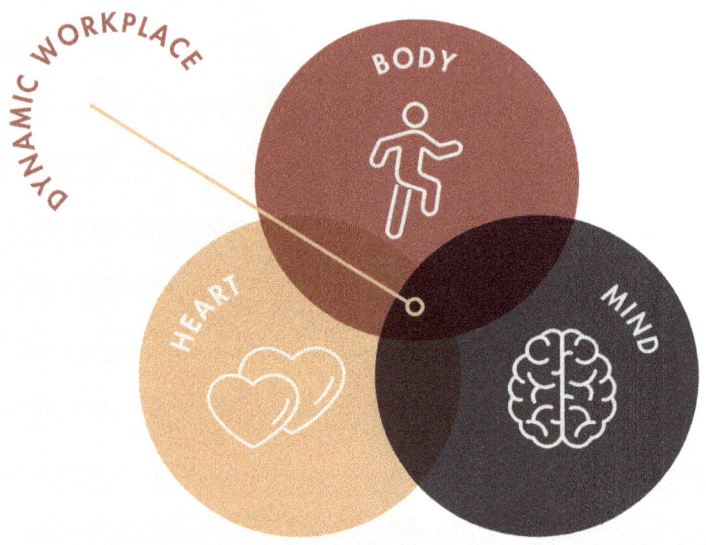

DYNAMIC WORKSPACES ARE:

- Agile, adaptable, flexible, and responsive to the user.
- Magnetic, attracting people to them with an irresistible gravitational pull. Places where employees want to be, clients want to visit, and everyone wants to be part of
- Infinite, bountiful, and brimming with potential. A place where the sum of the whole is greater than its parts.

Imagine a workplace that felt this alive!

NOW TAKE A MOMENT AND COMPARE THAT VISION IN YOUR MIND TO YOUR CURRENT WORKPLACE...

Is there a gap?

LET'S TALK ABOUT HOW WE CLOSE THAT GAP.

Cultural Environment

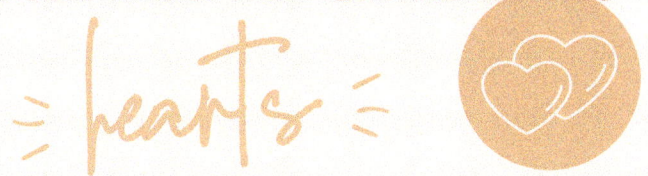

Let's start with the first pillar, the heart. As we explored in Chapter 2, we know that, as humans, we are hard-wired for belonging and connection. We have a primal need to belong, engage with others, and feel like we fit in – and when we don't, we feel excluded, isolated, and even experience physical pain.

To establish this sense of togetherness in our modern workplaces, we need to build connections, not only to one another but also to the organisation we are part of. This connection comes from understanding our own purpose and that of our organisation. We want to feel that our work is meaningful and contributes positively to the world. And when our shared values, stories and a common vision tie us together, we feel like we belong. It fosters our sense of community.

Your organisation's purpose and story inform your brand experience. It elicits emotion, creates connection, and builds magnetism. Your brand experience is about articulating your organisational DNA, the relationship between what is vital in your business, who you uniquely are and the feeling you want people to have when they enter your space. It's about embedding organisational DNA, your unique mark, and your fingerprint into the workplace.

It's about consciously designing the experience you want people to have when they do business with you, the emotions you want to elicit. How do you want them to FEEL? By drawing on your story and your whole reason for being, you can embed the Heart of your organisation into your space. And when you embed your Heart into the workplace, it will lead to unprecedented leaps in performance.

Physical Environment
body

Now let's talk about the body, where we start embedding our emotional objectives into the physical environment.

You physically interact with a space through your body, taking a sensory journey. That journey is punctuated with sensations we feel, the sounds we hear, the materials, colours and textures we see and the emotions that arise as we move through a space: excitement, energy, fun, inspiration, and curiosity. It is how the room responds to the user's needs and how it flexes and adapts to suit the tasks at hand. The body is how we influence behaviour and use our environment to guide alignment with organisational values, creating a workplace that people are excited to come to.

If the heart of a dynamic workplace is how we emotionally interact with it, then the body of a dynamic workplace is how we physically interact with it. These considerations go way beyond just the floor plan. As we learned in Chapter 3, it is about how each piece of the space flows into the next. It's the zoning that guides the interactivity within each space. It is the variety and choice of spaces employees are offered to work within; the physical materials, finishes and structures encapsulate and frame the spaces. These all guide how you feel in the space and, in response, how you behave and perform.

Technological Environment

mind

This brings us to our third pillar, the mind of our workplace: the technology that makes this all possible. A tech environment is how we plug ourselves into the workplace. How we unite, contribute and share our ideas creates a network of connectivity between people and places, tying our culture to the physical space. A network establishes a hive mind, where people's collective thoughts, ideas and opinions come together, continuously building on each other quickly and without friction.

The entire purpose of technology is to simplify and enhance our experience of life, reducing friction points. Each job we complete throughout our day entails several steps, a series of actions, or a process to be followed. Each of these steps creates what we call "open loops" in our brains. These loops remain open until the final step has been completed. With automation, we can reduce the number of open loops in our minds, removing steps in a process, and reducing our cognitive load and the friction between us and the environment. Technology facilitates a seamless use of space, enabling us to enter a flow state more easily. And we know that when we are in flow, our brains can create new neural pathways, supporting creativity, and solving problems with new ideas, essentially making us smarter.

As we explored in the opening chapter, with the right technology, our environments can continuously collect data on how we interact with our space, providing a real-time feedback loop with accurate data on the performance of the space, utilisation, capacity and much more. This data enables us to continually evolve and adapt our workplace to maximise our people's potential, minimising the open loops and reducing friction.

When you embed emotion *(the heart)* with a thoughtfully created environment *(the body)* and then integrate the tech *(the mind)* to refine the operations and experience, you are making your workplace smart.

YOU ARE MAKING IT DYNAMIC.

YOU ARE CREATING THE WORKPLACE OF THE FUTURE AND ONE OF YOUR ORGANISATION'S CHIEF ASSETS.

How our workplace environment impacts our experience of work

The workplace environment has a prominent role for organisations seeking to entice employees back to the office. After all, if your work experience at home is better than what your office offers, why would you want to bother going back?

For years before the pandemic, many organisations saw their workplaces as somewhere to "accommodate" their workforce, merely a space that brought people together under a single roof. These spaces didn't (and still don't) support the range of tasks required by their people, offering generic workstations and a few standard amenities to get the job done. Investing in the design and construction of the workplace was not considered a priority nor a lever for enhancing the performance of their people. But as I hope you see by now, it should be.

WHEN WE UNDERSTAND OUR EMPLOYEES' INDIVIDUAL TASKS AND ACTIVITIES, WE CAN BETTER UNDERSTAND THE SPACES NEEDED TO SUPPORT THEM.

By understanding the type of work your people need to perform, you can create an environment that enables their performance and enhances their work experience.

As we covered in Chapter 3, by exploring how flow, zoning and spaces guide our behaviour at work, we can ensure that we deliver the appropriate spaces. And offering a variety of workspace types is the number one differentiator between an outstanding workplace experience and an average one.

For example, if most of your people work collaboratively, a plethora of quiet individual workspaces would be counterproductive. Larger, open spaces that inspire collective conversations and places to brainstorm ideas and work in groups would be more appropriate. Conversely, if your people's predominant work activities are focused, individual tasks, fitting the workplace with interactive and collaborative workpoints would be highly ineffective.

For most organisations, the answer is a blend of these spaces, with a slight bent towards individual or collaborative space dependent on the industry and culture of the workplace.

TO WORK THIS OUT, YOU NEED TO LOOK AT EACH DEPARTMENT AND UNDERSTAND WHAT THEY DO AND HOW THEY DO IT.

> The Leesman Index is a workplace experience measurement tool, or as Leesman itself describes it, "we are workplace radiographers", measuring the impact of employee experience on performance.

CONNECTING PURPOSE TO PLACE

When we focus on the purpose our workplaces aim to fulfil, we return to building social capital, connecting people, and enabling collaboration and communication. Hybrid working, allowing the employees to work flexibly across other spaces, is another essential consideration.

According to Leesman's research[4], activities that are more collaborative in nature, require learning from others or more informal interactions, are more effective in the office, while individual activities such as reading, creative thinking and individual tasks are more effective from home.

THINK ABOUT WHAT YOU WANT YOUR PEOPLE TO DO IN THE OFFICE, AND BE DELIBERATE ABOUT THE EXPERIENCE YOU WANT THEM TO HAVE WHEN THEY ARE THERE.

How to create an outstanding *workplace experience*

HERE ARE THE TOP SIX DIFFERENTIATORS BETWEEN AN OUTSTANDING WORKPLACE EXPERIENCE AND AN AVERAGE ONE, IDENTIFIED BY LEESMAN'S INSIGHTS;[5]

Spaces that proactively support employees in these three ways rank as the highest differentiator for employee experience:

1. Thinking / creative thinking
2. Informal, unplanned meetings
3. Relaxing / taking a break

Workplace design makes a difference. Workplaces that incorporate these features deliver the highest rates of employee experience:

1. Variety of different types of workspace
2. Informal work area/s and breakout zones
3. Atriums and communal area

AND THE IMPACT OF CREATING AN OUTSTANDING WORKPLACE?

1. It's a place your employees are proud to bring visitors to
2. It creates an enjoyable experience
3. It enables your people to work productively

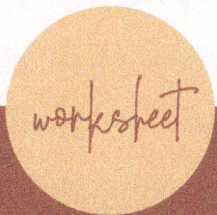

How to create an Employee Empathy Map

Empathy Mapping is a design thinking tool to guide the desired state of a user – in this case, your employees. By imagining how you want your employees to experience their workplace environment, you can consciously create that experience in adapting and/or designing the space. In each of the four quadrants, describe the experience you want your employees to have.

SEE
What do you want them to see? Is it collaboration, laughter, colour, concentration, or transparency?

THINK & FEEL
What do you want them to think and feel at work? Perhaps it's creative, comfortable, belonging, welcome, family, or energised.

DO
What do you want them to be doing? Engaging with one another, focused concentrative work, chatting, meeting?

HEAR
What do you want them to be hearing? What do the conversations sound like? Is there music or silence?

You should also consider the **Pains and Gains.** What are some of the pains your employees are currently experiencing, and how can you alleviate them to make their work life a little more frictionless?

Use this map to guide you in reimagining your workplace environment to create a more empathetic space that connects with your employees and their needs.

YOU CAN DOWNLOAD YOUR A3 PRINTABLE EMPATHY MAP FROM THE BOOK RESOURCES ON PAGE 9

Designing for *me*

The design of our workplaces in days gone by has been to provide individual workpoints with the least amount of individualisation! With the rise of activity-based work environments and the concept of "unowned" spaces, employees began to cling desperately to their owned real estate, connecting a desk covered in their personal effects with their identity at work, despite the space itself being highly generic.

As we reimagine our workplaces and shift into an environment of shared space, for "we" rather than "me", we can create areas far more responsive to the individual and their personal needs.

By creating spaces that cater to a wide variety of workstyle preferences, personality types and work activities through flexible, adaptable and shared work environments, we can offer more highly personalised choices in where and how we work. These choices are influenced by a range of personalised factors that we each have, ranging from our social demographics to our personality profiles.

Generations in the workplace

We presently have more generations in the workplace than at any other time in history. Ranging from the Baby Boomers who have spent their career vying for the corner office, to our newest Gen Z cohort who could operate a smart device before they could talk and are pretty happy to balance a laptop on their knees as they sit on the stairs.

What comes with this diversity of ages is a range of extremes, from how they work, to the tools they use, to the type of space they have become accustomed to working in and their expectations of employers in supporting these individual styles.

When designing a workplace that supports and enables all employees, you must first understand your workforce's generational mix and consider the likely transition of those generations over the term of your lease and the workplace environment.

Creating an environment that caters to a heavy demographic of Baby Boomers over a 10-year lease term will not support the transition of younger workers entering the organisation. Constructing individual offices supporting the isolated and hierarchical work environments familiar to Baby Boomers contradicts the flexible and agile environments desired by younger generations. As Baby Boomers move into retirement, you're left with a workplace environment that doesn't appeal to the next generation of talent, constraining your recruitment efforts in an already challenging market.

Or perhaps your organisation is structured in a way that requires the employment of seasoned, experienced people, so focusing on attracting Gen X employees into your business may be the best approach.

Or maybe your organisation is on a recruitment drive to attract the next generation of the best and brightest talent in the market.

WHAT KIND OF WORKPLACE WILL THEY BE LOOKING FOR?

Just as there is no "one-size-fits-all approach" to workplace design for any other aspect of your business, the same is true for supporting the generational mix in your business. You need to consider who your workplace supports and create an environment that attracts and enables them, increasing your retention.

Personality profiling

I find it particularly fascinating to understand the personality traits of the people I work with. What motivates people? How do they feel valued, respected and heard? What's their preferred communication style, level of detail or decision-making approach? Whether it is a prospective client, a business partner or a member of my team, understanding their personality is imperative to establishing a successful business relationship.

At COMUNiTI, part of our onboarding process is for our new recruits to complete a range of personality profiling tools and collate their unique personality into a poster that we then share and hang on the wall in our workplace (plus other digital platforms). These posters provide each of us with an insight into the world of our colleagues, capturing our Gallup Strengths, DISC profile, Myers Briggs, Love Languages and our unique set of values. As a company that strongly advocates for the use of values in business, it's vital for our team to understand their own, how they connect with those of the business and the alignment with our clients.

These profiling tools also give our team a common language for us to use in the business. When a colleague's love language is "words of affirmation," we understand that praising them for their work will fill their cup, making them feel valued. We get it when our introverted colleague needs some quiet time out on their own to recharge after an intense period of project delivery and client presentations. We know to be brief and to the point in our communication when dealing with a high "D" personality and to share the deeper details with our "C" styles.

THIS KNOWLEDGE PROVIDES OUR TEAM WITH A LEVEL OF EMPATHY, CONSIDERATION AND UNDERSTANDING THAT WE WOULD OTHERWISE NOT HAVE HAD.

These tools have helped us get to know each other fast, peeling back the layers and, in many cases, giving us language and insight into our behaviours that we previously could not articulate.

Knowledge of the personalities at work within your organisation can also illuminate how the style and design of your environment can influence individual behaviour and performance. The simplest analysis is looking at the range of extroverts to introverts. Extroverted personalities enjoy the company of others, thriving off the energy created, while introverts much prefer a quieter environment, feeling their energy depleted when in larger groups.

CREATING SPACES WHERE BOTH EXTREMES AND THOSE THAT TEETER IN THE MIDDLE CAN THRIVE IS IMPORTANT IN CREATING A WORKPLACE WHERE ALL EMPLOYEES CAN FEEL THEIR BEST.

Energetic, collaborative, shared work zones for those that thrive on the buzz and hum of conversation and ideas, contrasted with quiet, intimate, focused zones for those that prefer time to themselves.

The same applies to the personality of a team – not so much about the individual characters within each group, but more collectively the energy of the team itself, in response to the type and style of work required. Teams that need to perform detailed, concentrative, individual and highly focused tasks, such as accountants and data analysts, align more with the introverted end of the scale. While teams such as the marketing department typically are more energetic and collaborative, perform more group-oriented tasks, and sit towards the extroverted end of the scale.

CONSIDERING HOW THE TEAMS IN YOUR BUSINESS ENGAGE IN THEIR DAILY ACTIVITIES CAN PROVIDE YOU WITH A DEEPER INSIGHT INTO THE STYLE OF ENVIRONMENT THEY REQUIRE TO COMPLETE THOSE ACTIVITIES, BUT ALSO THEIR RELATIONSHIP TO OTHER TEAMS IN THE BUSINESS AND THE ENVIRONMENT ITSELF.

In my experience, sitting the marketing team next to the accounts team is not a good idea. Accounts will be distracted by the banter of the marketing team, and marketing will feel constrained by the need to "keep it down" around the accounts team, dulling both performances. It's also not a great idea to seat your accounts team next to the kitchen or cafe. In a naturally social and noisy space, the accounts team will be forever disrupted by their colleagues' chatter, comings and goings.

THESE PERSONALITY PROFILING CONSIDERATIONS FORM DEEPER LAYERS, BUILDING ON THE CONCEPT OF ZONING, FLOW AND THE VARIETY OF SPACES WE EXPLORED IN CHAPTER 3 AND PROVIDING GREATER INSIGHT INTO THE DESIGN AND APPLICATION OF OUR WORKPLACE LAYOUTS.

Understanding these personal preferences, workstyles and habits enables us to cater to a wider variety of individual needs in the workplace, further supporting and enhancing the experience of our employees.

Personality preferences

INTROVERTS

Recharge by spending time alone

Reflect before making decisions

Listen more

Enjoy one-on-one conversations

Introspective

Self-aware

Think before acting

Learn through observation

More social with familiar people

Highly perceptive and considered

Typically listen first, reflective thinkers

Prefer clear and planned change

Pause before decisions

Sociable in small groups

EXTRAVERTS

Recharge by socialising

Make decisions quickly

Speak more

Outgoing

Easily distracted

Action-orientated

Gregarious and expressive

Excellent communicators

Enjoy being the centre of attention

Brilliant connectors and communicators

Expressive and open

Enjoy change and spontaneity

Invigorated by group interaction

Learn by doing or talking

Team Profiles

| ENGINEERING | FINANCE | IT | LEGAL | ADMINISTRATION | OPERATIONS | HUMAN RESOURCES | CUSTOMER SERVICES | MARKETING | SALES |

MORE INTROVERTED ○------------------○ **MORE EXTRAVERTED**

Neurodiversity

Another layer of diversity extends to the physical and sensory diversity of people in the workplace. It's only in recent history that we have catered to diversity in the context of disabilities such as wheelchair accessibility and vision and hearing impairments, regulated under the building code AS 1428. However, diversity considerations are expanding in response to the growing awareness of neurodiversity of employees within the workforce.

Neurodiversity describes the idea that people experience and interact with the world around them in many different ways; there is no one "right" way of thinking, learning and behaving, and differences are not viewed as deficits.

The word neurodiversity refers to the diversity of all people, but it is often used in the context of autism spectrum disorder (ASD), as well as other neurological or developmental conditions such as ADHD or learning disabilities.[6]

Creating workplace environments that cater to a wide variety of personal working styles is not a new concept. However, it may have been approached previously by supporting various tasks and activities via workplace styles such as activity-based working.

What is emerging now is the need to support multiple environmental conditions that can influence the anxiety of individuals depending on their sensitivity to external sensory stimulation.

CEO of the UK's Universal Music, David Joseph, commented on the release of *Creative Differences*, the company's handbook for supporting neurodiversity in the creative industries:

> *Making your organisation ND-friendly is to the benefit of your entire workforce. Everyone should feel comfortable in bringing their whole selves to work."*[7]

In my work, I have observed a distinct cross-over between the design of environments to support the various personal work preferences and personality styles, to those proposed to support the needs of those with sensory sensitivities.

While workplaces are moving away from the personalisation of spaces, through the ownership of workpoints, we must enable individual control of the environment for those with neurodiverse needs to support their experience and performance in the workplace.

While *"don't provide personalised spaces but provide personal control"* sounds like a complex task, elegant and hybrid workstyles are already taking the first steps to address these individualised requirements.

GIVING EMPLOYEES AN ARRAY OF SPACES AND AGENCY OVER HOW AND WHERE THEY WORK IN THOSE SPACES THROUGHOUT THE DAY OR WEEK OFFERS A SENSE OF CONTROL OVER THEIR SURROUNDING ENVIRONMENT. EXAMPLES OF THESE SPACES INCLUDE:

- Access to rooms with their own lighting control. These spaces not only support deep concentration for the whole team but also enable individual control of sound and light.

- Designated areas in the work environment dedicated to quiet working, limiting ambient noise. Think library spaces with study carrels.

- Designated spaces for activity, collaboration and conversation.

- Private rooms where employees can retreat when they feel overwhelmed or stressed. These rooms can be multipurpose to support relaxation, meditation, stretching, etc.

OTHER CONSIDERATIONS INCLUDE THE FOLLOWING;

- Clearly defined spaces for socialisation and for working
- Clearly defined corridors of movement
- Using materiality and colour to guide behaviours
- Zoning and furniture typologies to cue the purpose of space

However, as with any workplace strategy, the objective is to make the workplace work for ALL your employees. And if that means that some of your team require a dedicated workspace to support their personal work performance, then you should work with those individuals to find a practical solution that aligns with the overall strategy.

And just like every other concept presented in this book, engaging with your team is the first step in understanding the needs of your people and what they need to perform.

EVERY ORGANISATION IS UNIQUE, SO THE MIX OF THESE SPACES WILL VARY IN RESPONSE TO YOUR COMPANY'S BRAND AND CULTURE, VALUES AND ASPIRED BEHAVIOURS.

If employees do not feel empowered to make decisions around how they work and the areas they use, then the provision of these spaces will fall short of the desired impact. It's essential to communicate your expectations and the permissions granted. A clear onboarding plan will help everyone understand how to use the space.

> **"Being allocated a quiet room I can go to when my tics are having a bad day helps. It stops me feeling like I'm disturbing my colleagues if I'm making lots of noise."**
>
> – CLARA, EMPLOYEE[7]

Diversity & inclusivity

WHAT IS THE DIFFERENCE BETWEEN DIVERSITY AND INCLUSION?

Great Place to Work, the global authority on workplace culture, defines the terms this way:[8]

> **DIVERSITY** is the representation of different people in an organisation.
>
> **INCLUSION** ensures that everyone has an equal opportunity to contribute to and influence every part and level of a workplace. That the contributions, presence and perspectives of different groups of people and values are integrated into an environment.

Why should this be important to businesses? Research demonstrates the business case for diversity and inclusion in the workplace where organisations have taken an intentional approach. Analysis from McKinsey[9] has shown that organisations with higher rates of gender, ethnic and cultural diversity are more likely to outperform less diverse organisations on profitability. And the greater the level of diversity the higher the likelihood of performance.

OTHER BENEFITS TO ORGANISATIONS FOCUSED ON CREATING DIVERSITY AND INCLUSIVITY INCLUDE:[8]

- Higher revenue growth
- Greater readiness to innovate
- Increased ability to recruit a diverse talent pool
- 5.4 times higher employee retention

Frans Johansson, the author of *The Medici Effect*, states that there is an inextricable link between the diversity of teams and innovation, explaining that there are three key drivers as to why.[10]

Diverse and inclusive teams create more unlikely ideas.

By bringing together people with a wide variety of backgrounds, you tap into a greater resource pool of experiences, beliefs, cultural norms and ideas that create an increased network of possibilities to achieve a solution. Johansson offers an example of this in practice, in which a hospital in the UK, experiencing a high volume of errors, analysed the operational performance of a Formula One pit crew. Implementing these learnings into their own operational process significantly reduced the rate of errors.

Diverse teams are better at making decisions.

When you have a greater diversity of people in the conversation, this diversity of thought, Johansson explains, stretches a team in ways that can be uncomfortable and highly effective. The varying inputs around the table represent a broader perspective of thought, by virtue of differing cultural backgrounds, beliefs, and experiences, reducing the potential of making a wrong decision.

Diverse teams are better at making innovative ideas happen.

Diverse teams bring a broader network to the table, enabling access to a more expansive group of resources. This means that ideas can be implemented faster by leveraging the group's resources.

These three drivers are further explained in the work of Juliet Bourke, author of *Which Two Heads are Better Than One?: How Diverse Teams Create Breakthrough Ideas and Make Smarter Decisions.*[11] As individuals, we each have a preferred way of thinking, and by nature, we are often drawn to others who think like us, otherwise known as the Similarity Attraction Bias. Bourke encourages us to create a diversity of thinking within a group by consciously seeking out individuals with diverse perspectives and approaches rather than simply seeking out differing thinking styles or personalities.

> Diversity of **perspective** is how we perceive or see an issue. With diversity, collectively, we see a more comprehensive view of the world, enabling us to see the whole picture.

> Diversity of **approach** is the "mental frameworks people use to solve problems once they have been defined." In other words, these are our own go-to, tried and tested approaches to solving problems. Awareness of our personal approach to problem-solving and those of others ensures that we can consciously create a diverse thinking group.

BOURKE CATEGORISES THESE SIX APPROACHES AS:

OUTCOMES   OPTIONS   PROCESS   PEOPLE   EVIDENCE   RISK

As leaders, 75 percent of us are typically focused on Options and Outcomes, with only 3 percent of leaders looking at or caring about Evidence and Risk. By ensuring a greater diversity of approaches within a group, all six will be more evenly represented, enabling a more balanced decision-making process.

75% of leaders Options and Outcomes focused

Only 3% look or careabout Evidence and Risk

Seeking out the contributions of a variety of people in the room provides a greater diversity of perspectives and approaches in decision-making. During meetings, former US president Barack Obama would invite the opinions of everyone in the room.

> *Obama then proceeded to call on every single person for his views, including the most junior people. "What was a little unusual," Obama admits, "is that I went to people who were not at the table. Because I am trying to get an argument that is not being made."*[12]

In this way, Obama enabled a voice for every individual, personality, perspective and approach in the room.

HE SOUGHT OUT DIVERSE OPINIONS TO ENSURE THAT ALL ASPECTS OF A PROBLEM, TASK OR DECISION WERE CONSIDERED, ENABLING HIS DECISION-MAKING OR SUPPORTING THE VARIOUS STANDPOINTS OF THE ARGUMENT.

Creating a diverse and inclusive workforce through conscious hiring is only the first step in enabling innovative thinking in our organisations. We then need to support it through management practices and the design of our environments.

The physical structures of our workplace influence and guide behaviour, encouraging or inhibiting gatherings, overhearing conversations or inviting others to contribute. Even the shape of a table can influence a room's power dynamic.

EVER WONDER WHY THE KNIGHTS' TABLE WAS ROUND? THERE IS NO "HEAD" OF THE TABLE, NO HIERARCHY OR POWER IMBALANCE.

Leveraging our environment to encourage equality and inclusivity, embedding the business' values into the physical space, and enabling a diversity of thought across the company all contribute to a feeling of belonging, enhancing operational performance. We have witnessed this effect in Mapien's workplace, with their people connecting on a social level in the cafe space and their teams' ability to both observe and overhear the work of their colleagues, promoting cross-functional collaboration, solving multi-disciplinary problems for their clients, resulting in significant uplifts in the work performed and profitability of the business.

We have observed the shift in individual behaviours at Hall Chadwick, as their clients linger in the cafe space, making themselves at home, engaging in conversations with other clients and their people, a response to the permissions embedded in the physical design of the space.

Designing a workplace that embraces the values and behaviours desired of your organisation, while naturally activating opportunities for your employees to engage in diverse conversations, will continue to expand the potential of your organisation's impact.

Your people, their behaviours and performance are all a product of their environment, so consciously creating a space that facilitates these interactions will further your diversity and inclusivity objectives.

The four types of worker

Furthering the conversation of employee diversity, establishing who your workplace is for, can help you understand the personas of your workforce and their individual needs in the composition of the work environment.

FOUR TYPICAL PERSONAS THAT I HAVE OBSERVED IN THE WORKPLACE ARE:

You may find that there are more or fewer personas that you can address. However, these examples provide a starting point for discussion around the various workstyles and the requirements of your people.

The Technician

The technician spends most of their time at their designated workstation relying on traditional work processes and formal workplace structures. The desk-centric worker's work processes and modes are relatively simple, straightforward and predictable.

Examples of Technicians:
- Data Analyst/Input
- Call Centre Employee
- Designer/Drafting Technician/Engineer
- Information Technology
- Accounts Officer
- Legal

The Collaborator

The collaborative worker is an agile worker who spends their day moving from desk to meetings and collaborative team settings with their colleagues.

Examples of Collaborators:
- Team Leader/Manager
- Account Manager
- Administration
- Human Resources
- Marketing

The mobile worker

The Mobile worker is an employee who has flexible work processes and arrangements. There is nowhere that these knowledge-based workers cannot perform their functions as the development of new IT infrastructure creates more flexible work practices.

Examples of Mobile Workers:
- Sales
- Project Manager
- Customer Engagement

The remote worker

Remote workers work out of a variety of settings, home environments, co-working locations and coffee shops.

Examples of Remote Workers:
- Today many of us are remote workers in some capacity with our newfound freedom to work from home.
- For others, this may be a function of our organisations with enhanced flexibility and a "global" talent pool.

By identifying the various personas in your workforce, you can construct a series of spatial typologies and space ratios to support your organisation's unique makeup.

WITHIN EACH PERSONA, THERE IS TYPICALLY A MIX OF THESE WORK ACTIVITIES:

- Desk-based work
- Collaborative work
- Quiet, focused work
- Mobile work

Developing a ratio of time that each persona spends completing these work activities contributes to a deeper understanding of the nature and style of spaces that your workplace is required to provide, enabling your people's performance.

Following are the employee personas identified in working with Entain at a whole-of-business level. These personas were established by reviewing the "job role" and considering the types of tasks and activities required. This review highlighted the volume of work needed at the desk and the ratio of collaborative and quiet spaces necessary to support the various personas.

When reviewed at a department level, it provided an even greater level of insight into the workstyle of multiple teams, prompting a deeper conversation about where people work and the purpose of the office.

THE OUTCOMES OF THIS CONVERSATION LED TO THE REVIEW OF THE ORGANISATION'S WORK-FROM-HOME GUIDELINES AND THE INTRODUCTION OF AN ADDITIONAL WORKSPACE TYPE TO EACH PERSONA, "WORK FROM HOME".

This resulted in the design of workplace attendance rhythms being revisited to see what work could be performed at home more effectively. Entain then tailored their approach specifically to the needs and operational objectives of each team. This meant that teams with a high volume of desk-based work came into the workplace less frequently – and when they did come in, the purpose of their visits shifted their spatial needs from individual desks to collaborative spaces for group activities. This shift led Entain to place greater importance on additional collaborative work zones, supporting a greater variety of collaboration styles and reducing the need for individual workpoints.

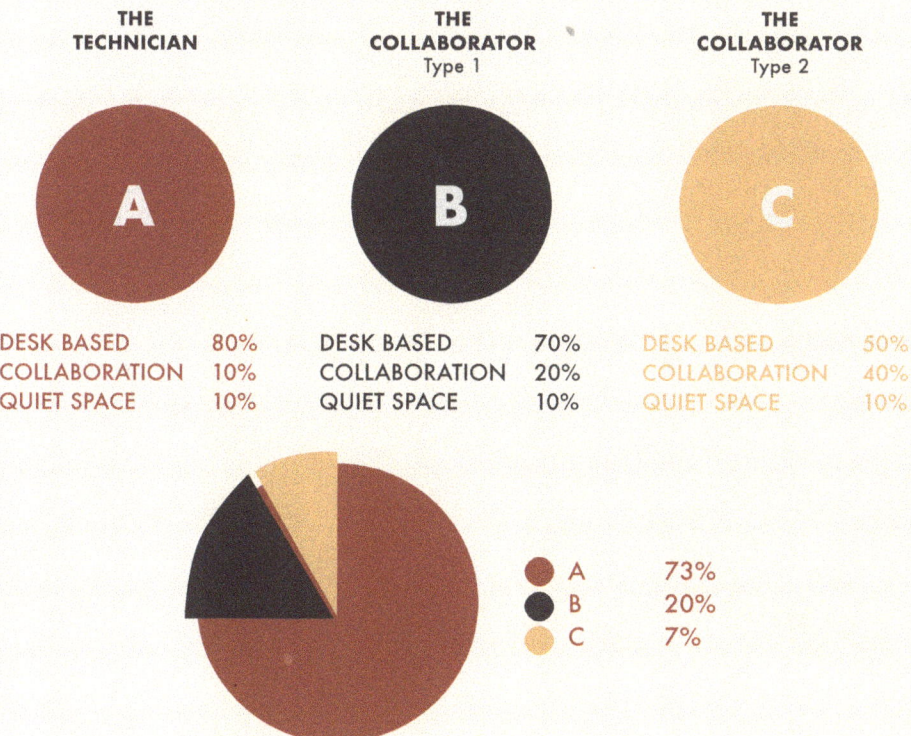

* At Entain, we identified only two of the four employee personas, The Technician and The Collaborator. However, it was also determined that there were two varieties of "The Collaborator" due to the variability of time spent collaborating, as reflected in the work activities breakdown.

worksheet

Identify your persona's

WITHIN EACH ORGANISATION, A RANGE OF ROLES MUST BE FILLED, REQUIRING A DIFFERENT TOOL KIT TO SUPPORT OPTIMAL PERFORMANCE.

These roles fall into a series of persona types. These personas require different spatial tools to enable your employees to do their job. When we have visibility over how these personas make up our organisation's employee mix, we can begin to shape our environments to provide these tools in the required ratios.

On the worksheet are the four personas typically found in each organisation. In the adjacent columns, reflect on your business roles and which column you feel they align to. Then determine the percentage of time each persona spends at their desk, collaborating with colleagues or in a quiet, concentrated and focused space doing individual work.

This activity will illustrate the quantity and ratio of support spaces your employees require to perform their roles.

This exercise can also identify the number of workstations/desks required should the organisation consider a more flexible and agile accommodation model that embraces a shared seating model.

Example:

COLLABORATOR

- Team Leader
- Account Manager
- Human Resources
- Design Coordinator
- Recruitment Exec

DESK 40%
COLLAB 40%
QUIET 20%

Making the workplace a place to be, with a hospitality-led *approach*

With organisations working hard to lure employees back into the workplace, now is the ideal time to take a fresh perspective on what it takes to elevate your workplace experience and create an environment that people choose to come to. The office's role has shifted from where we needed to "go to work" to somewhere that facilitates connection, collaboration, communication and learning.

WITH THIS PERSPECTIVE, LET'S TAKE A MORE EXPANSIVE VIEW AND LOOK AT HOW THE HOSPITALITY INDUSTRY, WHICH RELIES ON PEOPLE RETURNING TO THEIR SPACES AND SERVICES, DOES JUST THAT.

The hospitality industry covers a wide range of customer service operators, ranging from airlines to hotels, restaurants to bars. I have worked across them all throughout my career, designing and opening airline lounges globally for Etihad Airways, Air New Zealand, Singapore Airlines, Emirates, No1 Lounge and Virgin Australia, Amex and Plaza Premium, along with resorts such as Crystalbrook Byron (formerly The Byron at Byron), bars and cafes.

Taking the customer service elements of these operations and infusing them into a workplace environment is something that I have been working on since the late 2000s, with the first space embracing this enhanced amenity for their employees and guests alike in Ausenco's head office in South Brisbane.

Etihad Airways*

Air New Zealand*

Singapore Airlines*

No1 Lounge/Virgin Australia

Amex and Plaza Premium

Crystalbrook Byron**

Ausenco*

Tune into Episode 90 of the *Work Life By Design* podcast for the rest of our chat.

The idea of infusing hospitality into the workplace is one that Brad Krauskopf has taken a step further in the workplace industry through his nationwide coworking spaces, HUB Australia. Brad, HUB's founder, and his team are focused on delivering exceptional experiences to their members at every interaction, from a welcoming smile as you exit the lift to the curated program of regular events.

In my conversation with Brad in Episode 90 of the *Work Life by Design* podcast, we discussed how the office is far from dead and that people want to go to a workplace to work, socialise, connect and interact with others. However, they want it to be their choice to return to the office five days a week, not a mandate. Brad raised the question:

> *If you gave each of your employees $15K to pay for their personal office rent each year, would they give it back to you?*
>
> *Or would they go and rent a different office somewhere else?*

This is a pointed way of thinking about the workplace standard that you are offering your employees. If they would take that money and give it to someone else to satisfy their workplace needs, then your workplace is not enticing them back to the office.

One small change in language can create a big shift in our mindset. Rather than thinking about your people as employees, think of them as guests in your space.

HOW MIGHT THAT CHANGE YOUR PERSPECTIVE ON THE EXPERIENCE YOU'D LIKE TO DELIVER?

WHERE CAN YOU SHOW THEM BETTER HOSPITALITY?

The hospitality industry is about exceeding the expectations of guests, delivering quality service and a memorable experience, and creating a place people want to be in so they feel motivated to return. Hotels, airline lounges, restaurants and the like are rich with the qualities of lifestyle, community, connection and moments we aspire to by appealing to all of our senses.

Applying a hospitality-led approach to your workplace elevates the experience. It creates a unique work environment that promotes your brand and the culture of your business through curated services and amenities.

Every need is catered to at the HUB, from the fully serviced end-of-trip facilities, to a concierge to welcome guests and receive deliveries and a barista in the cafe. Events are celebrated, often with a "surprise and delight" factor.

But this experience doesn't start and end with the physical environment; it connects into and builds on the brand and culture of the business, what HUB wants to be known for and what they value. It also feeds into a frictionless and enjoyable digital environment, often our first interaction with the business. Consider how your employees experience the work environment you've created for them online and off.

WHERE MIGHT YOU SHOW THE YOUR EMPLOYEES A BIT MORE HOSPITALITY?

HOW COULD YOU SURPRISE AND DELIGHT THEM?

Some ways that you could introduce a more hospitality-led approach to you workplace include:

- Concierge services
    - Shoe repair
    - Dry cleaning
    - Parcel management
- Onsite barista and/or cafe
- Business lounges
- Spaces to support employee interests
    - Band/music room
    - Library
    - Recording studio
    - Games rooms
- Wellness rooms and relaxation spaces
- Curated events celebrating holidays and milestones
    - RUOK Day, with cupcakes
    - Wellness Day, with 15-minute massages
    - Valentine's Day, with "love notes"
    - Easter, with an egg hunt or simply a sweet treat
- Monthly drinks, lunches or breakfasts
- Wellness webinars
- Yoga, Pilates, stretch classes
- Tech support desk

With a bit of inspiration, you can create a workplace that is dynamic, ever-changing and attractive to employees, offering an experience that they can't get working at home.

THINK ABOUT YOUR BRAND AND CULTURE. WHAT ARE THE MOMENTS THAT MATTER IN YOUR BUSINESS, AND HOW COULD YOU ELEVATE YOUR APPROACH TO YOUR WORKPLACE?

So, how do we design the employee experience?

Curating your employees' journey through the workplace environment can enhance their overall experience. By consciously working your way through each moment of an employee's day, you can build in ways to elevate their experience of coming to work.

Taking our cues from the hospitality industry, how can you sweeten the "customer" (your employee) experience, surprise and delight them, and reinforce culture, brand and values, all while reducing friction, through each interaction they have throughout the day. And when we start thinking about their day, this starts well before they sit at their desk. As we are now in a world where we need to "earn the commute," that journey begins when they leave home, meaning that care needs to be given to *how* they get to their workplace, which in turn requires consideration of *where* your workplace is located.

ONCE THEY ARRIVE, WHAT ARE THE TOUCHPOINTS THEY EXPERIENCE, AND HOW IS THE BUSINESS GUIDING THEIR BEHAVIOUR?

If we consider the Mapien Case Study, the entire employee journey through the space was designed to guide the social interactions and work behaviours that the organisation wished to encourage among their people. As do Davidson, Hall Chadwick, Entain and our next case study, EDMI.

Reflect on these questions to ensure that your organisation's unique environment is tailoring an overall experience for your people.

- What is the journey that you want to guide people through?
- What experiences do you want them to have at each touchpoint?
- How do you want them to feel in those moments?

How to create a journey map

WHAT ARE THE TOUCHPOINTS THROUGHOUT THE DAY?

Think about the touchpoints that your employees move through in a day. Think about how things are done in your workplace now and how you would ideally like to see them. Depending on the size of your organisation, you may need to repeat this exercise for different teams, departments or roles to reflect the variety of journeys in your organisation.

Grab a piece of paper and mind map out the flow of your workplace. What do you do first thing in the morning? Then what? What's the last thing you do before you leave? How do you want your employees to move through their day? You might need to brainstorm a few scenarios to capture your people's unique workflows or commute options.

Now that you know what that flow looks like, how do you want them to feel at each moment, and what action can you take to influence that?

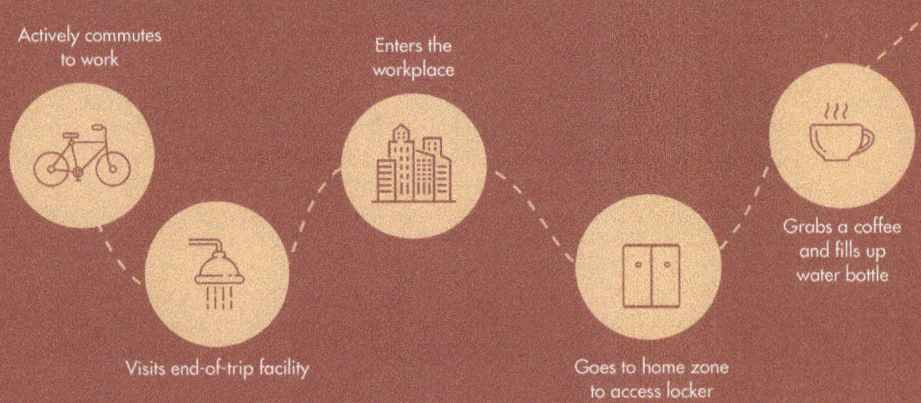

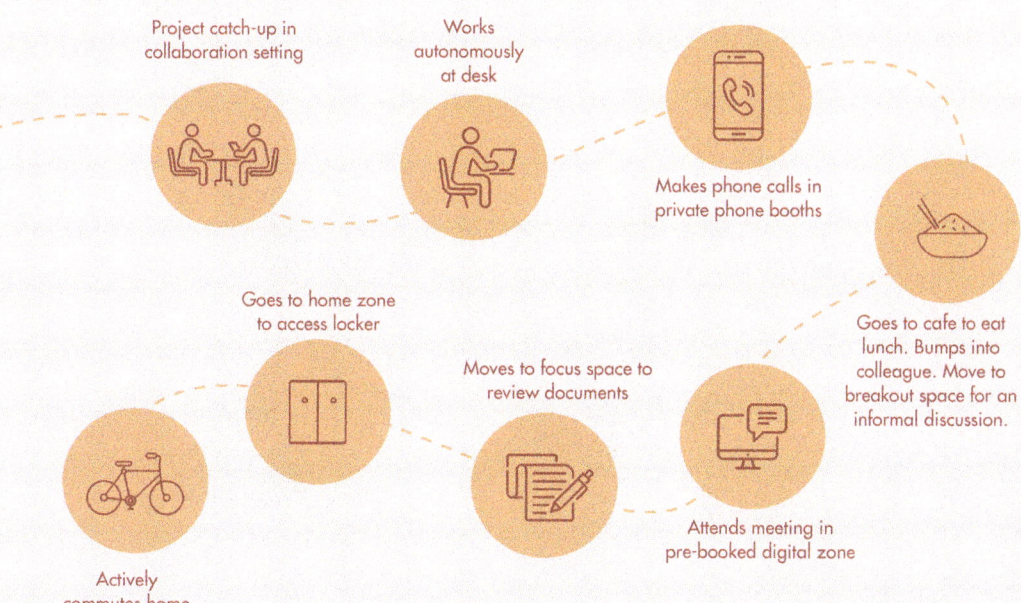

ACTIONS
Here are a few to get you started:

Actively commutes to work
FEELING – safe, energised, active.
- Workplace is located with easy access to bikeways.
- Building has secure bike storage.

Visits end-of-trip facility
FEELING – relaxed, refreshed, calm
- Clean, modern facilities
- Towel service
- Complimentary toiletries
- Secure lockers for active apparel
- Air diffuser with calming scent
- Hairdryers, hair straighteners
- Iron, steaming equipment
- Washing and drying facilities

Enters the workplace
FEELING – inspired, energised, connected to the organisation
- Corporate brand is infused into the colour and materiality of the space
- Style of the space reflects the behaviours of the company values
- Imagery reflects business objectives (e.g. artwork provides line of sight to the company "why")

Goes to home zone to access locker
FEELING – organised, arrived and ready to start their day
- Frictionless, e.g. locker access is issue-free
- Compartments in the locker for organisation
- Charging points in the locker for devices

case study
EDMI

Unless you live in an older home, you may have noticed that nobody comes around to "read the meter" to calculate your energy bill anymore. That's all thanks to a small box in your home that captures your energy usage and reports it back to your provider each period. That little box is a smart meter, and it was likely created by EDMI, a global energy solutions leader.

EDMI, led by Executive Director Andrew Thomas, came to us because their workplace did not reflect their technological progressiveness or contribution to the world's smart energy solutions. The business wanted a space that could unite teams, position them to attract top talent, and reflect their market presence as an energy solutions leader.

the task

When I first met EDMI, the office was located in a warehouse in a light industrial area of Brisbane's northern suburbs. The company's gradual acquisition of space throughout the building had segmented its teams across two floors, with a laboratory and workshop facility at one end and distribution warehouse at the rear. The staff facilities were austere, offering only a small kitchenette and a singular uninspiring "tea room".

The reception was nondescript, with no reflection of who EDMI is, what it does, or its impact on the smart energy and metering industry.

The work environment was cluttered; proprietary desks were arranged ad hoc to fit within the space, and desktops were littered with metering componentry, soldering irons, and the other tools employees needed to perform their roles. The business had clearly outgrown the building – in fact, its newest department had been annexed to another site down the road. What it needed was a space that supported future growth, enabled its people and reflected its brand.

the inspiration

To define the needs of EDMI's next property portfolio, we needed to address a few key questions. First, could we separate the office, warehouse and lab, or were there co-dependencies requiring them to be on the same site? Which teams needed to stay co-located with the warehouse or the lab?

Secondly, how did the various departments need to work, and was there a better way? How EDMI's employees viewed their space was an emotional challenge, and we needed to evolve their perspective on "how" they worked, to shift their mindsets from "my space" – where everything they needed to perform their role was on their desk – to "our space", a shared environment offering access to a variety of tools.

These questions then gave way to another, rather large, question: what is the most suitable location for each part of the business? Should the warehouse stay where it is or move? Should the workplace remain part of the warehouse? Does the lab need to be co-located with the workplace or the warehouse? Where are the customers located? Where do the employees live?

All of these questions fed into the decision-making process regarding how the property portfolio should be structured and where it should be located, and how those choices would impact the experience of current and future employees.

THE OBJECTIVE OF EDMI'S NEW PREMISE WAS TO PRESENT A MORE CORPORATE BUT HIGHLY TECHNICAL IMAGE OF THE ORGANISATION TO BOTH CUSTOMERS AND OUR PEOPLE. GIVEN EDMI IS AN ENGINEERING AND TECHNOLOGY ORGANISATION WITH COMPLEX FACILITY REQUIREMENTS, THERE WAS A SIGNIFICANT RISK IN BLENDING THESE TWO NEEDS INTO A SINGLE PROJECT. MELISSA'S PASSION, UNDERSTANDING AND KNOWLEDGE OF HER FIELD ENABLED HER TO NOT ONLY MANAGE OUR PASSIONATE ENGINEERING STAFF BY DELIVERING ALL OF THEIR FUNCTIONAL NEEDS, BUT DELIGHT EDMI'S ENTIRE STAKEHOLDER COMMUNITY WITH THE OUTCOMES PRODUCED AND THE COLLABORATIVE ENGAGEMENT THROUGHOUT THE PROJECT.

– ANDREW THOMAS, EXECUTIVE DIRECTOR

the solution

Our detailed analysis of the various operations led us to realise that the workplace could be separated from the warehouse, and the laboratory and workshop could be easily catered to in a commercial office tenancy. With this newfound clarity about the various portfolios, we could turn our attention to location. Geographical mapping of EDMI's clients and employees identified a strong need for an inner city location north of the river, easily connected by road infrastructure to the airport and shipping ports and on a direct public transport route to the north. This locational mapping positioned the business close to its clients and distribution needs while considering its employees' commute. The result was a narrowed focus on Fortitude Valley with a specific tenancy size to shortlist potential options.

The final tenancy was selected for its particular floor plate shape and size, which could accommodate EDMI's technical workforce on a single floor, support meeting and storage space, and house administration on the second contiguous level.

Above: The casual waiting area is nestled beneath the stairs, offering guests a comfortable place to sit before being escorted upstairs.

Below: The entry space facilitates contactless access to the workplace and direct access into the meeting rooms, without crossing the secure line.

CASE STUDY – EDMI

> "RATHER THAN FINDING A PREMISES AND THEN LOOKING TO SQUEEZE OUR STAFF IN, MELISSA AND HER TEAM DELIVERED A HOLISTIC OUTCOME THAT GUIDED US THROUGH THE ENTIRE PROCESS FROM GATHERING OUR REQUIREMENTS, TO SELECTION OF AN APPROPRIATE BUILDING, AND THE DEFINITION OF A WORKFLOW-BASED LAYOUT."
>
> – ANDREW THOMAS, EXECUTIVE DIRECTOR

the detail

The technical floor brought together the hardware, firmware and software teams, along with sales, product managers and solutions consultants into a singular space, eliminating the physical barriers of the previous tenancy. Large "L" shaped desks were replaced with electronic height-adjustable, bench-style workstations. The hierarchy was broken down, with no individual allocated an office. The workshop was expanded to provide a shared workspace for all individuals, reducing the need for desk-based tools. A range of collaborative workpoints was strategically positioned throughout the floor to create spaces for the two teams to come together and contribute to each other's meetings, without invitation but simply by overhearing conversations.

The aesthetics were inspired by the EDMI logo and the technical minds of its people. The Rubik's Cube proved the perfect metaphor, capturing the block-like form of the logo, the simple primary colour palette, and the cognitive thinking required to solve the puzzle. The metaphor influenced the various materials, colours and shapes employed throughout the spaces, ranging from grid ceilings to carpet inserts and dividing screens constructed from milk crates. EDMI's end client, the homeowners, are referenced in the brick cladding throughout and residential styling.

The result is a progressive workplace environment that encapsulates EDMI's brand and culture.

the employee journey

While the design of the space itself has a story to tell, so too does the transformative journey that EDMI's employees were guided through to inform and embrace the new design.

Engaging with EDMI's employees early in the process was critical to understanding the complexities of such a technical business and its unique property portfolio requirements. This engagement consisted of employee surveys and leadership interviews to uncover user needs, specific spaces, tools and equipment, and relationships within the business. Employee workshops teased out further details about the team's appetite for change and views on possible workplace solutions while providing them with a taste of what was possible in a new future.

It was also a delicate position to navigate, as some employees would stay with the warehouse and lab while others relocated to the new corporate head office. It was imperative that we were sensitive to the impact of this change on those who remained with the warehouse, so they wouldn't feel "left behind", "forgotten" or "not valued".

Those who were relocated would experience a big shift too. They were getting a vastly different workplace from what they were accustomed to and could no longer drive five minutes from their home to work, park and walk inside. They would now be required to commute on public transport, a minimum of 30 minutes for most.

As with any change, there are always individuals who do not welcome it, preferring to remain fixed to what they know instead of embracing a new future. One of these employees proved to be exceptionally staid in their view of where and how the workplace should be and should work. I affectionately reflect on this individual as my "anarchist" in the process. (More on him later.)

To bring the entire team on this journey, we planned a workplace showcase. The team met at the local train station, and collectively made the commute into the Valley. With the new office directly opposite the station, it enabled EDMI to demonstrate the change in habits required to get to the office. Once the entire team had arrived, pizza, donuts, and a plethora of treats from food and bar operators downstairs were handed out, introducing the team to the numerous food options nearby.

They then walked through the vacant floor space, which was marked out with tape on the floor to inform the various spaces and work zones. The material palette was laid out so that everyone could feel the new carpet, stone and fabrics that would form their workplace.

I then led them right back to where we began by reviewing their survey contributions and workshop input, and the data analysis and commercial realities that informed the decision and planning to this point. We talked through the floor plans, the materiality, the inspiration from the Rubik's Cube and the residential touches, along with intended uses, behavioral cues and general office etiquette. We discussed the change in workpoint style, the shared workshop and the shift away from on-desk equipment, everything they needed to familiarise themselves with the new environment.

This simply executed afternoon outing allowed the team to immerse themselves in the experience of traveling to the office, learn what was available to them for lunch and after-work options, explore what the space looked like, and imagine themselves in their new space. It shifted the mindsets of those individuals from one of fear, change, and unknowing, to familiarity, understanding and excitement. They could now prepare for the change, informed by the experience.

ANARCHIST TO ADVOCATE

Now, back to my anarchist. He was adamant that this relocation was a terrible idea, that the new workplace would be horrible and that staying at his large, cluttered and dark desk would be far better. This person shared his views in the employee survey, the employee workshops and again during the showcase. Clearly, he was not a fan.

As a connoisseur of coffee, however, this person was given the opportunity to select the cafe coffee machine, a gesture by the organisation to entice him.

I returned to the EDMI office several months after the business moved in and quickly found myself cornered by my anarchist. Immediately I was a little taken aback, and began to mentally prepare myself for the onslaught of criticism that was sure to come. However, to my surprise, nothing but praise came forth! He guided me over to the coffee machine and made me a coffee all while telling me how much he loved the office, how he enjoyed the commute and how it had changed not only how he worked but his team worked with other teams. It filled my soul with joy that day to see how genuinely this person's world had been changed, and how continuous communication along the journey had contributed to creating such a positive experience for that person, despite his deep reluctance.

HOW INVOLVING THE EDMI TEAM IN A CO-CREATION PROCESS UNITED A TEAM

But what about those who stayed in the warehouse and lab, the employees who didn't get to experience the new, bright, shiny space? If a workplace restructure is not managed carefully, it can leave some feeling like they have been left behind or, worse, forgotten about.

This consideration stayed front and centre as we transitioned a large portion of the EDMI team into their new inner-fringe location. To demonstrate the business's ongoing commitment to those who did not relocate, a refresh of the existing facilities was on the cards.

To ensure that the process was inclusive and the team owned the outcome, we engaged them in a co-creation workshop. First we explored the challenges of the existing facilities and then imagined how it could be different, which gave way to a united vision for the spaces that the whole team could get behind.

We then let them redesign the cafe space, a fixed area that opened out onto the rear driveway. It already had all the existing services so the makeover was aesthetically driven.

We then divided them into three groups, provided them each with a floor plan and set of "dollhouse" style furniture items, and set them to work. We also laid out a table of finishes for them to choose from: carpets, vinyls, tiles, fabrics and paint colours. Each group created their own vision for the space and shared it with the whole team. We then voted on the preferred design and colour palette.

Inviting the whole team to an afternoon of reimagining their space to suit their needs was an uplifting and joyful experience. The team loved the opportunity to contribute to the redesign of their own space and the mood shift was palpable.

Employees were guided through the design process using planning templates and material palettes.

The co-creation session enabled employees to play an active part in reimagining their workplace, providing a sense of inclusion and ownership over the finished space.

> **This was such a valuable investment of our time and resources. Bringing the team together and enabling them to contribute to the transformation of their space gave them a chance to collaborate, bond and brought them together with a single vision to enhance their work.**

– ANDREW THOMAS, EXECUTIVE DIRECTOR

The stair connects the two main social hubs of the workplace, the entry and waiting space with the GENIUS CAFÉ.

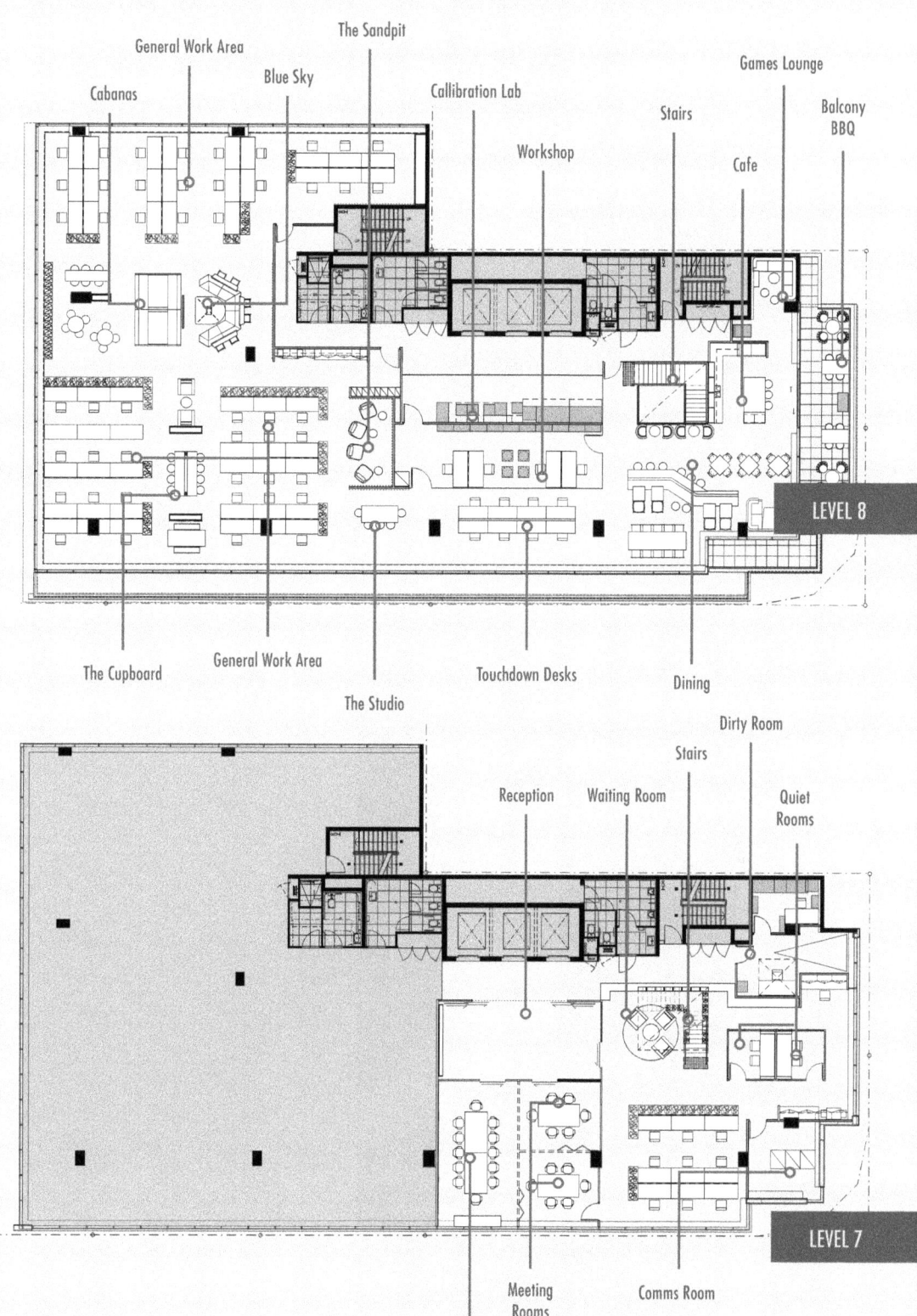

Above: The boardroom embraces the cubic design present through the space, inspired by the Rubik's Cube, through layered, acoustic cork wall panelling and whiteboards for brainstorming on the operable wall.

Left: Quiet rooms provide spaces for individual work, with coloured glass adding vibrancy.

Left: The laboratory is enveloped in glass to provide transparency into the core operations of the business.

Below: Open acoustic cabana's create flexible meeting spaces.

Left: Built-in seating activates the GENIUS CAFE, creating a "working cafe" — a space where employees can eat and socialise, and also work and collaborate.

THE STUDIO

Various meeting and collaboration spaces encourage connection, collaboration and socialisation.

GENIUS CAFE

THE CAMPFIRE

The BLUE SKY space provides for active collaboration and for the team to connect with international counterparts. Positioned in the centre of the floor, the space enables conversations to be overheard and contributed to.

The SANDPIT utilises full-height whiteboards and bean bags to support a more casual and interactive collaboration style.

Supporting your people *through change*

If there's one thing we have learned since 2020, it's that change is inevitable. With many businesses testing hybrid work arrangements, new work rituals and technology rollouts, change is being imposed on us at work and at home at a rate we have never experienced. Such evolution is full of uncertainty, but it also comes with great possibilities. In times like these, a change strategy provides structure and a reliable roadmap to a successful delivery – one that considers the project objectives and the human experience, expanding our vision of what's possible.

Creating a vision for your journey

Understanding your business through a deep discovery process is crucial to creating a change transformation program. This understanding goes to the very grassroots of your company, exploring employees and their work at a task level.

Throughout this book, we have laid the foundations for exploring your organisation and understanding your project objectives and people at a deep level. This process of discovery and understanding is crucial to developing a successful change strategy.

Insights such as how your employees perform their specific tasks, the tools they require to perform those tasks, and how they interact with other employees and their physical environment result in data.

The data extracted from this exploration is the basis for analysing how your environment can be designed to enhance employee performance and wellbeing. All help you to make data-led decisions on the types of space required, furniture typologies, and physical tools to enable your people to perform and thrive in the work environment.

As well as unveiling the core of your organisation's operations, it's equally important to discover the bigger-picture aspirations and the purpose of the "workplace", why we come to this place and the activities we want to foster within it. It ensures we capture a broader, more holistic vision of your desired outcomes. Such aspirations can come from a new branding experience, improved or enhanced culture, or complete organisational change. This deep discovery phase develops a clear vision of what lies ahead, identifying the tailored approach required to meet the organisation's aspirations and ensuring that your workplace has its own irresistible, gravitational pull.

Communication on the journey

A smooth transition relies on regular, direct communication to address employees' questions, anxieties and concerns, which requires consistent communication of an overarching message throughout the process. This message addresses the big picture questions, such as: What? Why? How? **AND THE ALL-IMPORTANT WIIFM: WHAT'S IN IT FOR ME?**

After communicating the overarching message, further messaging will reinforce this intention and get down to details – the HOW of change. Frequent communication will alleviate fear and confusion in employees and develop trust within the process. Keep in mind that communication doesn't have to be dull and strictly informative. Make it exciting! The tone of voice and vehicle you use to explain the change should reflect your organisational culture and will determine the buzz it creates.

Communication can take many different forms, such as a countdown, social gatherings like morning teas, lunch and learns or Friday drinks, videos, social media, company intranet, and perhaps one of the most important, Q&A. Enabling employees to voice concerns and know that they are being heard may be one of the most potent opportunities for success. Whether adopted or not, addressing your people's concerns and suggestions is an essential show of consideration.

The communication, platforms and strategies employed by your organisation may differ from another organisation. What's relevant is that it works for your business and your people feel acknowledged and considered.

Engaging your people throughout the journey

We know that our people are the biggest influence on the success of our business. So it goes without saying that involving them through the change process is critical. This engagement builds trust, a crucial factor in engaging and retaining staff through times of uncertainty and ensuring the employees feel synonymous with the outcome.

Identifying internal influencers, otherwise known as change champions, who will pioneer your overarching message can drive engagement to levels management cannot achieve. These change champions also become a safe touchpoint for other employees to ask questions and convey concerns.

Build excitement throughout the process to keep employees engaged with the outcome vision by sending sneak peeks of the proposed design, showcasing selected furniture items, putting up a finishes boards, and holding staff information sessions or an entire employee showcase, like we did with EDMI.

THESE APPROACHES CREATE A BUZZ AND EXCITE YOUR PEOPLE, BUILDING THE DESIRE FOR WHAT COULD BE.

Seqwater's CBD Hub supports a wide variety of workstyles for its staff.

A changing environment often means new spaces, tools and processes. Training and onboarding employees on how their new space can be used effectively and its benefits will help create a smooth transition and ensure a higher adoption of "how" the space can and should be used to maximise its potential.

WHEN EMPLOYEES UNDERSTAND WHY A SPACE IS DESIGNED, THEY WILL BE MORE RECEPTIVE TO ENGAGING WITH IT AS INTENDED, INCREASING THE OPPORTUNITY FOR YOUR PROJECT TO BE SUCCESSFUL.

A great example is COMUNiTI's project for Seqwater. When Seqwater introduced its CBD satellite hub, the hybrid workplace brought a range of new ways of working. With an extensive workforce, attempting to individually onboard all the existing employees and every new employee would have been a process set up to fail, so Seqwater opted for a short onboarding video. The video explains the inspiration for the workplace, the range of available zones and expected behaviours, and gives detailed explanations of how these spaces are to be used and the furniture settings within them.

www.comuniti.com.au/projects/seqwater

Seqwater's onboarding video received extensive positive feedback and reduced employees' apprehension about the new environment. It effectively communicates the why, how, and what, providing employees with a transparent and concise understanding of the space.

Humans are creatures of habit, and without an appropriate introduction to a new space, people will overlay old work habits, never realising the potential of the new work environment.

What experience do you want to create?

The environment our organisation occupies is a significant factor in the success of our business. It can enable a company's culture, entrench values, influence behaviour and enhance employee health and wellbeing. Creating a workplace is an incredible gift and one that should not be considered lightly. As you have learned through the pages of this book, it can also be an incredibly complex task and one that deserves time and care.

YOUR WORKPLACE IS AN OPPORTUNITY TO LEVERAGE YOUR EMPLOYEE VALUE PROPOSITION, MAKE YOUR BUSINESS A MAGNET FOR TALENT AND DELIVER AN EMPLOYEE EXPERIENCE THAT ALIGNS THE HEARTS, BODIES AND MINDS OF YOUR PEOPLE.

We are all *individuals*. We each have differing personalities, preferred workstyles, *varying roles* and task descriptions. Understanding the needs of your people is critical in designing a workplace to *best support* them, creating the right environment for optimal performance.

Chapter Huddle

CONNECT TO THE HEARTS, BODIES AND MINDS OF YOUR PEOPLE

THERE ARE THREE LAYERS TO THE EMPLOYEE EXPERIENCE WHEN CREATING A WORK "PLACE".

1. It's an employee's experience of working with your company.
2. It's an employee's experience of the physical workplace environment.
3. It's an employee's experience of change.

THERE ARE THREE ENVIRONMENTS INFLUENCING EMPLOYEE EXPERIENCE IN EVERY ORGANISATION.

1. Cultural Environment, the way people feel about your organisation and the purpose, values, behaviours and structures in place.
2. Physical Environment, the built space, what we see, touch, hear and smell.
3. Technological Environment, the virtual environment and tools people need to work (laptops, devices, software, systems and apps).

A DYNAMIC WORKPLACE CONNECTS THESE ENVIRONMENTS TO OUR PEOPLE, THEIR HEARTS, BODIES AND MINDS.

- Heart is the collective emotion of a space, otherwise known as an organisation's culture.
- Body is the physical environment, how it looks and feels. Like a body, is it put together for flexibility, agility and performance, or is it slow, rigid and fixed?
- Mind is the technology that brings the intelligence of the organisation together and makes it easily accessible, reducing friction.

DESIGNING A WORKPLACE TODAY IS A COMPLEX TASK, REQUIRING THE CONSIDERATION OF A MULTITUDE OF INDIVIDUAL NEEDS:

- Generational differences – we have more generations in the workplace than in any previous era, each with different work practices.
- Personality types – individual and team personality types require different types of workspaces.
- Neurodiversity – provide spaces considerate of employee sensitivities to enable individual performance.

Recruitment and management practices form two pillars in creating diverse and inclusive workplaces. The design of the space supports the effective execution of these practices.

KNOW YOUR EMPLOYEE PERSONAS.
Understanding the workstyles of your employees provides data that can inform and design the workflows and environments your people require to perform.

DESIGN YOUR EMPLOYEES' DAILY EXPERIENCE.
Delivering an exceptional workplace experience requires organisations to consider the touchpoints of an employee's journey throughout the day. Elevating the experience of these touchpoints is something we can take inspiration from the hospitality industry for.

CHANGE REQUIRES STRATEGY AND COMMUNICATION.
No matter how well-designed your workplace environment is, without effective engagement, consultation and communication along the journey, your workplace will unlikely realise its full potential.

ARE YOU READY TO TAKE YOUR EMPLOYEES ON THE JOURNEY?

ARE YOU READY? LET'S DO THIS!

CHAPTER SIX

let's put it into action

Planning, designing and building a new workplace, as you can see, is a complex task. There is so much to consider, manage, and execute. Most businesses get this opportunity once every decade if they're lucky! So be sure to make the most of yours. Armed with the knowledge you've gleaned from this book and with professional guidance, you can optimise this opportunity, creating an outcome that will dramatically impact your business and reimagine everyone's experience of work.

This book has been designed to enlighten, educate and prepare you to embark on the process of creating your next workplace. I want to ensure that you are informed about the choices, decisions and opportunities ahead so that you can guide the process and play an active part in it, rather than being a passenger.

So often I see organisations that have let their lease renewal run to its expiry with little to no thought about what comes next. They give no consideration to where their next workplace will be, what it needs to do, or how their business has evolved and, with it, their workplace requirements. They are left scrambling to make a fast leasing decision because the clock is ticking on their current lease, and they need to be out! This situation is stressful and doesn't allow the proper consultation, due diligence or planning to ensure that the next space is suitable for your needs. Making hasty decisions based on leasing "deals" or "ready to occupy" space results in people being shoe-horned in with no room to expand or swimming in space. With planning, you might find you don't need as much space as you thought, ultimately shifting the landscape on your leasing decision and opening up new opportunities around location, floor plate size and buildings.

In this chapter, we will start to tie the threads together on everything you have learned and map out the steps you can take to capitalise on this opportunity. We'll explore how to create a plan, assemble your team, share your vision and answer the all-important questions of "how much" and "how long".

So, are you ready to design your next workplace?

Start with a clear plan for _success_

Before you commit to a lengthy lease term that will not only have significant financial implications for your business but also impact the performance and efficiency of your people, you need to prepare yourself and the organisation for the journey with a clear plan.

If you fail to plan, you plan to fail.

For a project to be successful, you need to define what success looks like. Define the expectations, set the goals and measure the outcomes. These rules apply to any project, and the principles are the same whether designing a new workplace, implementing a new business system, renovating your home or building a hotel.

When I guide clients through this process, we develop a strategy and plan using the *Workplace Dynamics Blueprint*™. This Blueprint reviews each of the five pillars, capturing the gaps, opportunities and points of excellence that can be leveraged through the project. It communicates a clear vision for the project and the brand – the culture we wish to infuse into the fabric of the space, the values and behaviours we hope the workplace will embody, and the experience we want to evoke for everyone who walks through the doors. This vision is coupled with the practicalities of how much space is required to deliver on these opportunities, what areas and zones are required, minimum floor plate sizes and preferred geographical locations.

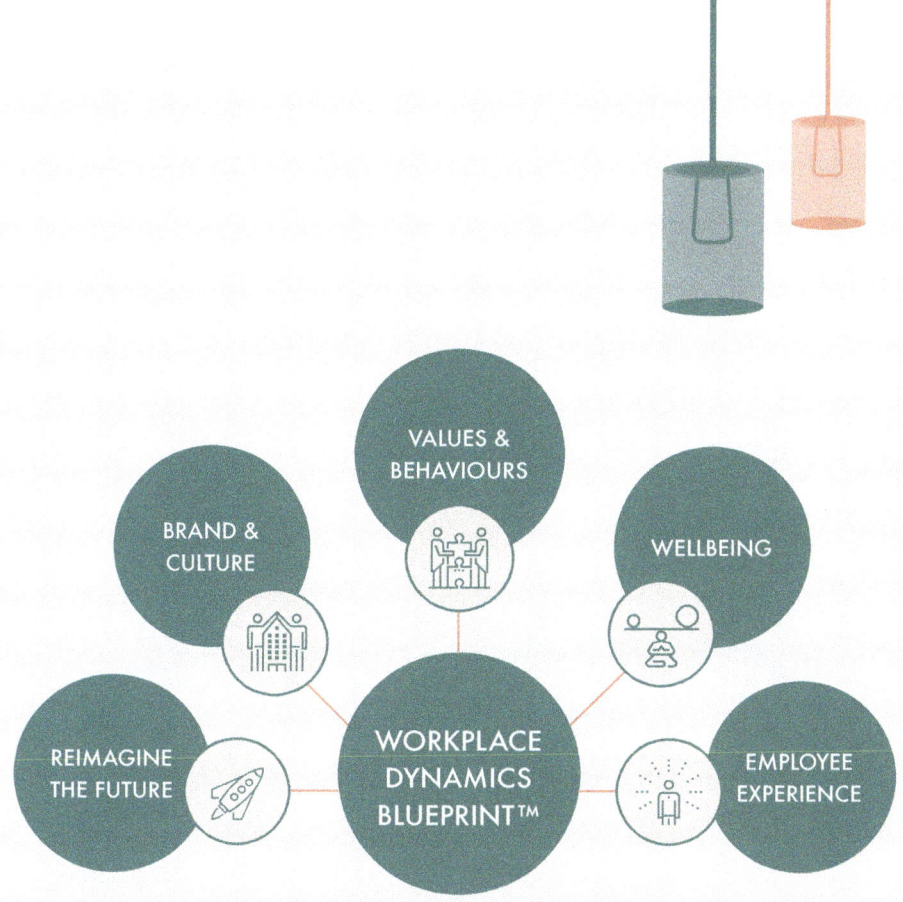

While you will be unable to round out this strategy without the support and guidance of your Workplace Strategist, you will be able to lay the foundations and ensure that you are informed when you engage with the market to assemble your team. This plan will help you establish the critical measurements of success, enabling you to ask informed questions and listen from an educated perspective. It'll equip you to delve deeper into the process and work with professionals to fill the gaps in the plan. My hope is that you will see your vision of success become a reality.

For any organisation, this can seem like an overwhelming task – but goals are achievable with a bit of tenacity and some planning. Using this book's earlier chapters to inform your thinking, work your way through each of these questions.

1 What are you trying to achieve?

WRITE IT DOWN.

At the commencement of a project, it's essential to get clear about what you expect to achieve. What will be your success measurements and KPIs?

After the project, what can you look back on to critically evaluate your achievement?

By considering these measurements now, you can focus your energy on the right areas of the project as you move forward. You'll have a clear endpoint in sight and can begin to plan out the most effective use of your time, energy and money.

In reviewing the earlier chapters, what is the overarching goal that you wish for your project to achieve? While you may need to address your workplace for the usual commercial reasons, such as lease expiry or growth, there are likely to be many other business goals you wish to leverage with this unique opportunity. Is it enhanced brand alignment like some of our earlier case studies? Improved employee experience? More effective workplace utilisation and operation?

PERHAPS IT'S A COMBINATION OF THESE AND MORE.

Whatever your goal, having a clear picture of the end result helps set your North Star for the entire project, ensuring everyone is focused on the same outcome. Using clear metrics, or KPIs, to measure your progress can also help establish the incremental change required to define success. What business factors might change as a result of achieving this goal?

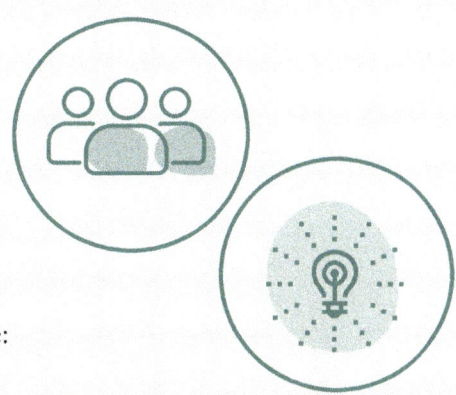

Some examples of success measures that I have worked towards with my clients are:

- Reduced sick leave
- Reduced employee turnover
- Employee attraction and recruitment
- An increase in the eNPS (Employee Net Promoter Score)
- Improved inter-departmental communication
- Brand alignment of culture and values to the work environment
- Optimised space utilisation
- Enhanced business performance, speed of delivery, increased service offerings, increased profit, etc.

One key metric I suggest is: "how do you want to feel during and after this process?" This journey is not for the faint-hearted. It is often filled with humps, bumps, potholes and pivots along the way. But with the right team, you can work to minimise their impact and smooth out the journey. Consider how you want to feel when it's done, too. I hope you would like to be proud of the end result – along with a raft of other emotions. Be sure to include these as well. How you feel about the result is just as significant to the project's success as the business metrics you are looking to hit.

2 What does your future look like?

GET SPECIFIC.

Just as you would approach your strategic plan with a view of how your business may change in the future, it is wise to approach your workplace strategy with the same perspective. As your business continues to evolve, your space will need to adapt and perform differently, supporting the operation, communication and workflows that come with it. Simply replicating what you have now will not see your space become agile and nimble enough to adapt to the fast pace your business will likely experience.

And if it's been a while since you've revisited your strategic objectives and business goals, now is the perfect time!

Take a long-term view and begin by asking yourself these questions, among many more:

1. What will your business look like in five years?
2. How many staff will you employ?
3. Who will your clients be?
4. What technology may have been invented that changes how your employees perform their jobs and service your clients?

By understanding how all these elements will perform or evolve over the coming years, you'll have a better handle on what type of space can flex with your changing needs throughout your lease.

3

What does the picture look like now?

ESTABLISH THE BASELINE.

As with any journey, we first need to establish where we are to know where we are going! It's no good to have a destination pinned if we don't know our starting location. Otherwise, we could be heading north for a long time before we realise we should have been heading south! So with our definition of success captured, we need to look at our present state to establish a baseline for where we are going.

Start with a review of how you use your current space. Typically our offices morph over time to suit our changing business needs. However, they rarely support what we intend them to do. Meeting rooms get converted into offices, and support spaces become storerooms. A thorough review of how you presently use your space may reveal that it's not as efficient as you thought. Make sure you know what you really need.

In addition to observing your current space, we have been gathering data to establish this essential baseline. (Please revisit previous chapters to complete these exercises.) This data helps us see where we are, determine our next steps and provide a future reference for implementing our plans.

Capture these observations and your collated data so it is clear what's working, what's not, and the concerns with your present space. You can now revisit your measure of success and add some targeted metrics.

Remember not all goals need to be SMART goals. Specific. Measurable. Attainable. Relevant. Time-based. Sometimes a simple intention is more appropriate. Our intentions set our attention.

4 How are you going to get there?

BREAK IT DOWN.

It can be overwhelming to think of what bringing your next workplace to life will entail. It can be months or years in the making. However, when things seem bigger than us, it always helps to break them down and take one manageable bite at a time.

Every project has a series of steps that need to be followed, and jumping ahead to the end feeds into our sense of overwhelm. It's also fraught with danger. We may miss a step, forget a critical decision, and soon the wheels begin to wobble.

By breaking the project down into smaller tasks and setting interim milestones, we can create a greater sense of control and calm about how we will achieve the big goal.

Remember, you are not in this alone! Together with your team, both internally and externally, with a good plan and their guidance, you will get there. I'll introduce you to your team shortly in the coming pages.

AND… Don't Forget to Bring Your People on the Journey.

COMMUNICATION IS CRITICAL THROUGHOUT THIS TIME, AND AN EFFECTIVE CHANGE MANAGEMENT STRATEGY MAY ALSO BE REQUIRED TO HELP WITH THE TRANSITION.

But there is another huge opportunity that many companies mistakenly leave on the table: asking your people what they want to see in the new design can empower both the organisation and the employees. Exploring the employee's perception of how they could perform better may lead you to better understand the current inefficiencies in your present space. While you may feel you already have a good idea about these aspects, often there is a curveball you had never considered.

How do you eat an elephant?

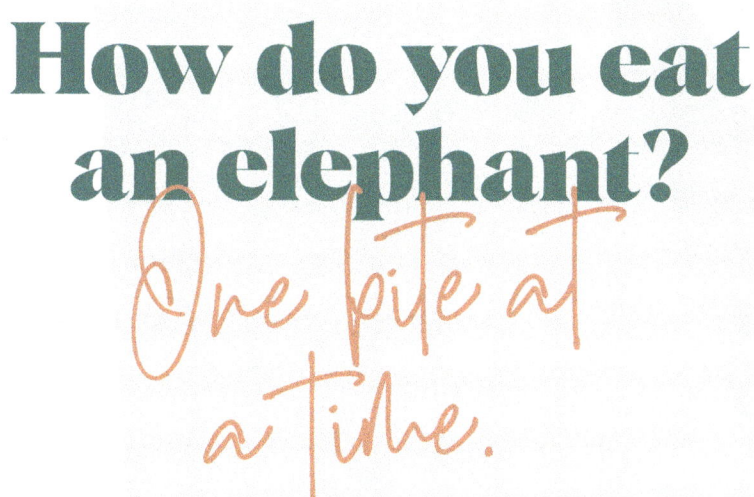

One bite at a time.

5 How do you know you've succeeded?

MEASURE IT AND ADAPT.

It's time to pop the champagne (or crack a beer)! You've done it! The new workplace is finished. Over the past months, you've clearly articulated your objective, imagined your future, understood your current state, set measurable targets, broken the project down into smaller tasks, and established clear milestones, all to get to this day!

Once everyone has settled into their new home, and it's back to business as usual, reaching the end of the project can often feel like it's the perfect time to close the book on that chapter. And while you can certainly begin redirecting your attention back to your day job, there are still a few more steps to ensure that you continue leveraging this project. It's time to evaluate the outcomes, absorb the learnings and iterate.

In order to ensure that you have achieved the goals you set, it's time to measure them. Has sick leave been reduced? Is the space being utilised more? Have you seen an uplift in your eNPS score? Are the teams communicating more? Have these changes increased profit?

Revisiting our success measures, understanding the movement and then analysing the cause enables us to make informed, data-led decisions about how the space is performing and impacting the performance of our people and the business. If you've introduced workplace technology, what is the data telling you?

IF YOU'RE NOT SEEING THE RESULTS YOU SET OUT TO ACHIEVE, WHAT CAN YOU DO TO CONTINUE TO ADAPT AND EVOLVE THE SPACE TO ENSURE IT'S OPTIMISING YOUR BUSINESS INVESTMENT?

As you sit with your glass of champagne and admire the outcome, reflect on that other important question… "How do I want to feel?"

SO… HOW DOES IT FEEL?

Now you have your plan laid out and are clear on the project's overarching objectives, it's time to clarify the details.

How well prepared are you to maximise your opportunity?

10 QUESTIONS YOU SHOULD ANSWER BEFORE ENGAGING THE MARKET.

You have a wealth of data within your organisation, and I have shown you how much through the earlier pages! Now it's time to bring it all together. Consider the questions below and collate the data outlined to better understand what your business looks like and how your aims can be translated into the physical space by your project team. Ask and answer the following questions before you engage with the market for your next workplace.

1

DOES YOUR BUSINESS STRATEGY HAVE A CLEAR OBJECTIVE ON HOW THE PHYSICAL ENVIRONMENT ALIGNS, ENGAGES AND INSPIRES YOUR PEOPLE?

Companies often centre their business strategies on the goals they want to achieve and the markers they use to measure success along the way – and designing your physical environment is no different. If you haven't considered how the environment enables or inhibits your people, you may be hurting more than you help.

Let's say your strategy is to decrease the time to process a sales order and dispatch the widget. Then you need to consider the present roadblocks. Where is the sales team located? What physical barriers are inhibiting the communication and collaboration of sales with production? Does the physical layout of your workplace silo them into two independent groups, with no opportunity to build cross-functional team relationships?

Such clarity is essential to designing a supportive work environment.

2 DO YOU HAVE DATA ON HOW YOU ARE CURRENTLY USING YOUR SPACE?

Awareness of how your workplace is presently being used is invaluable in understanding where more efficiency and expansion are required. Monitoring the actual use of space will give you a different perspective on how people are utilising it versus how they *believe* they are using it. Get clear on the data and use it as a base to make informed and measured solutions for the future.

3 CAN YOUR ORGANISATION ARTICULATE ITS BRAND STORY AND PERSONALITY BEYOND A LOGO?

Every organisation has a story about where it came from, why the business was started, how it has grown, the tough times it's ridden out, and the glory years. What's your business story? Is your business's personality masculine/feminine, metallic/natural materials, understated/loud? How do you want your business to be seen? What differentiates you from your industry competitors and tells the story of your business?

4 CAN YOUR BUSINESS CLEARLY ARTICULATE THE BEHAVIOURS THAT PUT YOUR VALUES INTO ACTION?

Once we know our values, we must then consider what it means to live those values, which means examining our behaviours. If your company value is "wellness" it would imply that you value health and wellness. Yet, if you have five printer locations throughout the office, enabling people to walk a mere 10 steps to collect their printing, you're communicating something else. Consolidating these in a central location and encouraging people to get up and get a little bit of daily exercise reinforces that the organisation values the health and wellness of the team. What message is your space sending, and is it conflicting with your values?

DOES YOUR ORGANISATION HAVE A WELLNESS STRATEGY ALIGNING WITH THE WORK ENVIRONMENT'S PHYSICAL SPACES?

Many organisations have developed systems around how they intend to support the health and wellness of their employees, covering physical, mental and emotional needs. But how does this translate into the physical work environment? What spaces, equipment or tools are provided to enable and encourage employees to engage with these strategies?

DOES YOUR ORGANISATION HAVE AN EMPLOYEE EXPERIENCE JOURNEY MAP?

What journey does each employee take in their lifespan with the company, including recruitment, onboarding, career development, training, promotion, and offboarding? What does that journey look like day to day? How do you wish to see staff engaging with their colleagues, clients and the business? A clear expectation of the experience you want your employees to have each day provides a platform to build your work environment.

DO YOU KNOW HOW INFORMATION FLOWS IN YOUR ORGANISATION?

Within organisations we have teams, and those teams need to communicate with other groups differently. Some may work closely, while others only need to interact once a month. So how do communication and information flow in your business? Understanding this data will provide insight into which teams should be positioned next to each other and how physical structures (walls, meeting rooms) could prevent communication between these teams and affect your business's workflow efficiency.

8. HOW IS YOUR CURRENT TECHNOLOGY INFLUENCING THE CULTURE AND OPERATION OF YOUR WORKPLACE?

Our best intentions for enabling our people and delivering on our desired culture can quickly fall short if our technology is outdated and clunky. If you want your people to work flexibly across the workplace, home and other sites, the technology needs to be mobile enough to do this. Too often, I've seen organisations aspire to create an untethered world of work for their team, only for it to fall down when the technology rollout is for desk-based computer systems and phones.

9. DOES YOUR BUSINESS UNDERSTAND YOUR PEOPLE'S PERSONALITIES, WORKSTYLE PREFERENCES, AND THE WORKSPACES THAT WOULD ENABLE THEM TO PERFORM AT THEIR PEAK?

Everyone is different, and we all have varying personalities and workstyle preferences. In the most simplistic terms, we each generally fall into introvert or extrovert, the way we handle external sensory stimulation. Some of us (like myself) move from one to the other throughout the day, depending on how we feel and the task at hand. By understanding the preferences of your team and the dynamic ratio of introverts to extroverts, you can be considerate of how the workplace is catering to the needs of all employees.

10. DO YOU HAVE A PLAN TO ENGAGE YOUR EMPLOYEES IN THE PROCESS?

Engaging your employees in the process at key points is a critical factor in the overall success of the final space. Inviting your people to provide input on what's working, what's not, and what would enable them to do their job better often uncovers insights management would never guess the business needed. Create a structured plan on how and when feedback will be invited and the communication plan to give them the decisions and intended outcomes.

Once these questions are answered, you're ready to engage with the market. Let's see who you're going to need in your support team.

Assemble your support team

Creating a new workplace for your business is a team effort. You will need to enlist the expertise of a wide variety of specialist consultants to ensure that you invest your time, energy and money well. Each role comes with its own specialties and superpowers, all adding value to the end product: a workplace that performs.

THE DIAGRAM BELOW OUTLINES THE ESSENTIAL CONSULTANTS YOU WILL NEED ALONG THE JOURNEY AND WHEN.

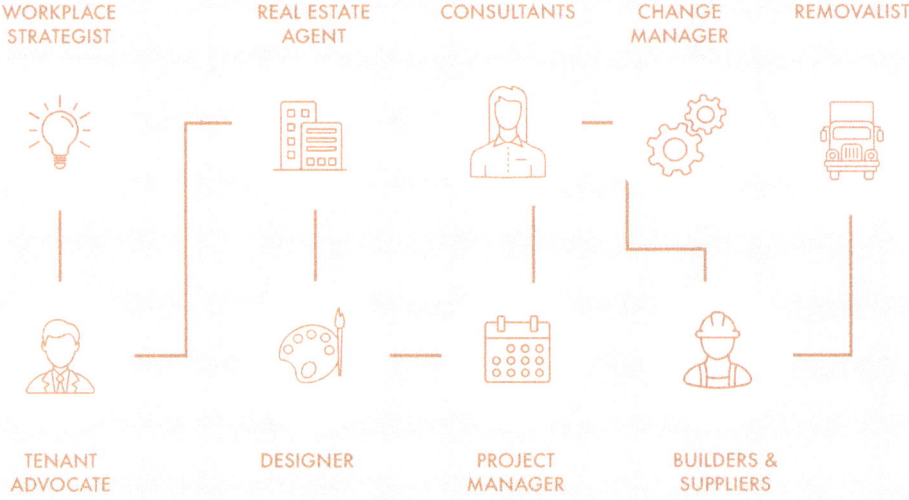

USE THE FOLLOWING GUIDE TO ENSURE YOU HAVE ALL THE ROLES NEEDED TO SET YOUR PROJECT UP FOR SUCCESS.

workplace strategist

The first people you need on your team are your workplace strategists. They are the people who will help you work out what your business needs to go to the market. Going out and looking at properties without a clear understanding of what your business needs is like going to the store to buy a suit without knowing what size you need, let alone the colour, style or brand. Sure, you can spend a lot of time visiting different stores, trying on a range of suits, working out what fits best and then having it altered to suit your unique body shape, or you can go directly to the tailor and have them customise a suit just for you.

Your strategist will support you in gathering, analysing and synthesising all the data we have gathered through the earlier chapters of this book. They will help you unpack what your organisation needs to move you forward into the future, with consideration of the best location, floor plate size for your required team dynamics, and surrounding amenities. Without this informed shopping list, you will have a raft of options, with no clear criteria for making your decision.

tenant advocate/representative

Armed with this clearly defined scope of requirements, it's time to engage with a tenant advocate/representative. The role of the tenant rep is to do precisely that: represent the tenant, *you*, in identifying a property in the market and negotiating the best deal. They facilitate the conversation between the landlords and real estate agents, cutting out all the properties that don't meet your requirements so you can focus your attention on those that meet your brief, saving you valuable time and energy.

The difference between a tenant rep and a real estate agent is who they represent. A tenant rep's role is to express your best interests as an incoming tenant, while a real estate agent works on behalf of the landlord. Their role is to lease the premises so that the landlord starts to see a return on their investment. The tenant rep is engaged and paid by the tenant, whereas the real estate agent is engaged and paid for by the landlord.

The risk of engaging directly with a real estate agent and not hiring the services of a tenant rep is that the structure of the incentivisation is not in the tenant's best interests and may lead you to secure a tenancy that does not service your needs adequately.

designer

With your shortlist of suitable properties, it's time to engage with your design team. Often when clients begin this process, their first thought is that they need an architect. While many skilled architects can create a workplace, an interior designer will be more adept at creating a place for people. Traditionally, architects design buildings and external structures. An interior designer creates from the inside out, working with the flow and interaction of people within the space.

Whichever direction you choose, the next step is to overlay your unique requirements developed by your workplace strategist onto the floor plans of the shortlisted properties. This process is often referred to as a "test fit", testing to see if you fit into the premises and how this looks and works with the shape and constraints of the building. Your test fits will enable you to make an informed decision on your selected property and for the supporting team to begin negotiating your leasing deal's commercials.

Establishing a good relationship with your designer is critical to the project's success, as they are involved for the entirety of the project, and 95 percent of your budget is determined in these initial phases.

Your designer will then support you throughout the process of concept design, design development and documentation to prepare a set of working drawings from which your space can be constructed.

project manager

Having someone on the team responsible for managing the program, budget and construction negotiations is absolutely necessary for any project. However, depending on the size and scope of the project, your architect or designer may be suitably experienced to provide this service. The role of the project manager is to support the delivery of the project from inception right through to handing over the keys and managing the project's closeout. It is a wide-ranging role with several key deliverables, covering cost management, program management, contract negotiations, construction and delivery quality, health and safety, risk management and general team coordination.

The term "project management" is used across industries. What's important to understand is that you require a project manager with construction experience and knowledge in the case of your build project. An experienced project manager in a software company may have a firm handle on managing the milestones of a program and budget; however, their experience in building a workplace is likely to be limited. Without a firm grasp on the established steps of delivery, the project is fraught with danger, so ensure that the person responsible for this role is experienced in all facets of project management relevant to the construction of your workplace.

Your project manager will be your eyes and ears throughout the project's progression. They are also your industry conduit, introducing you to the right builders, suppliers and consultant team you'll need to deliver your project.

They know how much things will cost and negotiate fees and contracts on your behalf to get you the most competitive market rate while balancing this against the quality of delivery and finished product satisfaction. Engaging with your project manager as early as your design team is an excellent step in ensuring smooth and well-planned project delivery.

Consultants

Aside from your designer and project manager, many specialist consultants may be required to support the delivery of the project:

- **SERVICES ENGINEERS**
- **CERTIFIER**
- **STRUCTURAL ENGINEER**
- **ACOUSTIC ENGINEER**
- **QUANTITY SURVEYOR**
- **STORAGE CONSULTANT**
- **DDA**
- **TOWN PLANNER**

Your project manager will be able to advise you of the required consultant mix for your project, depending on the scope, and connect you with those who specialise in the field of the workplace.

SERVICES ENGINEER
Reconfiguring the services on your floor is triggered by adding or removing any walls and the number of people you plan to accommodate. Without the appropriate documentation and certificates from licensed consultants, your building approval (required before you do most building work) cannot be issued. Depending on the existing services within the tenancy you lease, the consultants required include mechanical (air conditioning), hydraulic (plumbing), electrical (power and lighting), data, and fire.

CERTIFIER
In days gone by, you submitted your request to do building works to the local council for approval. Today this service has been replaced by private certifiers, expediting the approval process and providing you with a single point of contact for enquiries and explanations. They are responsible for ensuring the compliance of your finished workplace with all building codes and Australian Standards, including disability access.

STRUCTURAL ENGINEER

You might think of structural engineers as only being required to construct a new building, bridge or roadway. Still, the structural integrity of the building can be impacted by the design of your fitout. Floor penetrations for plumbing pipes, floor boxes and cabling all require holes to be created in the slab of your premises, which can impact the structural integrity of the slab. So hire a structural engineer for your own peace of mind and to meet your landlord's and certification requirements.

Seismic design is also a consideration for your fitout. Although the existing building is not part of your scope, the fitout works also require construction according to construction codes for seismic activity, impacting the installation and fixing of air-conditioning ducts, sprinkler pipes, suspended ceilings and wall construction.

ACOUSTIC ENGINEER

While an acoustic engineer is not required on every project, you may have more particular needs around soundproofing, reverberation, or even the desire for "white noise" in the work zones. An acoustic engineer can provide scientific advice specific to your project needs and design to ensure the adequate execution of materiality and construction methods to achieve your desired outcome.

QUANTITY SURVEYOR

Getting a firm grip on the cost of your proposed project is no doubt front of mind for you, and while your team will be highly experienced in delivering projects, having an independent assessment of the financial investment is critical in the design process. Getting an early evaluation of the project cost can avoid disappointment and the need for value engineering to occur at the last minute, impacting the program and the finished product.

Whether you engage with a quantity surveyor or liaise with a "friendly builder" to prepare your cost plan, it's advisable to do this at the project's concept stage and reassess at critical milestones before going to tender.

STORAGE CONSULTANT

If you haven't moved office for a while, are a paper-heavy organisation, or are looking to modernise your filing practices, you might need to enlist the services of a storage consultant. They can assess your existing situation and use their knowledge and experience to advise on practical ways to digitise and reduce the physical footprint of your paper storage, saving you valuable real estate costs.

DDA

Creating an equally accessible workplace is a crucial consideration for every organisation, and depending on your workplace design, alternative means of assessment may be required to fulfil your accessibility requirements. Your project manager will advise if your specific project requires their engagement.

TOWN PLANNER

This may sound odd, given that we are discussing fitting a workspace inside an existing building. However, I have encountered a few scenarios in which a town planner may be relevant to your project.

For example, if the building you are leasing is not "zoned" under the local council's planning scheme to support the use you intend to perform in the building, this will require a "material change of use" application to suit your intended business operations.

Alternatively, the requirement for external building penetrations may trigger the application of a DA due to the existing zoning of the property and its impact on the building façade.

In such instances, the help of a town planner can be enormously helpful.

Change Manager

Often with creating a new workplace, there is a significant shift in how the space operates compared to the previous work environment. As with everything, things change, evolve and improve over time. Creating a new work environment is a milestone opportunity to reassess the continuous improvements the business has made over the past five to 10 years and preempt the further improvements and efficiencies required in the next 10 years. What you are really doing is moving people along a continuum in a 20-year leap!

When we think about your new workplace design like this, it's a dramatic and tumultuous shift in how we work. Adequately preparing, supporting and training people for the new workplace is a fundamental requirement to see its success.

Just as you would onboard a new employee into your business, you will need to onboard people into the new workplace, setting out guidelines, expectations and ground rules for the use and operation of the space. This will cover everything from ways of working to communication and collaboration methods, technology use and storage of personal effects.

Engaging people in the process will support buy-in and the successful execution of the project. Whether you execute this internally or with the support of an external professional, it is highly recommended that this role be supported by the project team.

builder

This is where it all starts to become real! Appointing a builder to deliver your project is a critical step. Whether you do a market tender or negotiate with a preferred builder, your project manager will guide you through the process and assist you in identifying suitably qualified contractors for the project.

Your builder will be responsible for engaging and managing all the subtrades under a head contractor arrangement, providing you with a single point of accountability. They will also purchase all the furniture, appliances and equipment required to complete the project.

Establishing a good rapport with your builder is essential, as they will be with you long after the project is finished. While they might be intently building your dream office for a solid eight- to 14-week period (or longer), the relationship extends beyond you moving in with a 12-month defects liability period, where they are required to attend to anything that's not quite right.

removalist

Whether you are staying put and upgrading your current facility or moving to a new shiny home, the logistics require careful planning to ensure that Karen doesn't lose her keyboard. Packing, moving and storing equipment, furniture, files and personal effects is, in my opinion, one of the less enjoyable aspects of the process. Having someone who specialises in this space is a beautiful asset to a project, removing any stress and concern associated with damage and loss in the process, especially if you are relocating across multiple floors with hundreds of people.

As you can see, many people are invested in making your project an outstanding success. As the saying goes, "many hands make light work."

SO TRUST IN THE PROCESS AND THEIR EXPERTISE TO MAXIMISE YOUR RETURN ON INVESTMENT AND OPTIMISE THIS OPPORTUNITY.

Often clients can get swept up in the excitement and want to dive right in or feel that going with the DIY version will save them a few dollars. In my experience, this approach does not end well. There are reasons why these professions exist. Depending on the scale and size of your business, you may not require the entire suite of services, but their advice is likely to see you create an outcome you couldn't have achieved if you went it alone.

BUT, BEFORE YOU GO HIRING ANYONE, YOU NEED TO PREPARE YOUR WORKPLACE BRIEF, SO YOU CAN COMMUNICATE YOUR VISION FOR THE NEXT WORKPLACE.

preparing your Workplace Market Brief

The data you have captured throughout this book can now be synthesised into a digestible document to share with the market so you can engage your team of professionals.

This document is a high-level snapshot of your desired workplace, capturing the nuances unique to your business and communicating your desired outcome. It forms the foundation you and your team of professionals will continue to build on as they each bring their areas of expertise to the table.

SOME OF THE THINGS THIS DOCUMENT SHOULD CAPTURE ARE:

1. WHO YOU ARE AS AN ORGANISATION.
2. YOUR VISION FOR THE PROJECT.
3. A HIGH-LEVEL OVERVIEW OF YOUR BRIEF.
4. YOUR ANTICIPATED CONSTRUCTION BUDGET.
5. KEY PROJECT MILESTONES THAT NEED TO BE ACHIEVED (SUCH AS THE LEASE EXPIRY).
6. YOUR PREFERRED LOCATION.

ALONG WITH MORE DETAILED INFORMATION SUCH AS:

1. **THE SPACE YOU CURRENTLY OCCUPY, ALONG WITH YOUR CURRENT AND FUTURE STAFF PROJECTIONS.**
2. **THE WORKPLACE STYLE YOU'D LIKE TO CONSIDER – TRADITIONAL, OPEN PLAN, HYBRID.**
3. **SPECIFIC BUILDING AMENITIES – SHOWERS, BIKE RACKS, ETC.**
4. **ANY SPECIFIC ORGANISATIONAL PREREQUISITES – EXTENSIVE STORAGE, A DATA CENTRE, CALL CENTRE, ETC.**
5. **ANY OTHER DETAILS THAT WILL INFORM YOUR PROSPECTIVE PARTNERS IN PREPARING A PROPOSAL FOR YOUR CONSIDERATION.**

By clearly documenting what you are trying to achieve and the data you have already gathered, you can communicate your expectations for the project and enable the market to respond more accurately. This will make selecting and hiring your partners more streamlined and ensure you are all on the same page from the outset.

Use the briefing template to begin to compile your workplace market brief. And remember, while you may not have all the answers to complete the template, these are questions you will continue to answer as you progress through the project.

HEAD TO THE BOOK RESOURCES ON PAGE 9 AND SCAN THE QR CODE TO DOWNLOAD THE WORKPLACE MARKET BRIEFING TEMPLATE!

11

Questions you need to ask your prospective *designer*

Once you've got your Workplace Strategist onboard, your strategy is rounded out, you've gone to market, and you are now assessing your shortlisted tenancy options, it's time to find your design partner. Engaging your workplace designer is a critical step in the process, as they are responsible for seeing your vision and strategy become a reality. They will translate the data, strategic objectives, brand, culture and employee experience into a carefully curated environment that optimises your business operations and communicates your unique value proposition to employees and clients.

They will play an intimate role in the project delivery over the coming months. Getting to know them well and feeling comfortable with them personally and professionally is critical to a successful working relationship.

By quizzing your prospective designer with the following questions, you will be able to better understand their capability, experience and how aligned they are with your organisation's values and if they will be a good fit for you and your business.

1. EXPLAIN TO ME YOUR PROCESS FOR ENGAGING WITH THE BUSINESS AND OUR PEOPLE.

TICK ONCE ASKED

How the designer proposes to engage your team will differ from studio to studio. Some may require a few dot points to create a brief, while others will have a more detailed and hands-on workshop-style approach.

A higher level of engagement enables the designer to gain a deeper understanding of your business to deliver a design that responds to your organisation's unique needs, resulting in a more bespoke and tailored outcome that will provide long-term business value. Understanding this will enable you to see who aligns best with your expectations and will also impact the designer's fees: more involvement = more time = more value.

2. WHAT CLIENTS HAVE YOU WORKED WITH IN THE PAST? PLEASE PROVIDE REFERENCE DETAILS.

TICK ONCE ASKED

Like any business decision, having quality referrals from past clients will always be a great point to measure the client satisfaction of those before you. How did they do? What could they do better?

3. WHAT HAS BEEN YOUR FAVOURITE PROJECT TO WORK ON AND WHY?

TICK ONCE ASKED

As designers, we all have a favourite project we worked on, whether due to the great relationship we developed with the client or the endless budget. This question will give you an insight into what "lights up" your designer and how they intend to service your project.

4 WHAT HAS BEEN THE BIGGEST FAILURE IN YOUR CAREER, AND WHAT DID YOU LEARN FROM IT?

TICK ONCE ASKED

We all make mistakes, some bigger than others. The bonus for you is that we hopefully have learned from that mistake, and it's not likely to happen again on your project (fingers crossed). If your designer brushes this question off and isn't forthcoming with any mistakes, this would be a big red flag for me for two reasons.
1. They aren't willing to own up to their mistakes, and it's likely they aren't taking away any learnings either.
2. They aren't willing to push themselves to do something a little different; they play it safe, which means your project will look just like their last three clients' projects.

5 HOW WOULD YOU DESCRIBE YOUR DESIGN STYLE?

TICK ONCE ASKED

This is a big one for me. I believe that as designers, it is not our role to design for our own style and taste but that of our clients. Many designers have a signature style, which makes them highly attractive to potential clients, "I want what she's having!" Know your preferred approach and ensure that the designer you hire fits your desired outcome.

6 EXPLAIN TO ME THE PROPOSED TEAM FOR THE PROJECT AND THEIR EXPERIENCE.

TICK ONCE ASKED

More resources do not mean a better outcome. Having a well-rounded team to deliver your project is far more critical than having a group of 20 people. Larger firms may have a team that isn't focused on workplace projects and often have a large proportion of junior team members who haven't yet earned their stripes. And you'll often only have a few people working on your project anyway. After all, "too many cooks spoil the broth."

7

WHAT LEVEL OF INVOLVEMENT ARE YOU LOOKING FOR FROM US AS A BUSINESS?

TICK ONCE ASKED

How much time is your designer expecting you to invest in the project? What tasks are they expecting you to fulfil and are therefore not included in their scope and fee? Each designer will have a different expectation about the number of briefings, design meetings, presentations and the information you will need to provide. Understand this so that you aren't over-committed during the process or incur additional costly variations for scope creep.

8

DESCRIBE YOUR COMMUNICATION PROCESS BETWEEN YOURSELVES AND US.

TICK ONCE ASKED

What does the communication process look like? Will this be a conversation, or will your designer be directing traffic? How are they going to keep you updated on progress? Is it a meeting, an email or a task list? The communication style you expect may not align with your designer's.

9

WHAT IS YOUR ORGANISATION'S APPROACH TO MANAGING OUR PROGRAM?

TICK ONCE ASKED

Time is the other critical factor in delivering your project. You've likely got an impending lease expiry, a busy business period or a high-profile event, so your project needs to be completed within a specific timeframe. There are a lot of steps that need to be completed and stakeholders involved in delivering the project. How will they ensure they meet their milestones and don't impact the rest of the team?

10

HOW DO YOU HANDLE DESIGN ERRORS AND THE COST IMPLICATIONS DURING CONSTRUCTION?

This one more pointedly inquires about past errors and how they proactively handled them to not become your problem or cost. Did they incorrectly specify the wallpaper code or forget to document that piece of joinery? What happened, how did they handle it, and what was the cost implication to the client?

11

WHAT IS YOUR ORGANISATION'S APPROACH TO MANAGING OUR BUDGET?

Argh… money! It's always a sensitive subject, as it should be. You're investing A LOT of money in this project, and you must ensure your designer will spend it wisely. How are they going to ensure what they design meets your budget? How will they manage your excitement by adding new and wonderful things to the project along the way? What tools are they going to use to track and communicate your budget? Who will they engage with to help them establish and manage the numbers?

Not every designer will be money savvy, so get clear on who will support them to ensure you don't get any nasty surprises. The last thing you want is to make wholesale changes and shatter your dreams when you get the tender costs back – that just leaves everyone deflated and dissatisfied.

The two big questions every client wants the answer to...
how much? & how long?

When I first start engaging with a client, the two most commonly asked questions are, "how long is this going to take?" and "how much is it going to cost?" As I'll explain, there are a number of variables that influence the answer to both these questions.

Underestimating the answer to either of these questions is sure to see your project derailed before you've even begun.

How long does it take to design and build a workplace?

IT DEPENDS...

The short answer is "it depends". Many factors contribute to the time you and your team will take to plan, design and build your next workplace. Everything from the size to quality and market conditions will be a factor. What you can count on is, like everything, it's likely to take longer than you expect!

Each project will move through the same phases and milestones; however, each project's timeframe will be different. Once the lease has been executed, you could expect to complete a smaller fitout in as little as four months, with larger projects taking up to two years.

THESE ARE TYPICALLY THE HIGH-LEVEL MILESTONES THAT YOUR PROJECT WILL HIT ALONG THE WAY, ALONG WITH MY USUAL GUIDANCE AS TO THE TIME REQUIRED FOR EACH PHASE*

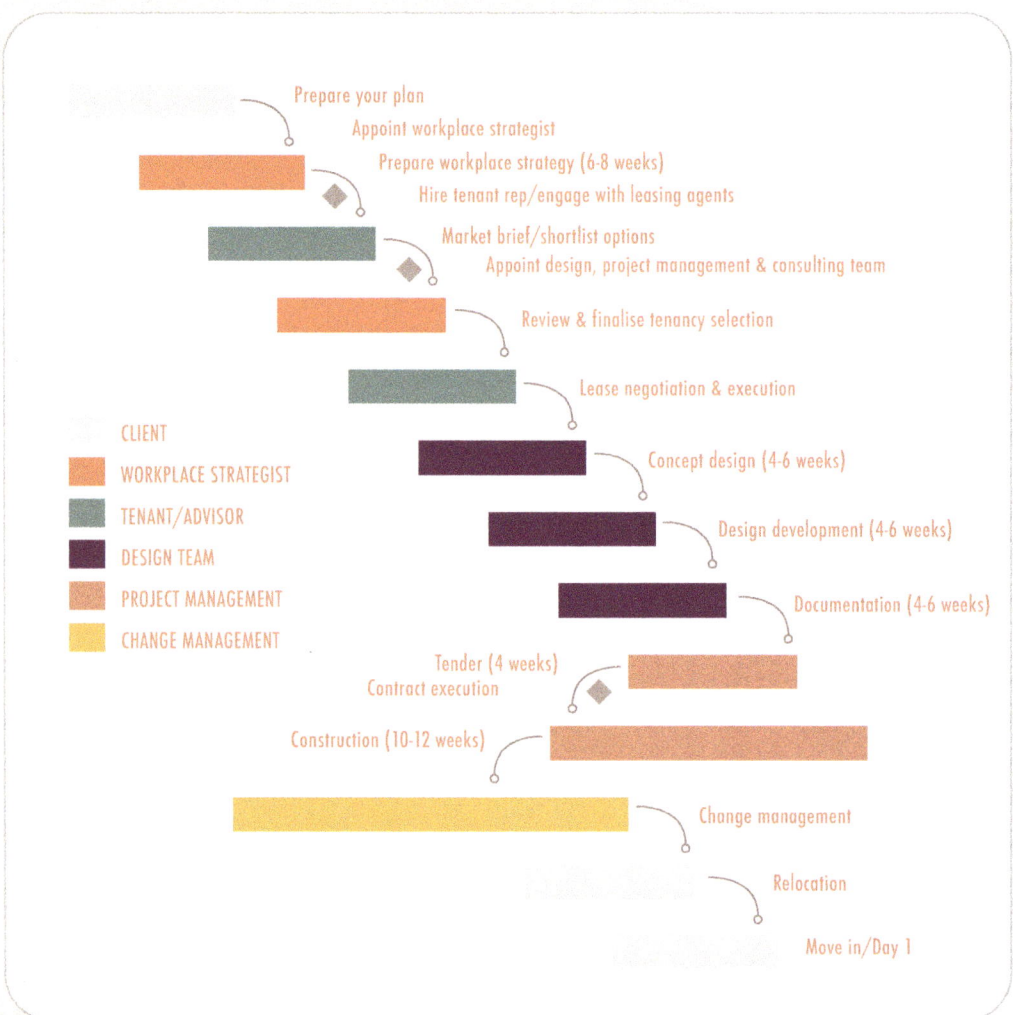

*Program based on a project under 1000sqm and with an average cost of $1800/sqm. Variability of either will result in changes to the anticipated program.

Here are some challenges and complexities that will influence how long each phase will take to complete.

Workplace strategy

While the size of your business is the prominent factor in influencing how long this phase will take, a number of other more nuanced factors can draw out this phase. Ranging from the availability and accuracy of data to the opportunity to coordinate the diaries of the right people at the right time, through to the impact of other business programs occurring concurrently. These factors can subtly or dramatically influence how long it will take to complete this phase.

While it may only take six weeks to develop a strategy when the required data and people are readily available, it can often take as long as six to 12 months to gather and validate this data before an accurate strategy can be created.

Market engagement and lease execution

I regularly see clients overlooking the time it will take to find suitable premises. Once you know what you want and engage with prospective landlords to identify the right tenancy, the process of shortlisting, lease negotiation and execution can take six to 18 months, sometimes much longer. Re-signing your current lease and remaining in your existing premises can be a prolonged exercise to negotiate the best deal.

Being prepared for your impending lease expiry, and starting the process early, will give you the time and flexibility to ensure that you have explored all your options thoroughly rather than having to make spontaneous decisions under pressure.

Concept design, design development and documentation

These three phases are the critical execution phases of what your finished workplace will look like. These phases encompass the coordinated skills and services of a range of people, including your designers, services engineers and various other consultants, to formulate clearly documented plans, schedules and specifications from which your workplace can be built.

THROUGH THESE PHASES, YOU CAN EXPECT THE FOLLOWING:

CONCEPT DESIGN
This phase of the project is where you will start to see your vision for the project taking shape: the overarching design metaphor, materials, finishes and furniture direction, test fit planning and conceptual sketches of critical spaces. It is also the first marker to establish project costs and realign your project to your organisational expectations before getting too deep into the project.

DESIGN DEVELOPMENT
Once everyone agrees on the proposed design style and aesthetic and is comfortable with the proposed budget, it's time to flesh out the design in greater detail. This phase will see the evolution of critical spaces, formulation of joinery concepts, and expansion of materials, finishes and furniture required to complete the design, along with coordination of services (mechanical, electrical, hydraulic, fire) to support the design, compliance checks with the certifier and technical detail development with the structural and acoustic engineers. The completion of this phase will see a more refined set of documents that delves deeper into communicating the design of the space. It will also be the last opportunity for you, as the client, to visually see the design conceptually before the documents transform into a set of technical plans and specifications. It's also the final checkpoint to evaluate the budget before the final documents are prepared for tender.

DOCUMENTATION

This is the final phase in the design process, where your design and consultant team develops technical drawings, specifications and schedules to communicate the desired outcome to prospective builders. The quality and accuracy of these documents will influence the tender pricing and the range of variability in the submitted tenders.

Some of the factors which can influence the length of time it takes to complete this project phase are the following:

- Size and complexity of your project. The more complex your project is, the more time it will require to complete the design and documentation.

- Level of finish and quality. The higher the level of finish and expected quality of the completed workplace, the more designing, detailing and documenting is required, thus increasing the length of time to complete

- Technical requirements specific to your project. Any bespoke elements requiring more significant technical consideration will also increase the length of time due to research, sourcing and design to the particular need, eg project control rooms, specific AV or media, and high levels of acoustics.

- Specific tenancy guidelines, building code and compliance requirements. Depending on the selected building and your desired design, there may be increased time and coordination required to develop the design in accordance with specific requirements. Such items may include mandated conditions by the landlord through their tenancy fitout guidelines, or fire egress distances may be impacted by the shape of the building and the position of the core.

Tender and contract execution

The period your project manager will allow for the tender phase will typically be influenced by the size and complexity of the project but will also consider the current market conditions. The time of year or an unexpected uplift in the number of projects in the market can influence the time your project will require to obtain a fair and accurate market price. While two to four weeks may be a reasonable amount of time, subject to the above, four to eight weeks may be more realistic.

Tender reviews and clarifications, going back and forth with the tenders and the project manager, can also influence the amount of time required to ensure an accurate "apples for apples" comparison of the submitted tenders, taking as little as a week up to four weeks, depending on the variability and number of items.

Before picking up the tools on site, the final step is to ensure that a contract is in place between the builder and your business. Both the proposed agreement and the negotiation that is likely to take place between your respective lawyers can influence the length of time to agree on terms and sign on the dotted line. While this could be as little as one week, it could also take several months. Circulating the proposed contract at tender can alleviate these delays, allowing contractors to respond when submitting their offer.

Construction

The time it will take to see all the planning and design for your next workplace take shape is highly influenced by the size, complexity and level of finish. A simple small space with limited built form, joinery and services relocations can be completed in as little as six weeks, while a larger workplace environment that has a number of meeting rooms, extensive AV, bespoke joinery and a high level of finishes and detailing can take several months on-site to complete.

Your project manager will guide you through this phase, advising on a suitable time frame that works for your business and ensuring adequate time for the builder to deliver the project to the expected standard. However, possible delays may impact your completion date, ranging from material, furniture and product delays to availability of trades, with each of these challenges navigated by your project manager.

Money money, money!

Starting a new project is always exciting – coming up with ideas, looking at what other people have done, and thinking of all the great new things you will have. And then the inevitable thought comes: how much will this cost? Like any project, building the workplace of your dreams will cost money. That cost can vary, but one thing is for sure: you can't buy champagne on a beer budget.

IT'S ALSO IMPORTANT TO REMEMBER THAT IN THESE EARLY PHASES OF PLANNING, HAVING THE RIGHT TEAM AROUND YOU IS CRITICAL TO THE SUCCESS OF YOUR PROJECT.

While you may only be 5 percent of the way through planning for your next workplace, you have already made decisions that have committed more than 65 percent of your capital costs. So it's critical that you have the right team advising you.

Ensuring you have people with the right skills and experience guiding this phase is critical to successfully managing your budget. Remember, saving a few thousand dollars on your consultant team could cost you tens, if not hundreds of thousands of dollars later.

INVESTING IN THE RIGHT TEAM FOR THE PROJECT WILL SAVE YOU MONEY LATER. CHOOSE WISELY.

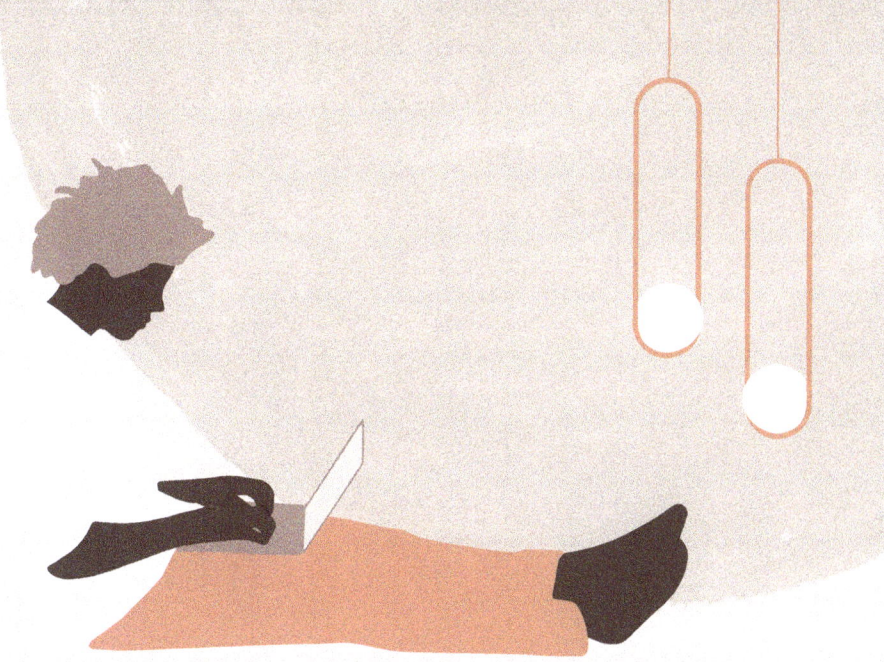

EQUATION OF INFLUENCE OF PROJECT EXPENDITURE ON COST[1]

INFLUENCE ON COST

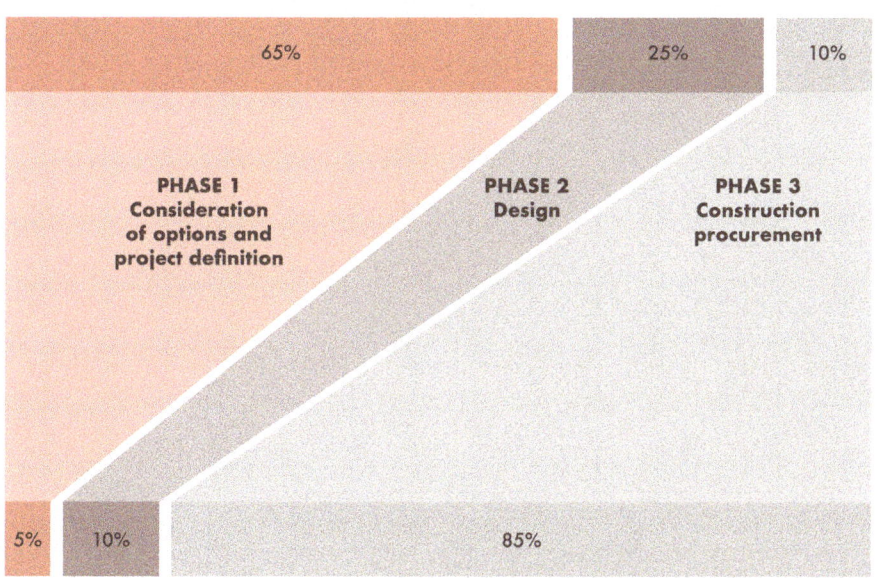

| 65% | 25% | 10% |

PHASE 1
Consideration of options and project definition

PHASE 2
Design

PHASE 3
Construction procurement

| 5% | 10% | 85% |

While every project is different and influenced by a range of factors (I'll get to these), here are a few metrics that can help to set your expectations for your next workplace.

INDICATIVE BUILDING COSTS[2]

Industry	Cost per net lettable area (NLA)*
Government department	$1,500 to $2,200
Professional services firms	$1,800 to $2,500 Tier 2 and 3
High-end professional services firms	$2,400 to $3,600 Tier 1 legal and accounting firms
Corporate	$1,600 to $2,400

*These costs are a guide only and influenced by a range of factors as outlined below. Excludes GST, AV Equipment, IT equipment, removalist costs. Accurate at time of printing.

Typical professional fees cost	8% – 12%
Typical workspace per employee	6-13m² (NLA / employee headcount)
Typical workspace per workpoint	10-13m² (NLA / workpoints)

Note: the area per employee and per workpoint are influenced by the workstyle approach, for example allocated seating versus hybrid model of un-allocated seating.

SO, WHAT ARE SOME OF THE CONSIDERATIONS THAT WILL INFLUENCE HOW MUCH YOUR PROJECT WILL COST?

There is a range of concerns that impact the final cost of your project. Outlined below are several that will support you in gauging the potential investment that you will need to consider in creating your workplace.

Size and scope

The size and scope of your project are huge factors in how much investment you will require. Here are two ways it happens.

THE TOTAL OFFICE AREA WILL DIRECTLY INFLUENCE THE $/SQM RATE.

The larger your space, the more cost efficiencies you will achieve. The costs of high-value investment spaces like receptions, boardrooms, kitchens/cafes, and comms rooms are spread across the total office space.

Let's look at the opposite scenario for a clearer picture. Smaller tenancies still need these high-cost centres but often fewer of the open-plan work areas, which overall cost less. In the project's totality, fewer small investments don't offset the big-ticket ones.

THE WORKPLACE LAYOUT CONTRIBUTES TO THE $/SQM RATE.

Your total project cost will rise if you require lots of meeting rooms and offices with minimal open-plan areas. This is because of the number of walls and doors built and the necessary alterations to support this layout. More walls mean more changes to the air-conditioning systems. This also means additional supplementary air systems to provide fresh and cool air, relocation of light fittings and installation of extra fire sprinkler heads to ensure that the space adheres to fire safety standards.

THESE IMPLICATIONS ARE "UNSEEN" COSTS – THEY HIDE IN THE CEILING!

Quality

Here is typically where the champagne taste on a beer budget comes into play. Office space is often leased in a "made good" state: new carpet, ceiling tiles, painted walls, and so forth. So we need to consider how much of this existing fitout we will change.

Are we going to remove ceilings, expose services or add feature ceilings? Will we remove sections of the carpet tiles to lay ceramic tiles in the entry, add a more durable finish such as vinyl in the kitchen area, or install a plush carpet in the boardroom? All of these alterations to the existing finishes have a direct cost impact.

And then, we consider the choice of finishes and materials to construct your office. Do you want stone benchtops or laminate? Are we going to paint the walls with standard-grade paint or clad them with proprietary finishes, wallpaper or specialist paint finishes? There are various material options, and each selection will influence your total project cost.

Furniture is also a significant contributor to the bottom line of your office fitout cost. Workstations come in all shapes and sizes with numerous accessories and electronically height-adjustable varieties. Task chairs can range from $100 to more than $1000, and then there are the loose and occasional furniture pieces for the cafe, breakout areas and reception. The options are endless, and your preferred style will determine your cost direction.

Time

The last major influence on the cost of your project is time. Let's break it down into two points.

TIMELINE
The price depends heavily on how quickly you need to complete your project. You may be looking at escalation costs if the project needs to be designed within a compressed timeframe or a double shift if the build time needs to be sped up.

HOURS
Some parts of the project may have to be done out-of-hours to reduce disruption to other building tenants. This can incur additional costs. It will depend on where your office is located and the guidelines imposed by your landlord.

Many variables influence the cost of your office fitout project. But by creating an accurate scope, an agreed level of finish and an expectation of time, we can arrive at a precise estimate. This can be further verified by developing a cost plan with a builder or engaging a quantity surveyor early in the design phase. Ultimately, you should consider it an investment, not merely an expense.

Your workplace is a business asset and, when done well, one that will deliver ROI. It will become your second home for the next decade or more. So it's good to invest in getting the workplace right for your people. After all, your people are the most expensive asset in your business, and workplaces are built for them. Create an environment where they can thrive, and your business will thrive too. It makes good business sense.

YOUR STORY IS THE REFLECTION POINT FOR EVERY *decision*

As you embark on your journey to create your Next Workplace, remember if one thing is unique to your business, it's your story. Who you are, where you came from, where you are going, and what you care about. Your industry is full of other businesses that do what you do, but they don't do it the way you do. They don't do it for the same reason you do. They don't have the exact same departments, values, goals or history. These are all the ways in which your business is unique and inimitable. Allow your story to guide each decision, and use it as a reflection point that ensures your design remains aligned with your company and the desired outcome.

YOUR WORKPLACE IS YOUR OPPORTUNITY TO EMBODY ALL OF THESE ASPECTS, AS IT, TOO, SHOULD BE ENTIRELY UNIQUE TO YOUR BUSINESS.

If you take anything from this book, let it be to embrace the idea that your work environment is the physical experience that you can design for your people and your clients. It is the vessel that holds the five pillars underpinning your organisation's unique dynamics: your future, your brand and culture, your values and behaviours, your approach to wellness, and your employee experience. Your workplace is so much more than an "office". It is your opportunity to influence people's experience working with your company at every touchpoint. •

How you make *people feel* is your true *legacy*

References

CHAPTER ONE

1. Automatic, accessed March 2021, https://automattic.com/how-we-work/
2. Matt Mullenweg 2020, *Matt Mullenweg*, accessed March 2021, < https://ma.tt/2020/04/five-levels-of-autonomy/>
3. Deputy Team 2016, *Deputy*, accessed March 2021, < https://www.deputy.com/blog/history-of-9-to-5>
4. Kim Lachance Shandrow 2015, *How the 9-to-5 Came to Be and Why It No Longer Makes Sense*, Entrepreneur, < https://www.entrepreneur.com/living/how-the-9-to-5-came-to-be-and-why-it-no-longer-makes-sense/249299>
5. Dr Sean Gallagher, Swinburne Centre for the New Workforce 2019, *National Survey Report, Peak Human Potential: Preparing Australia's workforce for the digital Future*, Swinburne University of Technology, accessed February 2021, < https://www.swinburne.edu.au/media/swinburneeduau/centre-for-the-new-workforce/cnew-national-survey-report.pdf>
6. The Office Chronicles, Are Physical Offices Dead? With Tracy Hawkins, Twitter 2021, podcast, Kursty Groves, 1 January 2021, accessed November 2021, < https://podcasts.apple.com/au/podcast/the-office-chronicles/id1547249791?i=1000504281226>

CHAPTER TWO

1. Dhingra, N et al, 2020, *Igniting individual purpose in times of Crisis*, McKinsey, < https://www.mckinsey.com/capabilities/people-and-organizational-performance/our-insights/igniting-individual-purpose-in-times-of-crisis>
2. Emmett, J et al, 2020, *COVID-19 and the employee experience: How leaders can seize the moment*, McKinsey, < https://www.mckinsey.com/capabilities/people-and-organizational-performance/our-insights/covid-19-and-the-employee-experience-how-leaders-can-seize-the-moment>
3. Sander, E, 2019, *Time for a Kondo clean-out? Here's what clutter does to your brain and body*, The Conversation, < https://theconversation.com/time-for-a-kondo-clean-out-heres-what-clutter-does-to-your-brain-and-body-109947>
4. 12 Surprising Ways Clutter is Ruining your Life, 2017,Huffpost, < https://www.huffpost.com/entry/12-surprising-ways-clutter-is-ruining-your-life-infographic_b_59160aace4b02d6199b2eee5>
5. Jackson, F & Matos, K, *Employee Survey Comments: Everything you need to know*, Culture Amp, < https://www.cultureamp.com/blog/employee-survey-comments>

CHAPTER THREE

1. Wikipedia, n.d, *Nudge Theory*, accessed 22 September 2022, < https://en.wikipedia.org/wiki/Nudge_theory>
2. Sunstein, C & Thaler, R 2021, *Nudge: Improving decisions about Health, Wealth and Happiness*, Final edn, Penguin Books
3. Saghai Y, 'Salvaging the concept of nudge', *Journal of Medical Ethics* 2013;39:487-493.
4. The Decision Lab, *Defaults*, accessed 22 September 2022 < https://thedecisionlab.com/reference-guide/psychology/defaults>
5. Ruby, A, 2018, *The Eudiamonia Machine – An office space concept for the 21st Century?*, Accessed March 2021, https://blog.fentress.com/blog/the-eudaimonia-machine-a-space-concept-for-the-21st-century

CHAPTER FOUR

1. Brim, B & Robison, J, 2020, *What Wellbeing Means in the Coronavirus Era*, Gallup, accessed October 2020, < https://blog.fentress.com/blog/the-eudaimonia-machine-a-space-concept-for-the-21st-century>
2. Knight, C et.al, *The Loneliness of the Hybrid Worker*, Solan Review, accessed July 2022, < https://sloanreview.mit.edu/article/the-loneliness-of-the-hybrid-worker/>
3. Mann, A, 2018, *Why we need Best Friends at Work*, Gallup, accessed October 2019, < https://www.gallup.com/workplace/236213/why-need-best-friends-work.aspx>
4. Culture First, Special: How to design experiences that increase connection 2020, podcast, Culture Amp, accessed November 2020, < https://www.art19.com/shows/culture-first/episodes/7f06f041-33f4-4db7-bc97-ea0784ceed91>
5. Microsoft 2021, *Work Trend Index Annual Report: The Next Great Disruption is Hybrid Work – Are we Ready?*, Microsoft, accessed June 2021, < https://www.microsoft.com/en-us/worklab/work-trend-index/hybrid-work>
6. *Busting the Mehrabian Myth*, 2009, Creativity Works, online video, accessed October 2022, < https://www.youtube.com/watch?v=7dboA8cag1M&t=161s>

7. *Future Forum 2022, Future Forum Pulse: Executives feel the strain of leading in the "new normal"*, Future Forum, accessed July 2022, < https://futureforum.com/research/pulse-report-fall-2022-executives-feel-strain-leading-in-new-normal/>
8. *Wellness at Work, 2022 Report*, Employment Hero, accessed July 2022, < https://employmenthero.com/wellness-at-work/>
9. Dr Lim, H, 2018, *Loneliness is a health issue – how do we ensure programs to tackle it are successful?*, Relationships Australia, accessed July 2022, < https://relationships.org.au/loneliness-is-a-health-issue-2013-how-do-we-ensure-programs-to-tackle-it-are-successful/>
10. *Social Isolation and Loneliness 2021*, Australian Institute of Health & Welfare, accessed July 2022, < https://www.aihw.gov.au/reports/australias-welfare/social-isolation-and-loneliness-covid-pandemic>
11. Dr Goodwin, K, 2021, *The Impact of Hybrid Work on Productivity and Wellbeing*, accessed July 2022, < https://drkristygoodwin.com/hybrid-work/>
12. Alexander, A et.al, 2020, *Reimagining the postpandemic workforce*, McKinsey, accessed July 2022, <https://www.mckinsey.com/capabilities/people-and-organizational-performance/our-insights/reimagining-the-postpandemic-workforce>
13. Attema, J et.al, 2018, *The Financial Case for High Performance Buildings*, San Francisco: Stok, LLC < http://stok.com/financial-case-for-high-performance-buildings/>
14. Wikipedia, n.d, *Social determinants of health*, accessed July 2022, < https://en.wikipedia.org/wiki/Social_determinants_of_health>
15. Klepesis, N et.al, n.d, *The National Human Activity Pattern Survey (NHAPS): A resource for accessing exposure to environmental pollutants*, National Exposure Research Laboratory, U.S. Environmental Protection Agency, accessed July 2022, < https://eta-publications.lbl.gov/sites/default/files/lbnl-47713.pdf>
16. *Health, Wellbeing & Productivity in Offices: The next chapter for green building*, 2014, World Green Building Council, accessed July 2022, < https://worldgbc.org/wp-content/uploads/2022/03/compressed_WorldGBC_Health_Wellbeing__Productivity_Full_Report_Dbl_Med_Res_Feb_2015-1.pdf>
17. WELL Certification, n.d, accessed July 2022, < https://www.wellcertified.com/certification/v2/>
18. Tzarimas, C, et.al, 2018, *Physical Activity in the Workplace: A Guide*, Exercise & Sports Science Australia, accessed July 2022, < http://exerciseismedicine.com.au/wp-content/uploads/2018/05/EIM_Workplace_PA_Guide.pdf>

CHAPTER 5

1. Gallup, Employee Experience Framework, diagram, accessed August 2022, < https://www.gallup.com/workplace/242252/employee-experience.aspx>
2. Morgan, J, 2017, The Employee Experience Cheat Sheet, *Medium*, August 2022, < https://medium.com/jacob-morgan/the-employee-experience-cheat-sheet-infographic-c0d6257dbcb8>
3. *Hopes and Fears 2021*, PWC, accessed October 2022, < https://www.pwc.com/gx/en/issues/upskilling/hopes-and-fears.html>
4. *Leesman 145K webinar*, 2020, Leesman, accessed December 2022, < https://vimeo.com/480857274?embedded=true&source=vimeo_logo&owner=40754439>
5. *The world's best workplaces 2019: Unpacking lessons from the top*, 2019, Leesman, accessed August 2022, < https://www.leesmanindex.com/media/LeesmanInsights-Book-SP-2019-Digital.pdf>
6. Baumer, N, 2021, *What is Neurodiversity?*, Harvard, accessed October 2022, < https://www.health.harvard.edu/blog/what-is-neurodiversity-202111232645>
7. *Creative Differences: A handbook for embracing neurodiversity in the creative industries*, 2020, Universal Music UK, accessed October 2022 < https://umusic.co.uk/Creative-Differences-Handbook.pdf>
8. Bush, M, 2021, *Why is Diversity and Inclusion in the Workplace Important?*, Great Place to Work, accessed October 2022, < https://www.greatplacetowork.com/resources/blog/why-is-diversity-inclusion-in-the-workplace-important>
9. Dixon-Fyle, S et.al, 2020, *Diversity Wins: How inclusion matters*, McKinsey, accessed December 2022, < https://www.mckinsey.com/featured-insights/diversity-and-inclusion/diversity-wins-how-inclusion-matters>
10. Johansson, F, 2020, *Why Diverse and Inclusive Teams are the Engines of Innovation*, Great Place to Work, accessed October 2022, < https://www.greatplacetowork.com/resources/blog/why-diverse-and-inclusive-teams-are-the-new-engines-of-innovation>
11. Bourke, J, 2016, *Which two heads are better than one?: How diverse teams create breakthrough ideas and make smarter decisions*, The Australian Institute of Company Directors, Sydney
12. Lewis, M, 2012, Obama's Way, *Vanity Fair*, accessed October 2022, < https://www.vanityfair.com/news/2012/10/michael-lewis-profile-barack-obama>

CHAPTER 6

1. Skelton, M, 2019, *Workplaces of the Future: Effective, expressive & exciting*, Davis Langdon/Slideshare, accessed November 2022, < https://www.slideshare.net/micskelton/infodata-workplaces-of-the-future-1303278>
2. Collaborative Cost Management, <https://collaborativecm.com.au>

About the author

Melissa Marsden is a workplace dynamics strategist reimagining work environments to drive high-performing teams. With her unique Workplace Dynamics Blueprint™, Mel guides organisations to envision a magnetic workplace that draws people in, aligning their hearts, bodies and minds. She helps her clients create an environment that positively influences behaviour and performance, inspiring human potential.

Mel's business acumen has been recognised by the Australian Institute of Management and Telstra Business Women's Awards for her leadership and transformational business strategy process. Her design excellence has been recognised by the Design Institute of Australia, Good Design Awards, Alistair Swayne Foundation, and Indesign Magazine.

As the Founder and Director of COMUNiTI, bringing more than 20 years in the industry to the task, Mel guides business leaders, corporates and professional services firms to navigate these unfamiliar times, transforming workplaces from the inside out. With a client list including Air New Zealand, APA, Entain, Hall Chadwick, Rugby Australia, Sunshine Coast City Council, and many more, Mel has helped her clients elevate their employees' experience of work and deliver measurable ROI to their business.

Mel is available for keynotes, workshops and leadership coaching. She is also the host of the popular *Work Life by Design* podcast.

You can learn more at **www.melissamarsden.com.au**

Acknowledgements

Reimagining the workplace has been a passion of mine since I started as a designer in this industry many moons ago. The silver lining that the pandemic created was that now many others share my passion and seek to find ways in which they, too, can reimagine the spaces in which we work to ignite imagination and inspire human potential.

While I have gathered my thoughts in this book over the past four years, the philosophies and frameworks I share have evolved through each client interaction, employee workshop, project creation and countless conversations with friends, colleagues and partners for over 20 years. So many voices have inspired the words within these pages.

I am incredibly grateful to my clients who have entrusted me with transforming their workplaces and allowing me to share their stories so that we can all learn. To those who have contributed via a conversation to bounce a theory, to fact-check an idea or to run your eye over a chapter, I am incredibly grateful. You each have helped me solidify my ideas and given me the confidence to put my thoughts into words.

The Next Workplace is a complex journey, and my editor Ann Maynard has skillfully encouraged me to stretch that bit further, to simplify my language, and it is thanks to her that the quality of this text is what it is. And my designer Emily Karamihas is a creative genius! Never could I have imagined something so beautiful. This book has brought my vision to life in a way I could never have anticipated.

This book presents a timely opportunity to reimagine our workplaces, ride the wave of change that the pandemic set in motion, and embrace a new frontier. The timing compelled me to finish the book, which required skillful juggling as we welcomed our son into the world. I am so appreciative of my husband, Michael, for never doubting my ability to see this through, for putting up with my procrastination, and for supporting me in stealing the hours I needed to finish it. To my daughters Malika and Bailey, and your brothers Isaac and Nash, the work I do, I do to create a better world for each of you.

Work Life by Design *podcast*

Ready to create your work life by design rather than by default?

Engaging conversations with those leading the way to reimagining work in a new era, Host Mel Marsden taps into the knowledge and insights of academics, business leaders and champions of change to explore what it takes to make work, work.

A podcast for People & Culture leaders, C-suite execs, entrepreneurs, designers and anyone interested in elevating their experience of work!

Our environments have the power to positively influence our behaviour and performance, inspiring our human potential. Together, we can all reimagine our workplaces.

www.melissamarsden.com.au/podcast

About COMUNiTI

COMUNITI IS A WORLD-CLASS TEAM OF SPECIALISTS CREATING HIGH-PERFORMING WORKPLACES WHERE PEOPLE CONNECT, TEAMS PERFORM AT THEIR BEST, AND BUSINESS THRIVES.

COMUNiTI reimagines workplaces across the globe and creates valuable ways to bring brands to life, connect people, and empower teams to perform at their best.

Drawing on data and insights, the highly skilled COMUNiTI team work with you to unlock the intelligence already within your business to create high-performing workplaces tailored to your brand story and team's needs.

We've delivered projects for global corporates such as Air New Zealand and local businesses from Brisbane Airport Corporation to Hall Chadwick, Mapien, and Entain, driving outstanding results, with 90% of employees reporting increased job satisfaction which in turn has delivered enhanced wellbeing and improved peer relationships and happiness at work.

WE BELIEVE A WORKPLACE THAT TELLS YOUR ORGANISATION'S STORY HAS A POWERFUL MESSAGE BEYOND WORDS.

And a connected and supportive workplace aligns individual behaviours with organisational values, so teams thrive and perform at their best.

www.comuniti.com.au

About the Workplace Dynamics blueprint™

THE ROLE WORKPLACES PLAY IS CHANGING. NO LONGER ARE THEY WHERE WE NEED TO 'GO' TO WORK, 'TO WORK'.

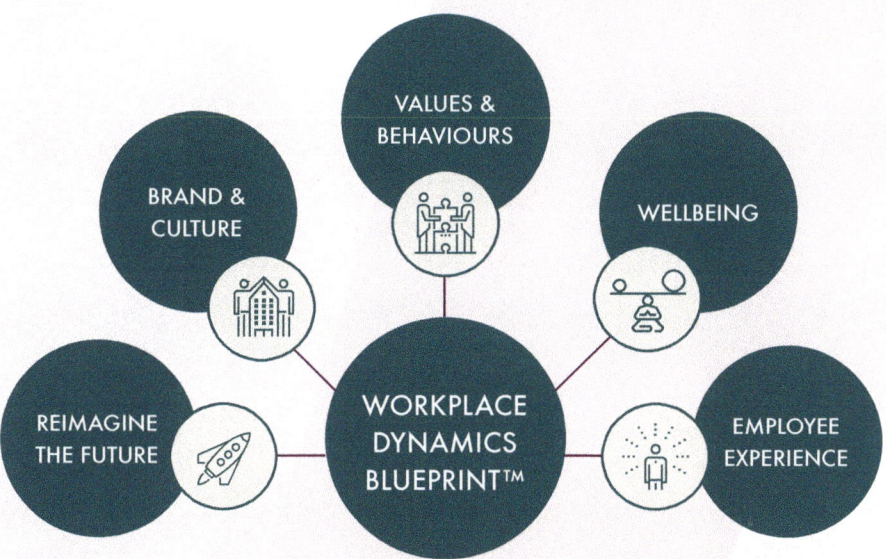

Well-designed workplaces should facilitate connection and belonging, and truly connect to your organisation's vision and values. Based on the five pillars that underpin workplace dynamics in every organisation, this blueprint will help you optimise your environment for employee experience and performance, delivering value to your bottom line.

To find out more visit:
www.comuniti.com.au/services

VISIT THE *website*

www.ingramcontent.com/pod-product-compliance
Lightning Source LLC
Chambersburg PA
CBHW040743020526
44107CB00084B/2872